False Flags over Europe

A Modern History of State-Fabricated Terror

by Nick Kollerstrom, Ph.D.

FALSE FLAGS OVER EUROPE:
A Modern History of State-Fabricated Terror

Published in London, England, October 18, 2018.
Length: 270 pages, 110,000 words.

Library of Congress subject areas:
Intelligence service--Israel--History.
State-sponsored terrorism -- Europe.
Terrorism--Israel.
Terrorism -- Political aspects -- Europe.
Terrorism -- Religious aspects -- Islam.

Bali Bombings, Kuta, Bali, Indonesia, 2002.
Charlie Hebdo Attack, Paris, France, 2015.
Gladio (Organization).
London Terrorist Bombings, London, England, 2005.
Madrid Train Bombings, Madrid, Spain, 2004.
Malaysia Airlines Flight 17 Crash, Ukraine, 2014.

BIC Subject Area Codes:		BISAC Subject Area Codes:	
History		**History**	
HBJD	European history	HIS015080	Europe / Great Britain / 21st Century
HBJD1	British & Irish history	HIS027180	Military / Special Forces
HBLX	21st century history	HIS037080	Modern / 21st Century
Political Science		**Political & Social Science**	
JFHC	Conspiracy theories	POL036000	Intelligence & Espionage
JPV	Political Control & freedoms	POL037000	Terrorism
JPVN	Propaganda	POL049000	Propaganda
JPWJ	Political subversion	POL064000	Corruption & Misconduct
JPWL1	Political assassinations	SOC049000	Jewish Studies
JPWL2	Terrorist attack	SOC058000	Conspiracy Theories

Synopsis:
All across Europe, awful 'terror' events are happening. But who is doing them? The media will tell you, who are the perpetrators - but a different view is here argued. Muslims are, generally speaking, innocent - they are NOT doing these events.

State-fabricated terror across Europe follows on from the great progenitor event of 9/11 - which was not what it appeared to be. These events are theatrical. They are designed, and their purpose is Eternal War - just like George Orwell predicted.

We here analyse fourteen of these big 'terror' spectaculars. This is alas the main art-form of the 21st century. You need to know, how crisis actors are bring used to fool you.

Dedication

Over the years, a monthly *911 Keeptalking* group has been meeting in London, which has focused upon these issues. It was a successor to the old 9/11 truth group which broke up in 2010. These chapters have emerged from seminars within the group. I dedicate this book to the good people in it.

We must stress the idea, unfamiliar and suppressed as it is, that the vast majority of international terrorism conducted on a spectacular scale is indeed state-sponsored terrorism.

Webster Tarpley.[1]

Most terrorists are false-flag terrorists or are created by our own security services. In the United States, every single terrorist incident we have had has been a false flag, or has been an informant pushed on by the FBI.

Robert David Steele — a 20-year Marine Corps infantry and intelligence officer, and former CIA clandestine services case office, speaking on the Max Keiser show.

Rage, rage against the dying of the light

Do not go gently into that good-night

Dylan Thomas

CONTENTS

Prologue

9/11 was the transcendent phony event ushering in this new millennium.

The collective intelligence of the British people does alas, *not* extend to comprehending who was responsible for designing and perpetrating that event. Even the motive to try and do this is absent.

The modern meaning of state-sponsored terror involves the state *killing its own citizens* for the purpose of creating an illusory narrative. As the film *V for Vendetta* asked in this context, who could be so wicked?[2] Can one answer that dire but inescapably relevant question?

This book is a meta-political text, concerning the fundamental process that politicians in the western world are not prepared to see - or at least not allowed to talk about - whereby illusion is fabricated.

The Enemies of Mankind create delusion, to instil fear in the public, and prepare them for whatever new war is planned. US and UK politicians behave as if they had no other option, but to promote and deal with the hate-images that are thereby conjured up. Our capacity to apprehend what it means to be human and to realise our hopes and dreams is extinguished in proportion as we accept these great war-ratifying untruths.

The perpetrators remain hidden, whereas the blame falls in a very public manner - this is the new art-form, made by *Those Who Create Delusion.* The very worst characteristic of the British people is thereby appealed to - the need for a collectively-shared enemy image, the need to demonise 'the Other,' the togetherness that is experienced though hating the Other.

What Is 'False-Flag' Terror?

False-flag terror is a term whose meaning has only become evident in this 21st century. Some kind of central, controlling force appears to be using this principle, this trick, or deceit, over and over again, but what is it? A scholarly political science course would need to grapple with this topic, if it is to have relevance. As a founding member of Britain's 9/11 truth movement, which began in the year 2003, I became involved in the deceptive tragedy of the London bombings of 2005.

False-flag terror is an intentional and mortal trick whereby blame is projected and made to fall upon an innocent third party. It has the specific and diabolical purpose of demonising an 'enemy' normally with the purpose of facilitating a war. It involves the State or elements of the State conspiring to kill its own citizens and that depends upon media collaboration, whereby the national media will project the required narrative. It leads to an increase in funding to the perpetrators, viz., the security services, the CIA, MI5, Mossad, etc., who use it to argue how necessary is their work. It promotes a dualistic and simplistic political landscape, of good-guys versus bad-guys, where the bad guys do evil *because* they are bad, and where truth-activists can be scoffed at as 'conspiracy theorists'- or, if that doesn't work, as a threat to national security.

It is an act of enchantment.

It is threefold, in that there is firstly a perpetrator, who aims to remain hidden, secondly a victim, and thirdly the innocent party on whom the blame falls. It used to be the case that some large or significant number had to be killed, so that the country experiences itself as under attack. Collusion of elements of the state security is needed to protect the guilty and frame the innocent.

These days the 'enemy' is Islamic, before which we look back to the European 'Operation Gladio,' starting in the 1980s, constructed to demonise 'the Reds', i.e., Communists, which successfully prevented the Italian Communist party from becoming part of a coalition government in Italy. How, after all, would NATO have been able to maintain its purpose in Europe, if the Communist Party were seen to be forming a part of Italy's government? So NATO officials - some of them - did the terrible thing, in secret.

Once the public trust has been thus betrayed, the people and groups responsible can in futurity be blackmailed and manipulated. Thus the 21ˢᵗ century kicked off with NATO in Brussels agreeing to fight in Afghanistan - thereby nullifying the North Atlantic Treaty of 1949 on the basis of which it was founded - in a trice, on no evidence whatsoever.

The European story of state-fabricated terror started around 1969 with what was called 'Gladio' or the Strategy of Tension: NATO's presence in Europe was used to keep people frightened of Communism. This was well exposed in 1990 by an Italian government investigation, and covered brilliantly by Daniel Ganser's book[3] then more recently by that of Richard Cottrell.[4] We touch upon it briefly here. Once the Soviet Union collapsed in 1991 that enemy image swiftly vanished and the Communist menace could no longer be invoked to explain what dozens of American bases were doing all around the world. A new demonised enemy had to be nurtured and gestated, which wasn't easy and took a whole decade - a process which has involved *state-fabricated terror*. A new Aeon of Darkness thereby opened which is where our story mainly begins, *centred on* and revolving around the terrible event of 9/11.

A US expert, formerly a CIA clandestine Services Officer, described the process as:

> A false flag event is one in which the alleged perpetrators, their motives, and the outcome are fabricated. It generally includes very real dead people and often includes very real terrorists, using very real bombs and bullets, but the entire script, the enabling logistics, and the prepared narrative that quickly follow are designed to meet the need of the deep

state and its financial masters - both of which are very international in nature, with no national loyalties to speak of...[5]

That tells us that such events are quite internationally - or even globally - organised and that we may be unlikely to find the actual perpetrators.

False-flag terror is something that has largely come over to Europe from America. Why should that be? There is an awful simplicity in the answer:

> No country in the world would want to attack America.
>
> America wants war for its imperial designs.
>
> The US population does not consent to unfair aggression.
>
> Therefore, state-fabricated terror has to be arranged.

There is more to it than that, of course, in that America needs an external enemy to function: with Communism gone in 1991, centripetal forces would have disintegrated the US had not the supreme new terror-event seared its soul with the most dramatic spectacle ever seen - in order to create, *the Phantom Menace.*

A colleague R.R. was working on the Channel Four News program back in November 2001. Various well-known TV producers were sitting around, before the program went out, and sharing a good laugh over the absurd new 'fatty Bin Laden' tape the Pentagon had come up with. This was shortly after the bombing of Afghanistan had begun, and this tape was meant to corroborate Bin Laden's guilt. It was the nearest thing to evidence, or a reason for bombing one of the poorest countries on earth, that America ever came up with. The character was meant to be a lookalike but could hardly compare with OBL's tall, wiry frame. He wore his ring on the wrong hand, got the month of Ramadan wrong, etc. After the Channel Four news team had all finished laughing, they put out the news report, deadpan - as if it were the real thing.[6] Do we have *any* national media that can be trusted? Or does only *Russia Today* remain?

An opposite view, to that here expressed, is found in the best-selling book *Voodoo Histories* by David Aaronovitch of 2010, which conveyed the mainstream media view. Why, of course, President Kennedy was shot by Lee Harvey Oswald, alone and unaided, and surely Lady Di died in an unfortunate car accident, and yes, Dr Kelly did just decide to take his own life; sure nineteen Muslims armed with box-cutters hijacked four planes on the morning of 9/11, and flew them into the Towers - and, yes, Muslims did 7/7, the Bali bomb etc. Going back a bit, yes Israel's 1963 attack on the *USS Liberty* was merely an unfortunate accident. Has any other book ever packed in *so much untruth* into a mere three hundred pages? It received glowing reports from the British media, because it ratified their own bird-brained view of 'terrorism'.

A *semi-metaphorical language* is here used to describe what is happening, with terms such as the Enemies of Mankind, Those Who Create Delusion, the necro-technocrats, the Axis of Evil (the military intelligence of the

US/UK/Israel), the Vampire Elite, and 'mirror logic'. This will hopefully enable us to focus upon the deep process going on rather than the names of transiently-forgettable politicians, and also help us to avoid 'ultimate' questions as to who is behind the process - where one should expect irreconcilably different views. Some, for example, may believe that the Jesuits are behind it all, or bankers, or the freemasons, or the 'Khazarian Mafia' or maybe shape-shifting reptilians from outer space! Such semi-metaphorical language may enable us to maintain a degree of calm, and also to reach consensus over the central issues.

The stories here presented have many transient and forgettable details, that vanish down the memory-hole, as they are supposed to, leaving an image of terror hanging in the air. Could this be a book that you *need* to read, but don't *want* to, because of all these details, names of people you don't want to remember, etc.? One can only reply that some kind of power appears to be seizing possession of our world, and it is a malign power, which cannot be fought by force of arms, but *can* be resisted by exposing the illusions it fabricates to the light of truth. We are sometimes able to find that, we are potentially able to see the truth - that is our strength.

We are here concerned to rescue a lot of close-focus detail around these events: before a crime is solved, a police department has all sorts of clues and leads pinned up on the wall. This work will be successful if it enables you to have a thoughtful conversation on the matter, by becoming well-informed about the central issues, but hopefully without pressuring you unduly as regards any conclusion concerning who may be ultimately behind it. This work may not be conclusive about who is really 'behind' these dreadful events, which more exciting books will reveal to you. I am privileged to no secret knowledge.

These are events which work by deception, keep the people living in fear, and promote right-wing government.

The Gunpowder Plot: LIHOP or MIHOP?

According to the orthodox, old-fashioned view Salisbury *discovered* the conspiracy, a second judgement is that he *nourished* it, and a third that he *invented* it.

-Archbishop Matthew[7]

A proper teaching of the story of Guy Fawkes in a school history syllabus would here be an enormous help. It would maybe start with Lord Cecil, the Earl of Salisbury, surely the great mastermind who plotted in 1603 how to turn Catholics into the new national enemy - using, as we now know, barrels of dud gunpowder that could never have blown up. Ah, how a school history lesson would come alive, if only schoolchildren were allowed to debate LIHOP (Let it Happen on Purpose) versus MIHOP (Make it Happen on Purpose)[8] in this context! Lady Antonia Frazer's *The Gunpowder Plot* (1995) presented the LIHOP thesis whereby Lord Cecil apprehended a pre-existent plot, and *allowed it to proceed* for his own nefarious political agenda; whereas the more definitive

Enigma of the Gunpowder Plot (2005) by Francis Edwards argued the MIHOP case whereby Cecil brewed it up, he concocted it.

No terror was involved because no one was terrified, except the plotters. Two of the Gunpowder Plot crew were double agents and the rest were patsies - if we may use the modern nomenclature rather than that of the late Francis Edwards. The history that matters, today, *above all else,* is of that deceptive process whereby our future is being stolen away from us. Pupils would love to hear of this plot, because it helps to make sense of the world we are living in. King James I may have wanted some reconciliation with and friendship towards Spain, however the success of this plot took matters somewhat out of his hands and led to a century of war with Spain. Yes that's right, *a century of war with Spain.*

The intelligence agency enjoyed *too much power*: shortly after Cecil's death, a Mr John Chamberlain wrote about him:

> He juggled with religion, with the king, queene, theyr children, with nobilitie, parlement, with friends, foes and generally with all.'[9]

What an epitaph!

We may wish to meditate quietly upon the fact that the terrible year of the London bombings, 2005, was the 400th anniversary of the Gunpowder plot, saw the first definitive text about that plot published, and furthermore, saw the publication of Daniel Ganser's definitive text *NATO's Secret Armies,* about how postwar Europe has been ruined or had its democratic processes greatly undermined by secret clandestine armies. A terror-menace was mocked up to make sure that right-wing military held onto power. Both books concern state terror, one in centuries gone by, the other in our present. You may here wish to read Wikipedia's comments about how sadly deluded are the beliefs of Dr Daniel Ganser – not a view here endorsed!

Pearl Harbor in 1941 was a LIHOP event, because President Roosevelt knew it was coming, had goaded the Japanese into a situation where their honour impelled them to attack, had knowingly instructed part of the US fleet to stay bottled up in Pearl Harbor in Hawaii as sitting-duck targets, and had read the Japanese codes concerning their intention to attack. The perpetration of the event was by Japanese fighter-pilots. Thus we say that Roosevelt 'let it happen on purpose' so that he could break his solemn promises about not taking America into war.

To give another example, the prolific British Muslim author, Nafeez Ahmed, has written books about 9/11 and the London bombings, which well-describe the incoherence of the official narratives and how the spectre of Al-Qaeda was brewed up by the FBI/CIA in the late '90s, etc.; yet, at the end of the day, his books affirm quite clearly that Muslims did it.[10] Is that a LIHOP position? Not really, it's more a critique of alleged incompetence of the intelligence services for failing to stop an alleged plot. His books have been widely respected. He holds a university position and *has a career* - a mere impossibility for anyone wishing to express a MIHOP version of these events.

The Guy Fawkes plot was what is here called phantom terror, where a scary image is presented with no real deaths (except the perpetrators). In a very different context, Chapter 6 describes the Heathrow Liquid bomb hoax of 2006, a 'phantom terror' event, which rode on the back of real terror, namely the July 7th (or, '7/7') London bombings. To create fear is the aim. Hundreds of millions of pounds in lost flights by airlines resulted and huge passenger inconvenience, in response to this imaginary terror threat. It helped citizens to realise how lucky they were to have Tony Blair's government protecting them against such things. Peace movements and ministries of peace will continue to be *of no use whatsoever* until they understand these matters.

Phantom Terror

Using the demonised enemy-image, politicians can reach a degree of national unity that is otherwise hard to achieve. The enemy-image is demonised to represent 'pure evil' - they are bad, nasty, and we can all hate them with a clear conscience. This can work to an extent that we do not even need to ask what motive they may have had, they are 'the enemy,' period.

In this 21st Century, being the 'enemy' has a rather specific meaning, in terms of countries which are about to get bombed. That happened for example in the wake of 'Charlie Hebdo.' Here we are *not* concerned with the motive for bombing other nations: one might assume that, as mass immigration of Middle Eastern and African people into Europe is the immediate consequence of our bombing their countries[11,12], it must have been the purpose? All that here concerns us is that we live in a culture that somehow cannot live in peace, but needs war. The horror of this irradiates all other aspects of our culture. We here examine how *theatre* is constructed to establish and maintain the demonised enemy-image. This is the main art-form of the 21st century: state-fabricated terror. It is spectacular and spectacularly successful, and will continue to be so - *as long as the people believe it.*

It has the consequence of enhancing funding of the perpetrator-groups, e.g., the FBI, MI5, etc., as they claim enhanced 'security' is needed to protect society against 'terrorists': those responsible are rewarded. There is a terrible risk in doing this, of course, indeed the state risks everything; which in turn implies that the only real 'enemy' such a state has are the those truth-tellers who are able to perceive the awful tactics whereby the state conspires to kill its own citizens.

Al-Qaeda was dreamed up in the words of Adam Curtis as "a nightmare vision of a secret, organised evil that threatens the world. A fantasy that politicians then found restored their power and authority in a disillusioned age. And those with the darkest fears became the most powerful.'[13]

A bogus narrative has served to open up the vista of Eternal War, functioning as a kind of new founding myth. One may here be reminded of the first Star-Wars episode, 'the Phantom Menace.'[14] The phantom 'enemy' is conjured up by the black arts of deception. Nowadays, citizens tend to expect a worse tomorrow: we do not expect a better future, and that will continue to be the case as long as the bogus narratives of state-fabricated terror, the nightmares which the Empire gives us, are believed in.

Every state-fabricated terror event can be regarded as an intelligence test given to the people: *are you really dumb enough to believe this*? If you are, then your future will get worse: *you will have a worse tomorrow*.

From 2012 onwards, we will here argue, phantom terror events could apparently be fabricated *without any real deaths*, which was a lot *cheaper*. The required negative emotions could be generated by street theatre using fake blood, etc. Actors firing blanks were *good enough*. In the UK, only one TV station was prepared to have an honest discussion about the 'death' of Drummer Lee Rigby (DLR) in 2013 and that was *Rich Planet,* where Richard Hall debated with me on the topic.[15] That caused him to lose his Sky TV slot, owing to a single anonymous complaint.[16] As phantom-terror street theatre, the DLR event was successful, resulting in arson attacks upon mosques all across England, etc. One person who has blogged extensively on this topic, the tattoo artist, Chris Spivey, has been arrested by the police arriving at his home at two o'clock in the morning on an obscure charge of harassment, and given a suspended sentence that prohibits him from blogging on that specific topic.

Nobody died - I here argue - in the street theatre event in Artillery Road, Woolwich on 22nd May, 2013. I initially accepted the line that Drummer Lee Rigby really lived and really died, maybe the day before. (See Chapter 10.) Chris Spivey has taken the view that his identity is artificial and to be sure the various things we have been told about him do seem contrived and don't seem to add up. The people on the scene were *actors;* there were, e.g., no real local policemen on the scene. Britons need to insist that yes, we do need to talk about this subject.

Before deploring such theatre-of-horror manufactured on a London street, citizens may wish to reflect on how much they are enjoying horror stories and movies, and maybe take a more responsible attitude as to whether that enjoyment may be somehow causing their subject-matter to spill over into 'reality' on daily newspapers.

Incoherent Narratives

Belief in such stories will tend to cause a disintegration of the rational mind, of our normal ability to connect cause and effect: if, for example, the world is asked to believe that the 9/11 event - which involved the destruction of *all seven buildings* of the World Trade Centre complex[17] in New York over just a few hours - was accomplished by an old man with a laptop in the Tora-Bora mountains of Afghanistan. Shelfloads of books have been published endorsing this view, and yet it did not happen, *it was not so.*

We try to discern cause and effect, and are thereby dismissed as conspiracy theorists. In the United States, quite a large and massively successful truth movement developed, even having a 9/11 truth journal[18], but nothing of the kind exists in Europe. The purpose of this essay is to call for such, for a pan-European initiative, in evaluating the several and shocking *state-funded terror* (SFT) events. Such meetings could maybe take place in Italy, because that is the one country which has had the courage and integrity to go behind the scenes and investigate and publicly report on the terrible 'Gladio' events there[19] - but we're jumping ahead.

Normally, the stories we are given have *a senseless incoherence*. Returning to the Gunpowder Plot, what motive could the Catholic plotters have had? There were many Catholics in the Parliament who would have been blown up, and had their plot killed the king, the heir to the throne would have been Elizabeth, a Protestant. So, what was the point? The point, of course, was that merely days after on November 10th the brand-new King James Bible was first read out from a pulpit, with British Catholics being denounced. William Barlow, Bishop of Rochester, thundered that the *enemy*, meaning papists, was 'satanic' - and therefore by contrast the king was a godly figure. A simplistic dualism thereby appears, which the dimmest politician can employ to mobilise the masses. The 'wickedness' of Guy Fawkes goes straight into the Book of Common Prayer and stays there for a few centuries![20] The event was *successful* in terms of Catholic homes being burnt, laws being passed restricting their rights, etc. (See Appendix 2.)

Can a child become capable of rational logic, once taught that an old man on dialysis in a cave off in Afghanistan *caused* 9/11 to happen? Dying of kidney failure somewhere in the mountains of Tora Bora, Osama Bin Laden is said - despite his repeated disavowals[21] - to have masterminded the event of 9/11.

The most spectacular, most-viewed event in human history has *a totally incoherent* storyline. If two hijacked airplanes brought down the twin towers by crashing into them, then how come all the other WTC buildings were destroyed as well? It is as if the perpetrators had instructions that everything owned by Larry Silverstein had to be demolished, while everything else should remain intact. Thereby Silverstein solved his asbestos problem and got his insurance payout. No coherent connection exists between the images of two planes flying into the towers, and seven huge buildings being pulverised. *Can coherent thought endure under the impact of these fabricated-terror stories, the new art-form of the 21st century?*

An undamaged passport flutters down from the raging inferno of the 9/11 plane crash into Vesey Street, which runs between the World Trade Centre complex and Building 7, in New York, bearing a name of one of the 'terrorist' hijackers. I love these details, not least because of the haunting sense of mystery: a huge rectangle of buildings gets pulverised in New York City, comprising the World Trade Centre Buildings 1 to 6, the first two being the tall skyscrapers we have all heard about. (One more-or-less has to buy Judy Wood's *Where Did the Towers Go?*[22] to find out about what happened to the other four, which is not 'on the agenda' of politicians.) Outside that rectangle stood a trapezium-shaped skyscraper, 'Building 7,' which likewise collapsed on that day, seven hours after the others - in six seconds - leaving the buildings around it remarkably intact and undamaged. A study of the 9/11 event is the essential basis for investigating the unfolding in modern time, of false-flag terror.

Sitting through Britain's 7/7 Inquest, held in a marquee outside the Royal Courts of Justice in 2011, I noted that none of the passengers on the top deck of the Number 30 bus in Tavistock Square as were interviewed or cross-examined, could recall the large 'gentle giant' alleged to have bombed the bus, Hasib Hussein.[23] Are Londoners not bothered by such anomalies?

In storyland, the 19-year old Hasib Hussein pressed his detonator-button and found that, alas, he didn't get to Paradise, but was still standing in the underground coach. He had to trudge up the escalator at King's Cross and *buy a new battery* at *Boots the Chemist,* then eventually wandered over to the 30 bus and successfully blew himself up. Do Londoners really believe this? I am afraid they do. The holding of such a belief cannot fail to damage their cognitive faculties.

Standing in front of the Edgware Road (or Aldgate) tube stations, one notices that a large proportion of Muslims come and go, at least sixty percent of the populace. And yet four young Muslims - one of religious belief, the other three quite secular - were apparently consumed by a desire to blow up the London Underground - on July 7th, 2005 - at these very stations?

Public debate *has not been allowed* in the UK, concerning who perpetrated the London bombings. 'Truth movement' persons would win any such debate, having sensible arguments and evidence. The official consensus tends to be little more than an instruction to believe an *incoherent story*, plus a demonising of 'conspiracy theorists'. Decent citizens are meant to believe the perpetrators were brown and dead, whereas a 'conspiracy theorist' believes they are white and alive. (The Latin verb '*spiro*' means to breathe, '*con-spiro*' means breathing together) The people of England don't seem disposed to discuss this unsolved puzzle. While reading and watching endless fictional crime stories (yawn), they seem unconcerned to attempt to solve the biggest real-life attack upon England in our lifetime.

When the MH-17 plane was shot down in Eastern Ukraine, to take another example, the story that we were given bristled with anomalies and unanswered questions. Amidst the wreckage, the pile of pristine passports on the grass did not look at all as if they had fallen from the sky. People were quite rightly comparing this to the passport that fluttered down to Vesey Street on 9/11. Analogies like these are important - after all, the perpetrators of these events may even be the same.

An official Dutch Safety Board report emerged a few months later, giving the predictable judgement on who did it by blaming Russia. The sage, Paul Craig Roberts, formerly a chief advisor to President Ronald Reagan, expressed a somewhat resigned view about it:

> The reason that the West has no future is that the West has no media, only propagandists for government and corporate agendas and apologists for their crimes. Every day the bought-and-paid-for-media sustains The Matrix that makes Western peoples politically impotent.[24]

Did that report deserve any further analysis? I doubt it. This comment describes the predicament we are all in, the awful reason for not buying newspapers or watching TV.

The most important political-cultural act we can hope to achieve in this 21st century consists in *perception of truth.* Anyone endeavouring to do this, i.e., to ascertain what is really happening, will be called a 'conspiracy theorist'. We are indeed concerned here to theorise about conspiracies. However, the term has been given a derogatory meaning, especially as used by journalists. Presently (2016) the UK government is taking steps to prevent such views by developing the concept of 'non-violent extremism' which involves - as Prime Minister David Cameron propounded at his September 2014 speech to the United Nations - 'The peddling of lies: that 9/11 was a Jewish plot or that the 7/7 attacks were staged.'

His government has set up a 'national extremism database' because, as Cameron explained, 'to defeat the ideology of extremism we need to deal with all forms of extremism, not just violent extremism .... We must stop the so-called non-violent extremists from inciting hatred and intolerance in our schools, our universities, and yes, even our prisons.'[25] I gave myself up to Scotland Yard with a copy of *Terror on the Tube*, because as a law-abiding citizen, I felt that these words had to apply to me - but the police sergeant refused to arrest me. [26]

The Queen's speech of May 2016 pledged that her government will introduce legislation to tackle 'extremism in all its forms'. *What are the forms of extremism?* Reading this book might even count among them.

On Omitting 9/11

We try to follow the advice of the philosopher, Wittgenstein:

> *Of that which you know, speak clearly. Of that which you do not, remain silent.*[27]

As the millennium-determining event, 9/11 unleashed the dark *Moira* of America's destiny in its dedication to Eternal War.[28] Seeking out its predecessors, we turn to the 1993 World Trade Centre bombing and the 1995 Oklahoma Federal Building explosions. For both of these events, the judge at the trial would only hear evidence concerning a single 'lone nut' who was accused,[29] and so we will always lack adequate accounts of them. (There is a fine book on these precursor-events by Len Bracken.[30]) The Oklahoma Federal building looks as if it were demolished in the same way as the three World Trade Centre buildings would be six years later, through some destructive technology placed inside it. In both cases, an outside agent was made responsible so that 'blame' could be allocated. The truck blast at Oklahoma (blamed on Timothy McVeigh)[31] could not have done more than shatter a few windows.

None of us know the 'actual' truth of *What Really Happened*, on September 11th 2001 in America, all these years after the event - which is in itself quite mysterious. What has called itself the 9/11 Truth Movement fractured into a pragmatic core, which said, we are not to be distracted by the various baffling enigmas of what happened, but merely campaign on the slogan '9/11 was an Inside Job' and advocating Islamic innocence. The excellent series of books by the American theologian, David Ray Griffin, for example, uses such negative arguments, being concerned to ascertain what did *not* happen, and thereby show that the government's view cannot be correct. There is still no better intro book to give to your friends than his *9/11: The New Pearl Harbor*. But the more usual course of action would be first to discuss what had happened before trying to judge who did it.

In a crime enquiry, the first question has to be, 'What happened?' For example, how many buildings were pulverised at 'Ground Zero' on the date of 9/11? I frankly doubt whether one in five hundred could give a correct answer to that simple question. One hears intense and emotional responses and comments, with a majority believing that 19 hijackers armed with box-cutters 'did it' (never mind that eight of these proclaimed afterwards that they were still alive - identity theft isn't that easy). The answer here is *seven* - the seven world Trade Centre buildings owned by Larry Silverstein were all destroyed on that day, while the other buildings around them stayed remarkably intact.

Three skyscraper buildings were destroyed, the two main WTC buildings plus 'Building 7' which was actually just outside the main square or rectangle of the WTC complex. So you'll often get the answer 'three' if you ask your friends how many buildings were demolished. As far as politicians are concerned, of course, two buildings were destroyed on that fateful day, because that fits in with their childlike narrative concerning the cause of the event, viz., 'terrorists' who flew planes into the buildings. They did it because 'they hate our freedoms' as President George Bush memorably explained.

Seeking for a scientific explanation, most of the group *Scholars for 9/11 Truth* concluded that thermite (or, 'nanothermite') had done it, had transformed the Two Towers of New York's World Trade Centre into several hundred thousand tons of fine, white powdery dust a-blowing in the wind - in ten seconds. The problem here is that thermite is not an explosive, won't go bang, does not detonate, it generates no explosive shock wave. Once ignited it will sustain a high temperature, but is that really enough? And what huge quantities of thermite would it have been necessary to smuggle secretly into the Towers to do this? Fragmenting off this learned consensus was the Judy Wood school which averred that some *unknown* technology was at work. *Scholars for 9/11 Truth* rather broke in two as co-founder Jim Fetzer started leaning towards this Judy Wood option. More recently he has favoured the mini-nuke hypothesis. Strong passions are here involved - as indeed, they should be, over atrocities and cover-ups of this magnitude.

The whole phenomenon has during this 21st century come over to Europe from America. Many books have been written about these US constructed-terror events, but none on the Euro-events. Does Europe itself have the ability to *know* what has happened to it, what is happening to it - or not? Our subject revolves around *cognition*. One is here reminded on the myth of Europa and the Bull, if the Bull carrying Europa away represents the military-industrial complex.

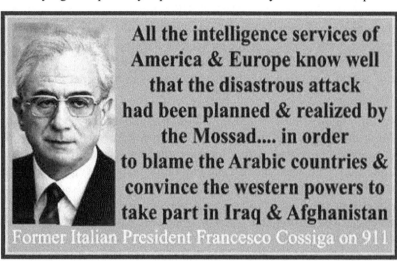

All the intelligence services of America & Europe know well that the disastrous attack had been planned & realized by the Mossad.... in order to blame the Arabic countries & convince the western powers to take part in Iraq & Afghanistan

Former Italian President Francesco Cossiga on 911

Fifteen years after the event, we find not a single European politician prepared to speak words of truth about the 9/11 event. I urge citizens of goodwill not to vote for any politician unless they are in some degree prepared to speak words of truth on this topic. Let's have a roll-call of honour here, of those who have spoken out - and often paid a price: Cynthia McKinney and Dennis Kucinich in America, former German Defence Minister Andreas von Bülow, the late Michael Meacher in the UK (in a guarded sort of way), in Belgium the ex-MP Laurent Louis and in Japan Yukihisa Fujita. The latter has called for an international inquiry. In Italy the former President Francesco Cossiga made the remarkable claim in 2007 that all intelligence agencies knew of Mossad involvement in the 9/11 atrocities.

Whoever did it now controls the world we live in… more or less. That supreme event of 9/11 altered history and shaped the course of this new millennium, extinguishing the worldwide hopes, which the human race was then holding, for a better tomorrow. Did it use some sort of para-science, some not-yet-invented technology that brought the Towers down? Fierce debates rightly revolve around this question, where I can only answer feebly: *I don't know*. I have yet to hear a debate about what brought the Towers down that got anywhere.

Reprobate elements of the US military intelligence conspired to perpetrate the event of 9/11. That is the simplest possible statement that can be made about that millennium-altering event. Deaths were real, but the story was bogus. It allowed the US entry into various Islamic nations to wreck them; and equally important, it achieved a degree of national unity for America that would have been otherwise hard to come by. Does America need an externally-defined enemy image to survive? It had for decades the Germans, and after that, the Communist menace, and when in 1991 that faded away, was its cohesion and unity threatened? Was it rescued by 'Al-Qaeda' the FBI's newly-created terror threat?

Evolution of State-Fabricated Terror

US state-fabricated terror, however, is not the focus here; and yet trans-Atlantic parallels are vitally relevant, insofar as the phenomenon itself may be coming over from America. Thus, the 2012 Sandy Hook 'massacre' supposedly involved twenty schoolchildren being gunned down in class, whereas it has become clear that in reality nobody actually died there and it was an elaborate hoax. The definitive (and, to-date, the only) book on the subject is *Nobody Died at Sandy Hook* (2015) edited by Jim Fetzer - banned by Amazon! - which explained that the event was *just a terror drill*, as requested and funded by the Department of Homeland Security. It did *not* as such 'go live', but its simulated terror did traumatise Americans.

It is helpful to compare such an event with, for example, the Drummer Lee Rigby event in London a year later. That had no real deaths, either, and was all done by actors. Every one of these events - every single chapter here - is a conjuring-trick mystery. They mostly promote the Islamic 'terror' menace, but Sandy Hook was about gun-control and the MH-17 shoot-down of 2014 served to demonise Putin (it was 'Putin's Missile' blared the headline, of the British tabloid, *The Sun*).

The books *Nobody Died at Sandy Hook* and *Nobody Died in Boston, either* (both 2015 and edited by Jim Fetzer) include contributions by the present writer. My decision to omit those events here was made partly because such fine accounts of US events exist in print and there is no need to duplicate them, but also because there are *so many* US events that it would greatly test the reader's patience. We endeavour to develop what has not existed before, a European discourse.

It is a *secret* story, of how state-fabricated terror has covertly developed and unfolded throughout Europe. Those perpetrating these terror-events seem to be concerned to destroy the integrity of the European cultures. By ratifying the attack on Islamic nations in the 21st century, by NATO and the USA - each nation in turn becoming allegedly a 'terror threat' - the vast flood of immigration into Europe - an EU Europe which has abolished any passport controls at national boundaries - has been unleashed. Disquiet has spread among European nations at the rapid influx of Muslims, whose rate of reproduction is far higher than that of the indigenous population.

The fate of Europe depends upon its ability to recognize and see through the bogus reasons for war, which in turn requires seeing through fabricated street-theatre done by feeble actors, such as the Drummer Lee Rigby event in London or the more complicated Charlie Hebdo event in Paris. These events generate hate - as they are meant to do - and then 'hate-crime' legislation is passed, which is designed to target alleged 'conspiracy theorists', who do not accept the official narratives, especially if they mention the role of Israel.

Trains blowing up in Madrid and London in 2004 and 2005 involved real terror, hidden perpetrators and the projection of Islamic guilt. Those events carried over into Europe the new 'Al-Qaeda' menace, and its concomitant 'War on Terror' meme - an exceptionally absurd concept if ever there was one. 'Hate-crime' comes as part of the package of the anti-terror legislation, which means that anyone ruminating on Israeli fingerprints which tend to be discernable in these events is liable to be accused, while the media are informed of the Islamic guilt on the very day of the event.

The helpful concept of how to plan your own disaster has come over from America. Two slides are here shown, from a slide-show of 2008 by the person who planned and designed the Boston Marathon bombing street-theatre performed in 2013.[32] For all the decent folks who have been believing what the TV news tells them, here's a quote:

> The people in those graphic, blood-soaked images were not the victims of the attack. You and I were. - Dave McGowan[33]

It is we who are hit by the emotional trauma, as we're given the awful story of what *didn't* happen. Were 264 people wounded in that dreadful event? Surely not!

We show just two of the slides, out of some three dozen, a guide by Homeland Security in planning your local disaster.

Why, Mephistopheles himself could not improve upon it.

In the year 2016 British citizens began to have to accommodate themselves to large theatre-of terror events on their streets, in shopping malls and a football stadium (Chapter 13). Britons are urged to tell their MPs that they *do not want* such planned disasters in civic areas.

Generally speaking, since 2012 the big state-fabricated terror events - *Drummer Lee Rigby, Sandy Hook, the Boston Marathon bombing, Charlie Hebdo, Westminster Bridge* - have no real deaths and are essentially street-theatre. Whereas earlier on, real deaths and real blood had been necessary, to generate the horror, whereby politicians could then expound on the 'war on terror' and how some new war had to be fought. More recently, crisis actors lying on the pavement, firing blanks, etc. are apparently good enough - and, a lot cheaper.

When in 1994 Israel blew up its own embassy in London, there were no deaths or serious injuries. Those working there conveniently happened to be out of the office when it happened, as we describe in Chapter 2. Years later in 2006 a *phantom terror* event took place, an alleged plan to blow up a load of planes in mid-Atlantic with liquid 'binary munitions'[34] kept in lucozade bottles. You probably don't remember that one, but it caused an awful lot of chaos at Heathrow airport, e.g., mothers were prevented from carrying milk for their children onboard. Do Britons now need the thrill of 'terror'? They seem to! The fiendish plot was discovered just in time - i.e., nothing actually happened - and then various innocent Muslims were rounded up and jailed. No material evidence, e.g., an explosive mixture, existed anywhere, which is why we call it 'phantom terror.' It could 'work,' i.e., be in some degree credible, because of the real terror the year before.

Our study concerns fourteen *state-fabricated terror events in Europe*. All but the first have alleged Islamic perpetrators:

1. Aug 1980   Bologna railway station bombing
2. July 1994   London Israeli Embassy blows up
3. Mar 2004   Madrid, four trains detonated
4. July 2005   London, four explosions
5. Aug 2006   London, Heathrow airport 'terror plot'
6. Dec 2009 Amsterdam Schiphol airport crotch bomber
7. July 2011   Oslo 'Breivik' terror
8. May 7 2013   London Drummer Lee Rigby
9. July 2014   Ukraine MH-17 shot down
10. Jan 2015   Paris, Charlie Hebdo
11. Nov 2015   Paris, Bataclan Theatre

12. Mar 2016   Brussels

13. July 2016   Nice, Munich

14. March 2017   Westminster Bridge

The table includes Israel bombing its own embassy, here described in Chapter 2.[35] Israel scored a propaganda victory by averring that certain Palestinian groups had done it.

The above will be the only list that you have ever seen of major European SFT

events. An undue number were in London, and with US-UK Intel working close together,[36] it should not surprise us that London has played a key role in hatching this diabolical 21st century tactic of political terror and deception.

The pace of these events is certainly accelerating, that's no secret. The Nice event featured a more brazen use of dummies than seen hitherto in such events, plus also it catapulted Mossad into the limelight in a somewhat unexpected manner. Normally the Mossad like to lurk in the background or remain wholly unseen in these events. But, that may be an appropriate finale to the present work.

Two American state-terror events are here of especial relevance: the Sandy Hook hoax in December 2012 and the Boston Marathon of April 2013. The year 2012 marked a decisive change, when crisis actors came to play a major role and real deaths became less necessary.

Crisis actors were first thoroughly used *in place of* any real deaths in those two US events. Readers may wish to doubt this - after all, did we not see real funerals with real caskets and mourning relatives on TV? The shocking story is well argued in the book *Nobody Died at Sandy Hook*. Life-size dummies were first used in the Boston Marathon event, plus prosthetic or artificial limbs to simulate wounds.[37] We need not ask why this was done - although presumably somebody must have reckoned that they looked more convincing than crisis actors lying down. We note the subtitle of the definitive book on the subject: *And Nobody Died in Boston Either: State-sponsored terrorism with Hollywood special effects.*

In the above sequence of European events, dummies start to appear from 2013 onwards: the Drummer Lee Rigby drama featured a rubber dummy thrown into the road, then the MH-17 crash had various dummies lying around on the crash site; the Paris Bataclan had dummies lying about on the theatre floor, after the event, as well a man carrying a dummy, as too did the Brussels event,[38] then the Nice event featured a dozen or more of them lying in the road. Thus it helps to view this unfolding sequence in its entirety. We need to understand what is being done, before we try to infer who might be doing it.

Training for Terror

A US company advertises its dummies as follows:[39]

> A cost-effective manikin when large numbers of casualties are required. They have little weight to them (8 kg) and would be perfect for a large, multi-agency exercise where a large number of casualties/bodies are required to be seen but not necessarily rescued - rather a scenario where emergency rescue teams have to be trained in the triage and management of multiple casualties.
>
> Think: aviation incident, train crash, terrorist blast, large building collapse, etc.

They are 'strong enough to be buried under concrete or steel lintels with no damage.' This is big business, and it *has come over* to Europe.

The US company *Crisis Cast Limited*[40] helps companies to acquire 'resilience' which means planning for the disaster - but where does the simulation end, and can we tell the difference? Its motto is, 'Nothing works as effectively in dealing with real-world disasters as rehearsal.' This company specialises in replicating mass casualty events, in 'Staging Reality.' Its 'emergency protocol disaster training' is carried out with 'internationally credited film crews', that bring their 'high-end stagecraft to life', through a frightening collection of 'role players, stunts, medical simulations and combat flashpoints' together with 'pyrotechnics, wardrobe, special effects, covert and aerial footage,' depending on the client's needs.

Crisis Cast will aim to develop a "joint ability to respond to the press," in a partnership with the company's clients through a multitude of social media platforms on the Internet. But, will it be made clear to the press that this is 'only a drill'? 'Our producers work with your trainers to create a 'script' that enables the roleplay actors to know when to trigger key developments in an evolving crisis management scenario. We brief and rehearse the team - where possible on location - but at least with video surveillance footage.'

Also noteworthy, *Cast* states that it has the ability to create "highly credible, dramatic scenarios to bear preparing your people for the worst," employing both "psychological and practical tools," in their disaster training - all the while making sure that roleplaying actors as well as crew have signed non-disclosure agreements (NDA's) before each scripted event. So the secret will be kept. Here's another passage depicting the kind of psychological implementation used to achieve a successful *Cast* simulation:

> Our roleplay actors are psychologically trained in criminal and victim behaviour. They bring intense realism to simulated mass casualty incidents on the battlefield, during kidnap and ransom and emergency evacuation situations and in hostile threat incidents in urban or public places.

In so doing, *Crisis Cast* 'provides learners with an irrevocable first encounter with the emotional challenges of any hostile incident:'

> The intricate dynamics within a staged crisis are witnessed when 'fictional' European countries are pitted against one another during riot-scene training with the Black Watch, 3rd Battalion, Royal Regiment of Scotland (3 SCOTS).

In his critique of what this company is offering, Patrick Henningsen asks, "Could this kind of 'training' also be used under a modern-day Operation Gladio?"[41]

Many of the events we here review feature not only crisis actors trying to look wounded, but also a template of the terror-drill happening, usually on the same day, which *appears to be controlling* the events. We've seen three slides from the US Boston Marathon event's official planning - but hardly less obvious were the carefully planned drills at say the Oslo-Breivik event, or the Paris-Bataclan event, or the Brussels event.

You might want to accept Olé Dammegard's view, that it's the *same team* doing these events, a sort of travelling terror troupe, a 'Rocky Horror show on steroids' as he put it. Here he is being interviewed by Kevin Barrett:

> Olé: I've come to realise after thirty years of deep investigation that what we're seeing is like a theatre group on a global terror tour being used by the powers behind the New World Order. I believe we are seeing the same people running around in SWAT team uniforms in Paris, Ottawa, Sydney, Copenhagen, and so on. The same crisis actors, the same media people in the background, the same marketing agencies, the same directors. We're looking at a small group, like a rock group on a global tour, repeating the same performance again and again, flown from country to country in military planes, then being transported to locations in buses, helped by local back-ups. I spoke to CIA whistleblower Chip Tatum about this, and he said it's not only possible, it's very probable.

Kevin Barrett: So, we're talking about a troupe of travelling terror troubadours, coming soon to a theatre of operations near you.

Olé: That is my deep conviction. and I've done a lot of work trying to identify people in the background, people in the uniforms. There's a reason why police SWAT teams these days are running round with face masks. It's because they don't want us to recognize them. They claim it's for their protection. But I say, what is the difference these days between what a so-called terrorist looks like and a SWAT team member? And I would suggest that this is why, when false flag terror attacks are carried out, the shooters - most recently in Paris and San Bernardino - are dressed in dark militia-looking clothes...[42]

Later on, in that interview, Kevin Barrett commented (apropos of the Paris event of 11/13/15; see Chapter 13): 'Another connection between the Paris and San Bernardino events is that in both cases, multiple witnesses reported that the shooter teams were white paramilitaries, not the brown-skinned patsies.' Various people made that comment - the San Bernardino 'terror' event happened in California a couple of weeks after Paris Bataclan, both being blamed on Muslims, while both had white shooters observed at the scene and reported. We won't be discussing that US event here, but that striking similarity might have aided Olé Dammegard in reaching his view.

In the 21st Century, the whole process works so well because of the silence of Muslims. Whenever some new terror event is reported, with wicked Islamic terrorists, we can be sure that no Islamic review or newspaper will emerge critiquing the story and casting doubt upon Islamic guilt. That just does not happen. If any 'truth' meetings are held, attempting to evaluate the event in retrospect, one can be fairly sure that no Muslims will be present, or at least it is very rare for them to be present. They are quiet, they stay quiet, they take the blame.

Following the Charlie Hebdo event (Chapter 11), there was one large meeting in London about the event, with about five hundred people present. It was organised by the *Stop the War* movement. Speaker after speaker (e.g., Jeremy Corbyn, Lindsey German, etc.) deplored the new war (the bombing of Syria) with hand-wringing frustration, and deplored the terror attack - but did we hear anyone deconstructing the event, or scrutinising what had just happened? No, we didn't, and moreover, no questions were allowed from the audience as if the organisers were nervous at what might transpire. The whole meeting was quite an emotional experience - as to how together we must oppose terror and support peace, etc. - but, *thought* was blocked out.

It reminded me of an earlier *Stop the War* meeting at Trafalgar Square - the usual terminus of London peace demos - at the 10th anniversary of the invasion of Afghanistan, i.e., in November of 2011: was there a single speaker who would cast doubt upon the ostensible reason for that invasion, viz., that Osama bin Laden dwelling in Afghanistan had caused the 9/11 event? No, there wasn't. Britain's

Stop the War movement seems to have the purpose of blocking out thought: it wants a lot of people marching on demos, it wants to oppose this and that, but will not seek out the causes of events.

Within days of the Charlie Hebdo event, a huge French battleship was dispatched. Presumably to 'fight terror' with 'the allies,' it was off to bomb Syria and start re-bombing Iraq! Might one not have expected the cadre of *Stop the War* intellectuals - politicians and published authors - to discern some intention, some cause-and-effect link here? Britain's *Stop the War* movement experiences amnesia over the conditions of its foundation: it was established in the week following the 9/11 event, and had aimed to stop the 'War on Terror.' Like its predecessor *Campaign for Nuclear Disarmament* (CND), it finds it so much easier to be *against* this and to *deplore* that - rather than to foster an intelligent deconstruction of the fictitious and fabricated phantasms put before the public to justify a war - which is what it ought to be doing. Then we'd have a peace movement that meant something.

> Thus 'truth activists' find that they are supported neither by left-wing nor right-wing movements. How strange that Britain's radical left-wing, Communist, socialist tradition - the latter always appearing to be in control of anti-war demos whenever they happen - has never any interest in deconstructing the terror events, not even 9/11! Supposedly anti-imperialist movements turn out to be based upon fossilised, hundred-year old socialist dogma, concerning the worker's revolutionary struggle which is not much help in this 21st Century and certainly won't stop a war.

This is a European text, an attempt to rescue *Europa*, the soul of Europe. But it does feature a few exceptions that I felt were somehow needed: the Israeli embassy in Argentina in 1992, Bali in 2002, Tunisia in 2015 (Chapters 1 and 3, plus Appendix 4). We here struggle to create a European focus and context for evaluating this subject, even though it may, in essence, have come over from America. That is a paradox, and as you can see we've already commented quite a bit of the 9/11 event in this chapter. The key phrases to ponder here could be 'The tactics of deception,' 'The technology of enslavement', and 'Theft of European sovereignty.'

The present text comes off the Web. A huge number of URLs have been deleted in the process - which could be accessed mainly from my *terroronthetube.co.uk* site. The Bali chapter comes mainly from two films from Down Under on the subject. *Fool me Twice* and *The Truth about the Bali bombings.*

Coming on to the most deeply-forbidden aspect of the whole topic, I have been shocked on drawing these essays together at the repeated theme of Israel-Mossad involvement. Lest I be accused of bias here, please note that my 2009 book *Terror on the Tube* about the 7/7 London event greatly played down the significance of this issue, consigning to a mere appendix all the evidence of Israeli security-firms involved in the event. Almost against my will this theme kept on asserting itself, hidden yet palpable. Some people, e.g., the brilliant geopolitical analyst, Webster Tarpley, just will not go there. But, without going there a study such as this would be totally valueless.

The 'Axis of Evil'

In my youth, I used to ponder the question of how the nuclear arms race kept going, against the wishes of the huge majority of the human race, and against even the will of a majority of citizens in the two nations leading that nuclear arms race, viz., Britain and America. I struggled with the concept of 'mirror logic' whereby those who were leading the nuclear arms race would always project their intent onto 'the Other' who was far away and could be demonised. What I called *Those Who Create Delusion* responsible for maintaining such a process - whereby all the hopes of the human race had to be subordinated to the goals of the military - were not, *as such*, liars. But, they would use the *mirror-delusion* process to ratify each new step.

The *necro-technocrats* acquired virtually unlimited funding by this process, and this meant that the scientific enterprise, which for three centuries had been regarded as a benevolent enterprise, became corrupted. Since somewhere around 1940 it had turned and gone over to the 'dark side.' A turning-point here was the Manhattan Project, a top-secret wartime project to make the A-bomb, halfway through which it became evident that the Germans did not have the Bomb, were not making it, which meant that the declared purpose of the whole enterprise had vanished; however, nothing happened - except that Professor Rotblat walked out of that Manhattan Project, because *it no longer had a reason.* The 'enemy-image' merely transitioned over from the wicked Nazis to the Communists, the Reds. Perhaps at that moment the scientific enterprise ceased to be governed by humane considerations, instead becoming the juggernaut we all know about, of military R&D with its own unstoppable momentum, its core of secrecy, its cadre of intel agents who give the delusional fear-stories to the politicians, who thereby become able to manipulate us through that fear.

As a science historian, I see how for three-and-a-half centuries Britain has pioneered the development of science in terms of the Baconian *knowledge-as-power*, and that has been a heartless knowledge, a materialistic *knowledge-without-wisdom*. Over those centuries of scientific progress do we find any case of a scientist declining an offer on grounds of its military implications? No, in fact we don't.

Here is a graph I produced some years ago from data in the UN Yearbooks.[43]

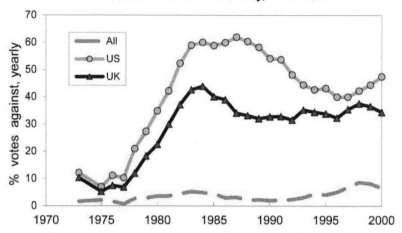

Every year the United Nations would produce a report of motions passed, and it would count separately all those motions given to the General Assembly by way of improving the world to promote world harmony and general well-being. That was what the UN was set up for, wasn't it? Counting these I noticed that every year there were two countries which voted *against* these motions, more often than any others. Clearly, you know which these are. They would vote against them for reasons of 'national security,' that sort of thing. The two other nations 3rd and 4th were Israel and France which also is not hard to guess. For three decades Britain and America were voting *against* motions for global harmony and well-being, more than any other nations. Over these decades, the US and UK have generally been the Number One and Number Two world arms exporters, although of late, Russia has been catching up (see figure).[44]

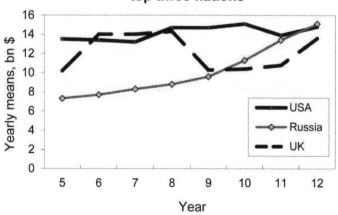

This has created a tail-wags-dog situation where politicians appear as little more than sales representatives of the military. In this 21st Century we have now become horribly aware of the consequence of this, whereby the military *creates theatre* to ensure its well-being and future access to funds, and a politician speaking against this, such as Robin Cook in the UK, can expect a shortened lifespan.[45] This book is about the theatre thereby created, a sort of update on Machiavelli concerning the danger of 'military intelligence.'

The late E.P. Thompson argued that we lived in a phase of culture that he called 'Exterminist:' *exterminism* was, he argued, a phase of civilization - maybe a terminal one - in which the military became so strong and dominant that a tail-wags-dog situation developed, where the politicians became little more than sales representatives of the arms industries.[46]

The tactics of deception *work,* and they work because of the fearfully high stakes involved. 'Surely, they wouldn't do that,' your shocked friends will ask. Just try asking that question to your Irish friends: 'O yes they would' will come the swift reply: they *have* done such things, and *will* again do so.

A 2016 report shows that the UK jails more people and spends more money on its prisons than any other country in the EU[47] and also has the highest EU rate of incarcerating its citizens, at 1.5 per thousand. These sad statistics are *directly related* to what we are here discussing: a dark secret state, which manages things behind the scenes. *How can young men (fifteen times more men than women in UK jails) be expected to tell the difference between right and wrong when they sense that terrific crimes are being committed by those in charge of the realm, who are then promoted for participating, who are honoured for their silence?*

Why did Britain want to acquire five million CCTV cameras, making London the most CCTV'd place on earth? There's *still* no evidence that they reduce crime. The average Londoner is caught on CCTV several hundred times *per day*. Yes, installed in car-parks they can reduce car theft - that is about all that has been established. The events that we here scrutinise are used to justify this undesired and horribly-proliferating surveillance technology. But, oddly enough, their crucial images always seem to be unavailable when these events happen…

Eternal War and False Flag Terror

There exists a *main sequence* of new millennium false-flag terror events, having alleged Muslim perpetrators, which we could outline as:

Table 1: Major 21st Century False Flag Terror Events

11/9/01	New York
12/10/02	Bali
20/11/03	Istanbul
11/3/04	Madrid
7/7/05	London

11/7/06   Mumbai

8/10/06   ***Heathrow Airport***

12/25/09   ***Amsterdam 'Crotch bomber'***

15/4/13   ***Boston Marathon***

22/5/13   ***Drummer Lee Rigby, London***

17/7/14   MH17 Shootdown, Ukraine

7/1/15   ***Charlie Hebdo, Paris***

13/11/15   Bataclan, Paris

22/3/16   ***Brussels airport***

14/7/16   ***Nice***

22/3/17   ***Westminster Bridge***

Those in italics are 'phantom terror' events where nobody or hardly anyone died so there was no actual terror, i.e., fear rather than terror was evoked - or, so I will here argue. Those in italics have what we might call dramatic street-theatre. It is not impossible that other events, the MH-17 shoot down and the Paris Bataclan Friday 13th event could also belong to this category, but it's too early to say.

We can be confident that these events are 'state-sponsored,' meaning set up and created by the 'Axis of Evil', CIA-Mossad-MI6. In general, we cannot know to what extent one or another of these intelligence agencies is involved, as they are so closely interlinked. 9/11 established the image of Islamic terror, for a new kind of war, one 'that will not end in our lifetime' as Vice-President Cheney informed the American people - and, because this menace did not actually exist, but was a mere phantom-illusion, a sequence of follow-up events was necessary to maintain its credibility. Al-Qaeda was put together in the late 1990s by the CIA, in a world where no Muslim group called themselves by that name.[48]

As we entered the new millennium the US/UK became fully dedicated to Eternal War. The question then became not, "Will there be peace?", but rather, "How soon will the US/UK initiate the next war?" Israel is a creation of these two nations and is likewise just as fervently dedicated to Eternal War, indeed, may be said to have pioneered the concept. Until 1991 the Red Menace had justified the vast military budgets - Russia being one of the few sizeable countries in Europe that had never threatened or attacked Britain in its entire history -then the new millennium saw the unfolding of a new enemy image.[49]

After 1991, a decade went by with no defined enemy-image, rather awkward for the military: during that time the UK military budget hardly increased. But during that interlude, some important progenitor events were taking place, examples of what remains to ordinary folk unthinkable, viz., that one's own government (or renegade elements thereof) had devised deliberate terror-events-civilian assassination programs. Why would they want to do that?

The following comprises a minimal, but nonetheless essential, list:

Table 2: Some Pre-9/11 Synthetic Terror Ops

Bologna, railway station	1980
New York, WTC	1993
London, Israel bombs its embassy	1994
Oklahoma City, federal building	1995

Gladio

The ultimate subject you never wanted to know about - you had wished to spend your life on more edifying matters - is: who plants the bombs? A solidly documented starting-point here could be the August 1980 bombing of Bologna railway station.[50] It was successful in that, together with the kidnap and murder of the Prime Minister Aldo Moro, it stopped the Italian Communist party from entering the government; that was the aim. Those designing such events intend the blame to fall on left-wing groups or 'extremists,' which thereby consolidates the power of the right-wing military - in the words of Webster Tarpley, 'Terrorism in the modern era is the means by which oligarchies wage secret war against the people...'[51]

Italy was about to choose to bring its own Communist Party into a coalition government. America and Britain did not wish this to happen and were used secret structures of NATO to make sure that it did not. We choose three quotes.

Webster Tarpley:[52]

> 'If the Italian left of the 1970s and the German left of the same period sympathized with the Red Brigades or the Baader-Meinhof group/Red Army faction, they only showed their own gullibility, since both of these terrorist operations were created by and controlled by NATO intelligence.' The Bologna bombing was 'the biggest terrorist attack in Europe before the Madrid train bombings of March, 2004'.

Tony Gosling:

> Hundreds of innocent people have been killed in false flag terrorist attacks, particularly in Belgium and Italy, where Prime Minister Aldo Moro was kidnapped then assassinated for inviting Communists to join the Italian Government. These attacks were blamed on leftist groups such as the Baader-Meinhof, Red Brigades, etc. which came out of the 1968 student uprisings.... Horrific unprovoked massacres at supermarkets and railway stations, no wonder people want to forget them.

> But we do so at our peril as they explain many oddities with terrorism 'spectaculars' today. 'Gladio' False Flag 'Strategy of Tension' attacks have been going on throughout Europe under the watch of NATO Intelligence's *Clandestine Planning Committee* (CPC) since the 1960s.

It all became public with an Italian Parliamentary Enquiry in 1990 followed by one in Belgium. Make sure your local politicians, soldiers, journalists and police force are aware of Gladio, maybe by giving them a DVD copy of Allan Francovich's BBC *Timewatch* series.[53]

Noam Chomsky:

Put briefly, the "stay-behind" armies of Western Europe - originally organised to fight in the event of World War III - morphed into substantial clandestine political forces with deep roots in European police and intelligence agencies. According to parliamentary investigations, the stay-behind veterans of Gladio appear to have made and broken governments. Elsewhere, they provided channels for intelligence operations and other relationships largely unknown to the elected leaders of a half dozen democratic states. This is important stuff.

'Gladio' acted as leverage for US foreign policy. It extinguished hope,[54] ensuring that the populations of Europe would continue giving their surplus revenue to an ever-growing military. It was imperative that they continue to hate and fear 'The Enemy', would desire US military bases on their soil, and would not elect unduly independent governments. *Ah, how Europe might have developed, had Italy been allowed to incorporate its Communist Party into government!* Italy would at last have happily enjoyed a stable government reflecting majority opinion - while the rest of Europe could have calmly seen how a 'communist' party worked, and so would no longer have needed to hate and fear it - it would no longer have been the bogeyman 'over there.' Reds under the beds could have been exorcised and Europe might even have decided that it could manage to live without having an Enemy.

The EU Parliament did discuss the shadowy network which the Italians had called 'Gladio' in its 1990 debate on the subject. A MEP from Greece then told them:

Mr President, the Gladio system has operated for four decades under various names. It had operated clandestinely, and we are entitled to attribute to it all the destabilisation, all the provocation, and all the terrorism that have occurred in our countries over these four decades ... In fact it was set up by the CIA and NATO which, while purporting to defend democracy, were actually undermining it and using it for their own nefarious purposes.

The Italian MEP Falqui urged:

This Europe will have no future if it is not founded on truth, on the full transparency of its institutions in regard to the dark plots against democracy that have turned upside down the history, even in recent times, of many European states ... There will be no future, ladies and gentlemen, if we do not remove the idea of us living in a kind of double state - one open and democratic, the other clandestine and reactionary.

That is why we want to know what and how many "Gladio" networks there have been in recent years in the Member states of the European Community.[55]

How true! Those words remain as urgent today as when first uttered, and need to be engraved on the walls of some European ministry.

In the conclusion of this debate, the EU Parliament:

> *Condemns* the clandestine creation of the manipulative and operational networks and calls for a full investigation into the nature, structure, aims, and all other aspects of these clandestine organisations or any splinter groups, their use for illegal interference in the internal political affairs of the countries concerned, the problem of terrorism in Europe and the possible collusion of the secret services of Member States or third countries.'

> *Calls upon* the governments of the Member States to dismantle all clandestine military and paramilitary networks...

> *Calls on* the Council of ministers to provide full information on the activities of these secret intelligence and operational services.'

Fine words, but alas, only words! Had they been acted upon,[57] the succession of state terror events here reviewed could never have taken place. It is high time for non-governmental organisations (NGOs) to assemble in Europe, to investigate what are being called SCAD, *State Crimes Against Democracy*, and try to ascertain who the mystery perpetrators might be.

The whole story was published as *NATO's Secret Armies*,[58] by Daniel Ganser - or if you can't afford the £25 for this erudite text, a DVD is available of Allan Francovich's three *Timewatch* 'Gladio' BBC documentaries of 1992 - showing far-right NATO Special Forces gunning down and blowing up hundreds of innocent European civilians. Francovich died rather suddenly of a 'heart attack' in 1997 - itself a CIA speciality - while entertaining the view that train bombings were a NATO/Gladio specialization in the shadowy field of false-flag terror.

The 1980 bombing of Bologna station in Italy had the purpose of preventing the Communist party from coming into the government. It involved Italy's Prime Minister Aldo Moro being assassinated - but, by whom?[59] Not by the Red Brigade, that's for sure. For the far-right who perpetrate these events,[60] it is axiomatic that they will enhance the power of the military and strengthen the apparatus of state security.[61] Such events help the public to hate and fear the correct enemy.

Later, in the 1990s, the Italian state carried out a very thorough evaluation of what it called the 'Gladio' program, whereby certain elements within NATO had endeavoured to 'stop Italy from going communist.'[62] As Henry Kissinger remarked, 'I don't see why we need to stand by and watch a country go communist due to the irresponsibility of its own people'.[63] Italy thereby became the only European state to manage a public evaluation of its own state-fabricated terror.

'Red Bologna' then had the communist party working, quite effectively, in local government. How likely is it that some left-wing or communist movement would choose that very district for an attack? That story will never make sense.

No other European state-fabricated terror events have received anything resembling a credible investigation or enquiry as those of Italy. We, the public, are left with a host question-marks, and with the terrible implication of the event - that those in power over us do not have our best interests at heart but are following some other agenda.

The words of Machiavelli bear the same truth now as when he penned them nearly five centuries ago, if not more so today:

> I say ... that governments should fear those persons who make war their only business ... no one can be called a good man who, in order to support himself, takes up a profession that obliges him at all times to be rapacious, fraudulent, and cruel, as of course must be all those who - no matter what their rank - make a trade of war.[64]

It is the second of these three terrible adjectives which here concern us.

There seem to be *only two books* that deal with our topic, i.e., that have a European focus. One of these is the Ganser book; the other is by Richard Cottrell, *Gladio, NATO's Dagger at the Heart of Europe*. He was Conservative MEP for Bristol for ten years and it's surprising how much he picked up! We will be quoting quite a bit from this erudite and insightful opus. I will not be disagreeing with anything in either of these books. I doubt whether either of these authors would view themselves as 'conspiracy theorists'; rather they are describing 'deep politics.'

Eternal War

'Gladio' was a precursor to the July 7th and Madrid bombs in Europe.[65] The killers are indeed establishing a new empire of darkness in which no one will know the truth and everyone lives in fear. Orwell saw it all so clearly, in his novel *1984*:

> In some ways, she was far more acute than Winston, and far less susceptible to Party propaganda. Once when he happened in some connection to mention the war against Eurasia, she startled him by saying casually that in her opinion the war was not happening. The rocket bombs which fell daily on London were probably fired by the Government of Oceania itself, "just to keep the people frightened."[66]

As British MP, Michael Meacher, has perceptively written,

> The "global war on terrorism" has the hallmarks of a political myth propagated to pave the way for a wholly different agenda - the US goal

of world hegemony, built around securing by force command over the oil supplies required to drive the whole project. Is collusion in this myth and junior participation in this project really a proper aspiration for British foreign policy?[67]

MI5 did in effect destabilise Harold Wilson's government, when the latter refused to send British troops to Vietnam.[68] A comprehensive history of MI6 concluded that 'the modern intelligence service's prime purpose appears to be to generate fears.'[69] How true! But our intelligence services do more than that: after all, the nightmares have to incarnate now and then, taking bodily form.

As regards the racist enemy-imaging that now goes on almost daily in newspapers, you probably don't want to see the ever-growing list of thirty-plus nations bombed by the US since World War II, but here it is. Only one of them has a white-skinned population (Yugoslavia, including Croatia and Bosnia)! `

Table 3: *Nations bombed by the US since WW2* [70]

Japan	1945	Libya	1986-89
China	1945-50	Iran	1987
Korea	1950	Panama	1989
Guatemala	1954-1960	Iraq	1991-2003
Indonesia	1958	Somalia	1992
Cuba	1959	Croatia	1994
Vietnam	1961	Bosnia	1995
Congo	1964	Sudan	1998
Laos	1964	'Yugoslavia'	1999
Peru	1965	Afghanistan	2001
Dom. Republic	1965	Iraq	2003
Cambodia	1969	Pakistan	2004
El Salvador	1981	Yemen	2004
Nicaragua	1981	Libya	2011
Lebanon	1983	Somalia	2011
Grenada	1983	Syria	2014

Overwhelmingly, "bombable" nations have been of a darker skin colour. The Axis of Evil, the US and the UK, is white, from Whitehall to the White House, and its holy-communion-taking leaders go about their normal business of stealing the resources, demonising and bombing nations of darker skin colour.[71]

Admittedly, after Vietnam, *at least three years* went by without the US bombing another nation. Yes, it's hard to believe, isn't it (where the bombing of Vietnam and Laos ended 1973)?

9/11 and 7/7 Compared

On 20th November, 2003, on his visit to London, President Bush became trapped in Buckingham Palace where he was staying. Anger on the streets of London due to the Iraq war prevented him from being able to even wave at a crowd. At last, tomorrow's headlines were going to be about the US President having to cancel all British engagements due to public indignation!

But that couldn't be allowed to happen, of course: he and Blair were rescued by a bomb - in Istanbul, in a nearly empty British embassy.[72] The next day the news was: *Bush and Blair walk tall, defying terror, while foolish peace-protesters fail to apprehend*, etc.

On his next visit, two years later, it was London's turn. Bush arrived on July 6th, shook hands with Blair, and then, as on the previous occasion, a day later the bombs went off. The G8 summit was aborted, the hopes of the world to 'make poverty history' successfully side-lined, and the next month a whole raft of civil liberties were successfully withdrawn from us, the British people. Yes, *terror works* - state terror, that is.

Thereby, Britain has come to perceive itself as a self-bombing nation. Ordinary folk can believe in desperate Muslims immolating themselves. Let's not go into why this is credible - whereas, say, Afro-Caribbeans doing so would not be very credible - and sages like George Galloway can tell us that this is due to their despair over our bombing their nations. That is a very reasonable view, but happens not to be true. However hard one tries, one cannot find evidence of 'suicide bombers' anywhere in London that morning, whereas, there are good reasons for believing that certain bombs were placed under the carriages (or seats) on the morning of July 7th.

Most people are not willing to credit elements of their government with complicity in domestic terror. On days before and after the anniversary of July 7th in 2006, one noticed how Sky News and BBC News both continually presented images of three of the four alleged-bombers in their visit to London on June 28th, 2005, as recorded by CCTV cameras at Luton and King's Cross Thameslink.[73] The time-stamps had been removed to make them look as if they had been shot on July 7th, ten days later. Three of the four suspects had indeed visited London on June 28th for a day-trip. Al-Qaeda (assuming for the moment that it really does exist) cannot do this, it cannot make the BBC show fake CCTV footage for the purpose of deluding the British people. The stunt was successful in that around half of Londoners came to believe that they had seen CCTV footage of the 'Four' in London on July 7th - whereas in reality that was highly questionable. We live in a world where discerning what is real and what is not has become rather difficult and where seeing is no longer believing. Who would want to frame four Muslim youngsters who cannot defend themselves, with bogus film played and replayed in the background to ... news reports? *Who indeed?*

A year after July 7th, the Home Secretary finally admitted to Parliament that the 7.40 am train from Luton to King's Cross had not run that morning.[74] I, who had discovered this, was suddenly catapulted into the limelight. The Official Narrative[75] had claimed to have CCTV coverage of the lads getting onto that train, plus the witnesses in the train who noticed them, four Muslims with large rucksacks; then, finally, *after a year, we are told there was no such train*. It happened that all the trains from Luton to London that morning were severely delayed due to an unexpected accident, which meant that there was no other train that would have transported them between the announced CCTV pictures at Luton, and King's Cross. We would all like to have a Public Enquiry, but the powers that be will make sure we do not get that. We the public cannot be allowed it; the truth cannot be allowed to be revealed.

By Tuesday, 12th July, 2005, police claimed to have identified the remains of five bodies altogether, either from 'forensic evidence' or I.D. remaining nearby, and this happened to include *all but one* of the Muslim 'bombers.' Quickly, the trail led up North to Leeds. But ... if there were 56 bodies altogether, that count taken on the 12th was mathematically impossible. From a mere one-eleventh of the total victims, that three of the four of the previously-unsuspected perpetrators should happen to be included was too improbable, i.e., it was proof of the fabricated nature of the official story.

The public are shown a doubtful, photo-shopped image (of four alleged bombers entering Luton station), but in general failed to notice this. We are bombarded with untruth through our media, because journalists print what they are told, having no time to listen to both or all sides' point of view, but have to commit themselves in print right away. The truth that matters can be found on the Web, as an expression of the collective intelligence of the human race, whereas it is hardly to be found in a newspaper. A politician standing up on his hind legs and braying about the Islamic terror menace can be fairly confident of the ensuing news reports.

'Is this part of the exercise?' asked the NORAD official, at about 9.20 am, on September 11th, on hearing of the multiple plane hijackings. July 7th needs to be understood in the wake of 9/11, and this is primarily so in regard to the terror-drill that was going on at the time of this event, using the same tube stations, and the same morning - Peter Power's exercise. The terror-drill metamorphosed into the real thing, just as did the war-games and terror drills on the morning of 9/11: planes flew into buildings on the morning of 9/11, while radar operators were unable to tell whether the blips on their screens were real planes or just part of the game-simulation - as the game played out and USAF exercise-drills became real. The perpetrators get the cover they need. The No. 30 bus blows up on July 7th - not on its route, after having stopped, not at a bus-stop, in Tavistock Square, with all its CCTV cameras switched off-its whole top neatly lifts off.

For both events the world was informed as to who had done it within hours after it had happened, before the police could possibly have reached any conclusions. Then we were assured that no public enquiry into the event would be necessary. Bin Laden had done it, as Bush told America a day or so after 9/11. Britons were told by Blair that Muslims were responsible for the July 7th event at 6 o'clock on the very same day. Both announcements used the same script, claiming that an enquiry would divert essential resources from the 'war on terror' that had to be fought.

Tony Gosling has slammed the BBC over its reporting:

> July 7th: Through systematic bias and a criminally complicit government the BBC, which the public is legally forced to fund, has turned on us and become an accessory to the crime. Despite the wealth of evidence to the contrary, the Corporation's misleading and partial coverage is that of the discredited Metropolitan Police and MI5 anonymous 'narrative' line of unproven but 'obvious' Islamic guilt. After London's most devastating attack since the blitz, Londoners are told there will be no enquiry and to: 'trust us, they're suicide bombers'.

> The Corporation crossed a lethal professional line when it decided to refer to the four 7/7 suspects as 'suicide bombers'. By rubber-stamping Muslim guilt here in the UK, ignoring Peter Power/Visor Consultants' parallel exercise; the Netanyahu/Scotland Yard warning and other hard facts, the Corporation has taken on a leading role in an anti-Muslim pogrom. BBC actions now fly in the face of its motto carved on Broadcasting House, 'Nation Shall Speak Peace Unto Nation', as its one-sided presentation of the facts of modern terrorism plays into a Neo-Con/Zionist case for a religious war against Islam and for Islamic oil ... A professional journalistic blunder is committed with almost every new story of a 'suicide bomber'.'

A year after the 7/7 event, on the anniversary, we were told that Mohammed Khan's will had mysteriously appeared, and that it declared his intention of self-martyrdom. Finally, his widow Mrs Patel was shown it.[76] Four years earlier, the will of Mohammed Atta had been allegedly found in baggage somehow prepared for the 'suicide plane' but left behind, declaring his intent to martyr himself. No one got to see it. We discern a similarity of narrative here, with the same low-credibility, B-movie scriptwriters at work. Atta wasn't on the plane; Khan wasn't in London.

Many folk believe they have been shown pictures of the alleged 19 hijackers or at least of Mohammed Atta in one of the airports involved on 9/11 (e.g., Boston's Logan airport). They haven't-there were no pictures of any hijackers at any of the airports in question, nor evidence for any of them having been on the planes, except for the dodgy phone calls. What the public were shown instead was Atta at Portland Airport, Maine, on his way to Boston. Furthermore, analysis of the time-stamp shows the image not to have been taken that morning but probably on the previous day.[77] This is all distinctly comparable to the July 7th setup four years later, where a faked photo at Luton was all that was offered to the public, with efforts made to lull them into believing that they had seen images of the four in London on that day.

Britain has little by way of Muslim terror threat. It has angry Muslims, because we keep bombing their nations, but regrettably and all too often, British Muslims accept the blame and guilt they are offered. Muslims especially within the Stop the War movement should take a stand on this issue. From white, anti-war campaigners one hears the identical refrain: 'O, I'm not really into conspiracy theories' which translated means 'Shut up and take the blame.' Do you really want to take all that guilt? It seems to be an integral part of the Anglo-Saxon psyche, that the Enemy is needed out there, and it works in this age as a major social control mechanism.

Thierry Meyssan, manager of the French Voltaire Network intelligence service, surveyed false-flag terror events in South America. Israeli agents had usually caused them, he found, while Muslims got blamed:

> It is lamentable to be able to assert that all the enquiries into the terrorist attacks imputed to Muslims are inconclusive, whether it is a case of Buenos Aires, New York, Casablanca, Madrid or London. Although that doesn't prevent the neo-conservative governments and their "experts" from drawing sweeping conclusions. The US has a habit of modifying retrospectively the perpetrators of terrorist attacks against themselves, according to their real or imagined adversary of the moment. Now they are rewriting the history of other peoples' terrorist attacks. Finally, it is advisable to be vigilant with regard to warmongers who want to evoke the Buenos Aires attacks in order to categorize some or other group or government as "terrorist" and call for their eradication.[78]

Fake Terror

There are a various such events, sordid packs of lies, such as the 'Ricin Plot' used to prime the British people for the Iraq war (Chapter 6), but you might well not want to remember them. These are cheap events because nothing actually happens and nobody dies, but fear is (hopefully) generated. The dastardly plot to 'blow up 9 US-bound airliners' flying out of Heathrow by fiendish Al-Qaeda terrorists was unmasked just in time (no tickets, no bombs, not even passports?) but then a *Guardian* survey showed that only 20% of the British people believed the story! Hundreds of millions of dollars were lost over airport delays etc., due to ultra-tight security that suddenly became necessary. This nine-plane episode, widely compared to 9/11, had the important function of softening up the public during Israel's act of naked aggression against Lebanon.

An 'imminent' event was about to bring 'mass murder on an unbelievable scale,' according to the Deputy Chief of the Metropolitan Police in London (Chapter 6). 10th August, 2006 and 9/11 comparisons were all over the front pages. Britain's Home Secretary complained that some people still "don't get" why we had to abandon traditional liberties. Citizens were being arrested because they *might have been intending to* do something. 'We will now never know if any of those arrested would have gone on to make a bomb or buy a plane ticket,' as was remarked in the sole sensible critique to appear in the UK media, by Craig Murray in *The Guardian*.

Nafeez Ahmed posted up an exposé of this fabricated tale,[79] then a week or so after posting this, Ahmed's uncle was gunned down in Pakistan in front of his wife and kids. Ahmed has published a scholarly book about the July 7th bombings plus a highly regarded one about 9/11,[80] and his books contain in-depth analyses of how 'Al-Qaeda' groups have been set up and sustained by the CIA and MI6.[81] He is the only British academic to publish important material on our theme. As a Muslim daring to speak out on these vital issues, did he have to pay a price?

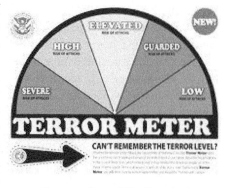

A progenitor of this non-event at Heathrow was MI5's bland announcement two years earlier that it had foiled a sinister plot by Al-Qaeda to fly a plane out of Heathrow and crash it into Canary Wharf. MI5 did not feel obliged to produce any scrap of evidence for this slur upon British Muslims. The tale had come from 'a collusion of imaginative government lobbyists and lapdog media collaborators,' as Prison Planet correctly noted.[82]

The media will print any false-flag terror story from an official source. Our last table can be reduced to merely four items; after all, they are events which did not even happen.

Table 4: 'Foiled' false terror in UK

Ricin plot	January 2003
'Crevice' arrests	April 2004

Canary Wharf   November 2004

9 Planes Heathrow   August 2006

Both Madrid and July 7th seem to have had military-grade explosive actually used, with later stories brewed up about amateur explosives which local 'terror-groups' could supposedly make. Still less credible was the liquid explosive used at Heathrow on 10th August, 2006 - or rather, which might have been intended to be used - to be mixed in the plane's toilet. A phantom is woven together, having a mere semblance of being, to instil fear. *The people have to live in fear* - that is the fundamental axiom of modern politics. The deaths are real, the perps walk away, scot-free, and the phantom of 'Muslim terror' hangs in the air.

All through the Cold War, the US/UK had projected its own diabolical designs upon the 'Other' beyond the Urals: whatever new mega-death weapon was to be assembled, it had to be done out of prudence, because the 'Other' was maybe already doing it. This delusion-logic mandated politicians to give ever more funding to the military, whose 'intelligence' was unaccountable and not transparent. The US/UK led more or less every step of the nuclear arms race.

Deep in the Anglo-Saxon psyche, there lurks a togetherness that is gained from that hate-and-fear image. People have been reared on films in which the enemy threatens our whole way of life, and has to be blasted to bits in the last reel. Ordinary citizens are grateful to their leader for telling them who to hate and fear - just as George Orwell predicted. Actually, this country has no need of an enemy. Ever wonder why all the hopes and dreams of your youth - about socialism as the sharing out of our common-wealth, whereby we could be happy together, yes that's right, be happy - why none of that ever happened? Who stole your dreams away and gave you all these nightmares? Muslim terror groups?

Nope, try harder!

1

Israel Bombs its Own Embassy
Argentina 1992

The Phantom Truck

On 17 March 1992, on a busy street of Buenos Aires, in the early afternoon, the three-story Israeli embassy was entirely demolished: 'a pickup truck driven by a suicide bomber and loaded with explosives smashed into the front of the Israeli Embassy located on the corner of Arroyo and Suipacha and then detonated. The Embassy, a Catholic church, and a nearby school building were destroyed.' - or, at least, that is *Wikipedia's* story. In fact, we shall here argue, no trace of any such car-bomb existed, nor was there any suicide bomber, nor did any witness testify to seeing one; nor were other buildings adjacent destroyed, but merely had windows broken. Quoting from a more reliable source:

> although the shock wave broke glass windows and plaster of practically all the buildings across the street from the Embassy - even blowing in the vitraux of a church across the street, which sadly fell on a priest and killed him - the only building structurally affected was the Embassy itself.

A car bomb soon became the official story, but would you really want to believe that its blast could have worked in so selective a manner? We quote further from this expert (Salbuchi[83]), below.

Two years later, a seven-story building nearby was reduced to rubble, belonging to AMIA, *l'Association Mutuelle Israélite Argentine*. Again, a car-bomb was alleged as the cause, but a US explosives expert who was part of the investigation, Charles Hunter, identified "major discrepancies" between the car-bomb thesis put forward and the blast pattern recorded in photos. A report drafted two weeks later noted that, in the wake of the bombing, merchandise in a store immediately to the right of AMIA was tightly packed against its front windows and merchandise in another shop had been blown out onto the street - suggesting that the blast came from inside rather than outside. Hunter also could not understand how the building across the street could still be standing if the bomb had exploded in front of AMIA.

The AMIA building blew up killing 85 innocent Argentinean civilians and wounding 230. Once again the casualties were mainly Argentineans and only a few Jews. Those killed were all Argentine citizens, and the whole tragedy fell strictly under Argentine jurisdiction. None of the Israeli personnel in charge of security were killed in either of the two terrorist attacks.

On the day the first explosion took place, President Carlos Menem officially requested the assistance of the FBI and CIA from the United States and the Mossad intelligence service and the armed forces of Israel. Why, how very thoughtful of the President. Years later, these same guys somehow turned up immediately after the Bali bomb in Jakarta to 'investigate' it - and that was without even having been invited.

It was soon alleged that car bombs had caused both of these events, despite a complete absence of witness testimony. A court hearing in 2004 continued to insist on the car bomb thesis despite the testimony of at least a dozen witnesses, who swore blind that there was no car bomb. This was dealt with in a section of the report headed "Those who didn't notice it" [i.e., the car bomb]. E.g., Gabriel Alberto Villalba: "He related that…. his glance being directed towards the police patrol car in front of AMIA, he saw suddenly an explosion which came out of the main entrance of the building, from the inside outwards, which covered everything," and "a ball of fire which came from the building towards the street".

Another witness, Juan Carlos Alvarez, was a street cleaner standing in front of the main entrance just where the car bomb was meant to have passed - he would have been knocked over by it - when the explosion happened. Miraculously, he survived, the doorman with whom he had been speaking only seconds before dying instantly. He also failed to "notice" the car bomb, laden with 300 kilos of explosive, turn at speed, its brakes screeching as it came straight at him. He paid a heavy price for his insistence: in an article which appeared in October 2006 he recounts how his treatment at the hands of the prosecutors nearly led him to suicide. He suffered terrible after-effects from the bombing and now lives in poverty in Buenos Aires without the medical support that he needs. Effectively, the court claimed that the failure of these witnesses to see the car bomb was attributable to post-traumatic stress rather than to the more obvious explanation that it simply wasn't there.

The investigation of the 1994 bombing by the Argentine judiciary, which had no political independence from the executive branch, has had little credibility with the public, because of a bribe by the lead judge to a key witness and a pattern of deceptive accounts based on false testimony.

Security Staff Unhurt

1996: Towards the end of the year a document entitled "Buenos Aires police are being scapegoated" is circulated, presumed to come from within the Federal Police. It questioned, in an ironic manner, the car bomb thesis, listing all the witnesses who say that there was no car bomb. It mockingly questioned how the car bomb managed to make it to the fourth floor, the epicentre of the 1994 explosion, and points out the exceedingly suspicious circumstance that none of the Israeli personnel in charge of security were killed in either of the two terrorist attacks.

May, 1997 The report of the National Academy of Engineers, commissioned by the Supreme Court, is heard. On the insistence of Beraja and DAIA this was held behind closed doors. However, the 77-page document came into the possession of Libre Opinion, who published a summary on their website. In their report, these experts expressed their absolute certainty that the explosions at the Israeli Embassy came from bombs within the building.

"The day after this session, the spokesman for the Israeli Embassy in Buenos Aires deplored these conclusions and accused the Supreme Court of anti-Semitism." Absolutely no witness recalled seeing the Renault van. The Israeli army turned up after the event, planted a flag in the rubble, and then one soldier 'found' a twisted fragment of Renault van. The existence of this phantom van has become central to such arguments. The final death toll was 29 killed, and 242 wounded. Several Israelis died, but most of the victims were Argentine civilians, many children.

The Israeli military, Shin Beth, presumably supplied the actual bombers. They held complete security at the embassy so no lay-person could ever have brought in a bomb of that size. The Shin Beth refused to allow an independent investigation of the embassy, only allowing Mossad allowed access to the site. The 1994 destruction of the seven-story AMIA building would have similarities to the Oklahoma City bomb two years later.

Wrecked from Within

We quote from a question which Jim Fetzer (who visited Argentina and became interested in the event) put to Adrian Salbuchi, on a radio discussion of 13.10.09):

JF: What similarities do you find with other attacks in the US on 9/11, in the UK on 7/7, and in Madrid on 3/11?

AS: Well, they all seem to have the same "fingerprint" so to speak. These false flag events all had near-perfect technical performance, where the buildings the perpetrators wanted to blow up and collapse, always did so - reflecting massive technological support and planning. In each case they left "loose ends" that could not be explained away - the inconsistencies showed through in a glaring manner. The stories all had episodes of planted evidence. Common people - the workers - died, while the elite - ambassadors, CEOs, governors, billionaires - were "luckily" out of the buildings at the time. Finally, they all served to support the "Global War on Islamic Terror".

Argentina needs the assistance of philosophers - rather than politicians, lawyers or journalists - who are able to tell the difference between what is real and what is not. The media sneer at those who study these events, as 'conspiracy theorists.' Media hacks, having sold their souls to Corporate Untruth, are annoyed at persons who refuse to do so. Analogies with the Oklahoma bombing of the Murray federal building, where the local FBI lived, are surely relevant: none were present in the building when it blew up, and the FBI received an increase in funding after the event.

Those perpetrating false-flag terror tend to receive an increase in their funding as a consequence of the event - partly to ensure that everyone stays loyal and quiet. Blame at Oklahoma was meant to fall upon some local Muslims, but this didn't go according to plan. The judge at the enquiry insisted on the 'lone nut' explanation, a certain Mr Timothy McVeigh, and all other testimony was ignored - and lost. Can Argentina prevent this from happening and rescue the true and relevant facts - before they vanish down The Memory Hole? Probably not.

'9/11 was an inside job' is a slogan, a motto, that is relevant to both Argentine terror-events. The bomb(s) were placed inside, not outside. If the two events of 1992 and 1994 were both 'inside jobs', then the two buildings both completely destroyed were wrecked from within - not by an external cause, viz., a Renault truck packed with explosives. If they were 'inside jobs', then the hypothesis would have to be, that Shin Beth the Israel army perpetrated the event and then (in 1994) planted the fragment of a Renault van.

The turning-point of the investigation had to be the publication in May 1997 of the National Academy of Engineers report, which determined that the Israeli embassy explosion had originated *from within the building*. It is important that the full text of this report be published and circulated around science departments.

There are analogies with the London Israel Embassy bombing ten days after the 1994 event in Buenos Aires. Here the blame was assigned to Palestinian sources. These two Embassy bombings were both successfully blamed upon enemies of Israel. The London Embassy was blown up by a car bomb (without excluding the option of a bomb also having gone off within the Embassy). If a mere ten days separated these two events, in Buenos Aires and London, is it not likely that the same agency was involved? 85 were killed in one event, none in the other. The latter was phantom terror in the sense that no one was badly hurt. Phantom terror is cheaper, but has to ride on the back of real terror. It aims to produce fear and terror, by reawakening the memory of what happened earlier.

In this new millennium, what called itself the 'Truth' movement came into existence, in the wake of 9/11, and this examines the global extent of false-flag terror, by those who seek to control our world: The Vampire Elite. Argentine philosophers need to use the insights gained by this movement to acquire a proper perspective on things, and remedy the mistake that their country has made, of blaming Iran.[84]

Atomic Collaboration

Jim Fetzer has sagely commented: "These events appear to me to have been orchestrated with the objective of undermining technical and scientific cooperation between Argentina and Iran in relation to the development of peaceful atomic energy." Indeed, that has to have been the real motive.

'IranCen' during 1987 - 88 signed three agreements with Argentina's National Atomic Energy Commission. The first of these agreements provided help in converting the U.S. supplied Tehran Nuclear Research Centre reactor to low-enriched uranium, and supply that uranium to Iran. That uranium was delivered in 1993. The second and third agreements were for technical assistance, including components, for the building of pilot plants for uranium-dioxide conversion and fuel fabrication. Under US pressure, assistance under these agreements was reduced.

In 1988 Nuclear Fuel reported that Argentina has contracts to supply a hundred kilos of nearly 20 percent enriched uranium to Iran, to be fulfilled by mid-1990. Argentina was continuing to provide Iran with low-grade enriched uranium and the two countries were in serious negotiations on broader nuclear cooperation when the bombing occurred.[85] In December 1991, the U.S. Embassy in Buenos Aires informed Argentina's foreign ministry that the United States could not accept the continuation of the contracts on nuclear cooperation with Iran. In January 1992, Argentina announced the suspension of the shipments of nuclear materials to Iran. But in February 1993, The IAEA confirmed that a shipment of nearly 20 percent enriched uranium from Argentina was to arrive in Iran within the year.

Moving onto 2002, absurd arrest warrants for former Iranian president Ali Akbar Rafsanjani and six other former top Iranian officials were issued after the United States had applied diplomatic pressure (Source here: Marc Perelman, the Jewish daily *Forward*, Nov 3rd 2002) The Bush administration used the indictment as part of its campaign to get Russia and China to support a Security Council resolution on sanctions against Iran.

Iran's alleged motive for ordering the bombing of the headquarters of the Jewish organisation AMIA on Jul. 18, 1994, is that Iran wanted to retaliate against Argentina for its decision to cut off exports of nuclear materials. That motive, asserted by former Iranian intelligence officer Abdol Mesbahi in a 2002 deposition, was repeated in a report by the Argentine Intelligence Service (SIDE), in September 2002.

Why would Iran, thousands of miles away from Argentina, wish to cause this horror? Arrest warrants were issued in Argentina for top Iranian politicians with no scrap of real evidence, but instead only an allegation. The allegation concerned the supposed bitterness of Iran over the cancellation of a civil nuclear-power program with Argentina. In 1991, Argentina was instructed by America to cease this exchange program, after it had signed several binding contracts with Iran and was thereby put into a quite stressful situation.

But, this program was evidently still ongoing, in that enriched-uranium was being exchanged, over the key period 1992-4. Iran was benefitting from this and needed that collaboration. No way could it have deliberately engineered such a bomb outrage to terminate this relationship. The US ambassador to Argentina at the time, James Cheek, commented in a 2008 article: "To my knowledge, there was never any real evidence of [Iranian responsibility]. They never came up with anything." But the case for Israeli complicity was strong from the start.

Argentina has a Spanish ancestry, and so after the Madrid bombings of 2004 some turned to the Madrid bombing to help make sense of the horror. Quoting from Israel Shamir: 'If you study the works of the Spanish investigator Del Pino, you can find out an uncanny similarity to the attack in Atocha. Would you like to meet the twin sister of the false Ford truck used in the attack on the Embassy of Israel and the false Traffic used in the attack on AMIA? Meet the False Backpack that the "silly terrorists left behind" in the Spanish station Vallecas'. In the early hours of the morning after terror struck the Madrid train stations, a planted rucksack was 'found' nearby and it had 'clues' that led the police straight to some hapless Muslims.

Voltaire Network (Thierry Meyssan) commented: 'While trying to provide grounds for the accusations against Muslims, the US is attempting to exploit the memory of the attacks perpetrated in 1992 and 1994 in the city of Buenos Aires. In fact, most encyclopaedias continue to attribute those crimes to Hezbollah or to Iran. Despite that, no one believes in those accusations anymore, and the Argentinean justice itself is currently turning towards an Israeli lead. Consequently, Washington is putting pressure to end an investigation that is becoming uncomfortable.'

To quote Adrian Salbuchi:[86]

> The case for a car bomb melted away when the State Prosecutor and the Court hearing on this case invited technical specialist surveyors from the Argentine National Engineers Academy to determine what caused the Israeli Embassy building to collapse. Their conclusion was that the explosion took place from inside the building and was not caused by an alleged car-bomb. To make matters worse for Zionist pressure groups, a passer-by had filmed from several blocks away the mushroom cloud that rose from that explosion, a characteristic effect that also pointed to an internal explosion.... Strong rumours surfaced that what actually blew up was an arsenal that the Israelis apparently had housed in the building's basement.

> The in-fighting among Zionists had as one of its bloody episodes the bombing of the Israeli Embassy and later the AMIA building in Argentina, which was perceived by the Zionist Nazis at the time as a symbol of Labour's stronghold. Why Buenos Aires, you might ask? Simple - because Argentine public security has always been, and still is, very weak, thus making both terror operations relatively easy with Argentine targets. ... The problem with Argentina is that over the past forty years our Nation-State has eroded so badly that it has ceased being a Sovereign Institution and become a highly dependent Colonial Administration entity. Now, how can you expect a totally dependent

nation like Argentina to have an "independent judiciary"? No way. Our judiciary does the bidding for those people who really control and run the country, where a global power network of think tanks, NGO's, lobbies and pressure groups has the final say.

This network includes not just entities like the Council on Foreign Relations, the Trilateral Commission, the Bilderberg Conference, and Chatham House, but also embedded within it are The World Jewish Council, AIPAC, the B'Nai B'Rith Masonic Lodge, the World Zionist Organisation, the ADL, and the American Jewish Congress, among many, many others. It is this power network that calls the shots and twists our government's arms! ... Naturally, the global think-tank network also drafts what the global media should report and say. They are those who decide who will appear as "good guys" and who as "bad guys" on CNN, Fox News, The New York Times, Washington Post, Financial Times, and so on. More still, they are the ones who decide what is and what isn't news!

A Mexican Clue

By way of a comparison, we turn to a well-forgotten incident, in The Congress Hall of Mexico, Mexico City, 11 October, 2001. Two Israelis sneaked past security into the Chamber of Deputies, Mexico's parliament, posing as cameramen, and aroused suspicion. Security guards frisked them. They turned out to be formidably armed, with 9-mm plastic Glock pistols (undetectable by metal detectors), nine grenades, several sticks of explosives, three detonators and 58 cartridges. The two terrorists, Ben Zvi and Smecke, were caught red-handed. And what was their punishment?

These were real plotters, aiming, like the legendary Guy Fawkes, to blow up (in this case, the Mexican) Parliament. Guy Fawkes and his gang were hung, drawn and quartered, for attempting so heinous a crime. But this couple - just went back home! Let's quote John Leonard - in what could be the sole English-language account published of this event: 'In a flurry of damage control, the Israeli Embassy interceded, Sharon sent a special envoy, strings were pulled, the story was spiked, and everyone went home.'[87] This edifying tale seems to have completely disappeared not only from the media but also from the web. You can only find it today on Rense.[88] *Thank God for Rense!*

As regards the motive for this foiled terror attempt, no personal or national motive was evident, nor was it revenge, but rather a part of a global strategy of terrorism. Mexicans, and South Americans in general were not keen on the forthcoming war with Iraq and saw it as totally pointless. This act of terror would supposedly have gotten them in the mood for it - or so reasoned The Vampire Elite. But, how could the tiny state of Israel have extended its hand as far as Mexico, plucking away the guilty culprits, and then have the influence to crush all media debate? Who could ever be so wicked, as to do such a thing?

The Zionist Mafia

Tell me, do the evil men of this world have a bad time? They hunt and catch whatever they feel like eating. They don't suffer from indigestion and are not punished by Heaven. I want Israel to join that club. Maybe the world will then at last begin to fear us instead of feeling sorry. Maybe they will start to tremble, to fear our madness instead of admiring our nobility. Let them tremble; let them call us a mad state. Let them understand that we are a savage country, dangerous to our surroundings, not normal, that we might go wild, that we might start World War Three just like that, or that we might one day go crazy and burn all the oil fields in the Middle East. Personally, I don't want to be any better than Harry Truman who snuffed out half a million Japanese with two fine bombs.

-Israeli Prime Minister Ariel Sharon[89]

A similar pro-terror view was expressed by another Israeli Prime minister, Yitzhak Shamir:

"Neither Jewish morality nor Jewish tradition can be used to disallow terror as a means of war… We are very far from any moral hesitations when concerned with the national struggle. First and foremost, terror is for us a part of the political war appropriate for the circumstances of today…"[90]

As to where such ethics came from, let us try going back to the Old Testament. The *Book of Exodus* avers that, 'I will send my terror ahead of you and throw into confusion every nation you encounter' (23:27). A predator-theft ethic is expressed in the *Book of Deuteronomy:*

And when the LORD your God brings you into the land which he swore to your fathers, to Abraham, to Isaac, and to Jacob, to give you, with great and goodly cities, which you did not build, and houses full of all good things, which you did not fill, and cisterns hewn out, which you did not hew, and vineyards and olive trees, which you did not plant, and when you eat and are full, then take heed lest you forget the LORD…(6:10-14)

The destruction of other cultures is mandated:

Then the LORD will drive out all these nations from before you, and ye shall dispossess nations greater and mightier than yourselves… Ye shall utterly destroy all the places, wherein the nations which ye shall dispossess served their gods, upon the high mountains, and upon the hills, and under every green tree. And ye shall overthrow their altars, and break their pillars and burn their groves with fire, and ye shall hew down the graven images of their gods and destroy their name from out of that place.   (*Deuteronomy*, 11:23 + 12:2-3)

The Deity explained the tactics of deception:

> When you march up to attack a city, make its people an offer of peace. If they accept and open their gates, all the people in it shall be subject to forced labour and shall work for you. If they refuse to make peace and they engage you in battle, lay siege to that city. When the LORD your God delivers it into your hand, put to the sword all the men in it.' (*Deuteronomy*, 20:10-13)

The *Book of Isaiah* is emphatic that other cultures *only have a right to exist* if they pay tribute to Israel:

> Therefore thy gates shall be open continually; they shall not be shut day nor night, that men may bring unto thee the forces of the gentiles, and that their kings may be brought. For the nation and kingdom that will not serve thee shall perish; yea, those nations shall be utterly wasted... Ye shall eat the riches of the gentiles.' (*Isaiah* 60: 11-12 + 61:6).

Instructions are given about lending money with interest: 'Unto a stranger thou mayest lend upon usury; but unto thy brother thou shalt not lend upon usury' (Deuteronomy 23:20). The *Book of Genesis* devotes a whole chapter to the question of how to take over control of the finances of a host nation (Chapter 47)!

Jewish attitudes towards Palestine are so well expressed by the Psalmists's words: 'Happy shall be he who takes your little ones and dashes them against the rock!' (Psalm 137) After all, 'Anything devoted to destruction is most holy to the lord.' (Leviticus 27:28) *There are at least a hundred passages on the OT, where the deity expressly commands others to kill.*[91] *Can planet Earth survive the existence of a nation that employs such a source of ethical guidance?*[92] These ancient texts, scratched upon leather scrolls in centuries BC, acquired an alarming new geopolitical relevance once the United Nations voted in 1947 for the existence of a 'Jewish State.'

A vicious kind of 'Zionist Mafia' appears to exist in our modern world, inspired by such ethics. Here are some helpful attempts to describe it by a colleague:

- Their ambition seems to go far beyond the desire for a Jewish homeland towards their own brand of world control. Their brand of world control does not seem to include the well-being of the existing world human population or the well-being of the world environment on which all our existence depends.

- These people, whoever they are, have a lot of similarities with the Italian Mafia. They are secret, they are ruthless, they loan money to people, they kill people when necessary, even their own kind. Their success depends on the public not being aware of their activity and accepting the guilt of those publicly blamed.

- In the early days of the Israeli State there was a lot of idealism and there was even socialism. The covert criminal militarism we see now was not part of the agenda.

- The core of the Zionist Mafia is probably a small number of persons; we can speculate as to who they are. At present, they have the whole world under a spell.

- To break a spell, it is recognized traditionally by magicians that one has to have a name, a word or group of words to focus on as a reference. Anyone can use the term 'Zionist Mafia', and it refers to the inner circle of activists who are running, driving, coordinating the current global conspiracy.

- The Zionist Mafia has considerable influence on American foreign and military policy, in the banking system, in the security business and intelligence services, and in supply of fuel, and in Pharmaceuticals.'

That notion of breaking a spell is important. Standard accounts of both Argentine events state matter-of-factly that a suicide driver blew up a truck, etc., while those who doubt this are 'anti-Semitic.' These trucks were as nonexistent as the Boeing airplane alleged to have flown into the Pentagon on 9/11. People are being induced to believe in another phantom.[93]

2
Israel Blows Up Its Own Embassy
London 1994

In 'Millionaire's Row' London, Israel's Embassy suddenly exploded. A witness on that day - July 26th, 1994 - reported that 'The blast appeared to come from the Israeli consulate but we were told to stay inside. Just by the sound, anybody in that building would not have had a chance.' (*Evening Standard*, 26 July, Donald McCloud). It went off around noon, yet strangely no one was killed, and the injuries reported were only light - although walls were blown out and a floor collapsed. There had, it turned out, been a prior warning: 'Senior Israeli officials had warned the Foreign Office of their fears of a bomb attack in London eight days before the embassy explosion, it emerged last night' (*The Times*, 28th July).

Israelis commonly have prior warnings

The attack came the day after King Hussein of Jordan and Israeli Prime Minister Yitzhak Rabin had met in Washington to declare an end to war with a historic peace handshake, and it successfully extinguished this hope. It transformed the rhetoric into that of Islamic terrorism, with vows not to let the 'enemies of peace' destroy the momentum, etc.:

> *There is no doubt in my mind that we face a wave of extreme Islamic radical terrorist movements in Arabic countries*

> - Yitzhak Rabin

The BBC News reported[94] on how, as well as destroying the front of the building in London, windows were blown out of the nearby Kensington Palace, and the blast was heard a mile away. How come no one was seriously harmed? 'The worst injury was a broken arm,' commented an eye-witness: 'The whole street shook.... The first thing we noticed was a huge plume of smoke, coming out of the top of the building'. Kensington high street was cleared by police within minutes.

A car bomb had been involved, and the car involved had been blown fifty yards by the blast, and only a charred shell remained. Access is strictly limited in this area of London, especially at the back of the Israeli Embassy, where the car was parked, raising questions about how the car had been able to be parked there. The street, Kensington Palace Green, known as 'Millionaire's Row', was as highly security-protected as anywhere in London. It was continually patrolled by armed police. A woman of middle-eastern appearance was alleged to have parked the car, then just walked off, before it blew up. (BBC News video 26 July 1994)

Citizens were at once told about who had done it, with the BBC news *for that day* announcing: 'Extremist Islamic resistance to the peace process led to the bombing of a Jewish community centre in Buenos Aires, killing 96, on 18 July.' *How could the BBC decide so quickly to link the event to something on the other side of the world?* After all, the massacre had happened ten days earlier. They might have been connected, but how? False-flag terror has the establishment media pointing to the guilty party, right away, even when its origin could not then be known.

Late that same day, a car-bomb went off outside Balfour House, the historic site where Zionist plans had been formulated. It was at midnight, when it was empty. 'The security, a police presence, was taken off Balfour House an hour before the explosion.' ('Justice Denied', 1999) A bomb going off after midnight may not be very surprising (i.e., early on the 27th July). Normally, around 90 people worked in that building, but at that late time of night only security guards were present. It destroyed shop fronts around and cars were smashed up, but again - no one was killed.

Blame falls on Palestinians

Many conflicting theories were put forward in the wake of the July 1994 bombings. It didn't take long for the police to disregard most and decide that the bombings had been carried out by Palestinians. Never mind that the Palestinians were one group not to benefit from the bombings, that there had been no similar Palestinian actions for twenty years, or that the organisation allegedly claiming responsibility - the 'Jaffa Unit' or 'Jaffa Team' of the 'Palestinian Resistance' - has never been heard of before, or since.

Soon, two Lebanese citizens were jailed for twenty years, for a crime 'they did not, could not, and would not have committed.[95] They were *not even around at the time,* and no one suggested that they had made the bomb, but they could not escape from the extreme vagueness of the 'conspiracy' charge. Quite simply, the Government needed a couple of patsies to put in jail so it could close the case. Samar Alami and Jawad Botmeh were convicted in December 1996 on the basis of circumstantial evidence, most of which related to their activities in support of Palestinians in the occupied territories.

None of the evidence connected either of them with any involvement in the Israeli Embassy or Balfour House bombings. There was clearly a bigger picture here: *the sophisticated way in which the bombings were carried out in the middle of London without leaving a clue, which indicated the work of a professional organisation or government.* The prosecution simply refused to acknowledge this fact and instead alleged that Samar and Jawad - well-known and popular Palestinian student activists - had acted alone with a small British-based amateur group having no connections to any large terrorist organisations.

Expert commentators, such In November 1996, the authorities brewed up a 'Public Interest Immunity' order to protect themselves regarding information obtained by Israelis and British investigators on explosive traces at the bomb sites: *it all had to stay secret.* The prosecution's continuing use of secret (PII) hearings to suppress vital evidence meant that Britons remain in the dark about the true story behind the bombings. But at a Court of Appeal, at the end of October 2000, the prosecution was forced to admit that the prosecuting authorities at almost every level - from the Crown Prosecution Service to MI5, MI6 and Special Branch, and all the way up to the Home Office - had been concealing vital evidence. The evidence pointed to the probability that a known terrorist organisation with no connections to Samar or Jawad was responsible for the bombings.

Robert Fisk, found it curious that such meticulously and professionally planned bombings in the middle of London *had not led to any fatalities* and wondered whether this might indicate Israeli involvement. Thatcher's government had shut down the Mossad's base in Britain back in 1987; pinning bombings such as these on the Palestinians would enable the Israelis to perpetuate their 'victim' image, whilst simultaneously playing on the popular racist stereotype of the Palestinians as violent enemies of peace. Other theories had the bombings related to those shortly beforehand in Argentina and Panama, that they were somehow connected to enmity between Israel and Iran.

Samar and Jawad were convicted, *where evidence of their political activities in support of Palestinians was portrayed as evidence of involvement in terrorism.* None of the evidence showed that either of them had any involvement in the London bombings - they merely had the misfortune to come across someone who was. None of the prosecution evidence against Samar and Jawad ever connected them with either of the London bombings or, indeed, with any bombings anywhere.

The prosecution accepted that Samar and Jawad had no links to any large terrorist organisations. To get around this obstacle, the prosecution decided that the bombings were carried out by a small, previously unheard-of, amateur group of disgruntled British-based Palestinians, including Samar and Jawad, but which had no connections to any larger organisations in Britain or abroad.

The Israelis confirmed that they received an early warning of a bomb. The Israeli Embassy is protected around the clock. Security cameras and armed police guards are constantly on patrol. Yet somehow the Audi carrying the bomb was driven up the heavily-guarded road and parked outside, and the driver walked off without a problem. Israelis claimed that the security cameras on the Embassy building were not working, thus thwarting attempts to see who carried out the bombing. *This is the signature of false-flag terror.*

The identity of the bombers remains a mystery. Both explosions were so expertly carried out, and with such high-performance explosives, that not a trace was left behind, leaving no clue as to what kind of explosive was used. Israeli teams came and took away samples from the bomb crater, but no one will reveal who they were, what they took, or what the results of their tests were. The role that Israeli government agents played in examining the scene of the blast at the Israeli Embassy is still unknown. As Michael Mansfield explained to the court, "Somebody undoubtedly did come from Israel. For some reason, nobody knows who they were, what they took away from the scene or what conclusions they came to."

A bomb crater? We could do with hearing a bit more about that! Normal car-bombs do not make craters in the road. The Bali bomb of 2002 did, but that was (as we'll see) hardly a normal explosive. The public has never been given any information about what explosive was used.

The Hero Steps Forward

Quite how far the cover-up went remains a matter of speculation. Leading Defence counsel Michael Mansfield, QC, put it like this, in the Court of Appeal:

'It is an astonishing and incredible failure in the duty of disclosure by those who are responsible....a catalogue of disasters, errors and failures by at least eight different individuals, at seven different stages, beginning with the domestic security service and going all the way up to the Home Office .... Had it not been for David Shayler, the CPS would still be saying to us that there is nothing further to be revealed.'[96]

At the end of 1997, a year after Samar and Jawad were convicted, the ex-MI5 officer David Shayler blew the whistle. He revealed that before the bombings, the security service MI5 had received specific warning from a reliable source of an impending attack on the Israeli Embassy, but had buried the information and failed to pass it on to anyone. Shayler also said that a senior MI5 manager believed that the Israelis had been involved, but that this evidence had also been held back. Shayler's revelations blew a hole through the prosecution case and went a long way to confirming that Samar and Jawad were innocent. Throughout the trial the Defence had been told that no such intelligence information from before the bombings existed. If the security services had been warned about the bombings, they might have an idea about who had really carried them out.[97]

Clearly, there had not been an intelligence vacuum, and a known terrorist organisation was suddenly and verifiably in the frame. As for Shayler's other revelation - that a senior MI5 manager believed the Israelis were involved - that might explain the many mysterious circumstances surrounding the bombings and subsequent successful get-away of those who carried them out, whoever they might have been.

What Shayler referred to seemed to be just the kind of evidence Samar and Jawad needed to prove their innocence. But, at this point, the British government intervened to suppress the information. In May 1998, Jack Straw, the Home Secretary, signed a public interest (PII) certificate to authorise the withholding of the evidence in question on national security grounds. The withholding of the Shayler-identified material was subsequently confirmed by a secret sitting of the Court of Appeal - with only the prosecution in attendance - in May 1999.

At that trial, the Defence was unable to investigate a car involved in a "dry-run" of the bombing some weeks earlier (at least, according to the testimony of a guard working at the gates of the road to the embassy), because police had conveniently lost the logs of the entrance to the road to the embassy. Uh-huh.

The Shayler evidence had two components to it, shattering the main prosecution case:

(1) In November 1997, he revealed to the media that MI5/MI6 had received a clear warning from a reliable source that the Israeli Embassy in London would be attacked in July 1994. This warning was crucial new evidence in the case, implying the July 1994 bombings could not have been carried out by Samar and Jawad.

(2) Further, in August 1998, investigative journalist Paul Foot established from Mr Shayler that there was another hidden piece of information. This is a report written in September-October 1994 by a senior MI6 officer involved in the investigation in which he concluded that Israeli intelligence could have been involved in the attacks.

Both pieces of evidence were withheld from court at the time of the trial. They contradicted the main premise of the prosecution, namely that an "intelligence vacuum" surrounded the bombings, which were carried out by a few London-based Palestinians. They are in accord with the fact that the highly professional and precise attacks must have been carried out by well-trained, experienced group or international terrorist organisation. As a reminder, the trial judge accepted that neither Samar nor Jawad belonged to a terrorist organisation.'[98] Shayler gave his story to the *Mail on Sunday* in November 1997.

A Midnight Blast

Why would a terrorist, planning to attack a historic Jewish building (Balfour House), *choose a time, 1 am, when it would be empty?* Did they want to avoid hurting anybody? Yes, I suggest that that was the aim. It was vital that no real deaths take place, because otherwise subsequent court hearings would have been a far more weighty matter. They could not then have gotten away with the mockery of justice - whereby two persons not even present were jailed and the case closed - with no real attempt to seek for who had done it. Also, it would not have been credible if the second blast had taken place in the daytime, again with nobody killed. Both events had to be taken seriously, because of the preceding and similar events in Argentina, which did have lots of real deaths.

Private Eye expressed a view in August 1998: "Soon after the bombing a senior MI5 manager wrote a note expressing his view that the Israelis had carried out the bombing on their own to embarrass the British government into providing more security for Israeli buildings and personnel." . . . . 'Did the Israelis bomb their own London embassy in 1994?' asked Paul Foot in *The Guardian,* 1.12.98.

In February 2000, a petition concerning the innocence of these two, with over 200,000 signatures, was presented to the Prime Minister at 10 Downing Street.

November 2002. The House of Lords, however, rejected an appeal by Samar and Jawad. The two innocent patsies were incarcerated until 2009.

High-Level Complicity

Another area of particular concern are the certain - albeit unseen - Israeli role, interests, and pressures. The individual who manned the camera at the Embassy the day of the bombing was not interviewed by police and was removed to Israel. An unspecified number of people removed samples and material from the crater left by the car bomb, but no one knows how many they were, what they took, or what results they obtained. The Ambassador himself congratulated police after the initial wave of arrests in 1995 even before the trial. Anything pertaining to their role in the investigation or their findings has been invariably excluded from mention or disclosure, as well as the warning that the Embassy itself received at the time. Further, the report written by a senior MI5 officer pointing to the possible involvement of Israeli agents in the bombings themselves was not disclosed. Thus, there are genuine fears that justice is being blocked by extremely high level political considerations.[99]

In false-flag terror, *the state is complicit in the crime* - which is the terrible aspect that ordinary, decent citizens find difficult, even impossible, to believe. The larger purpose of the crime is to justify war, in this case to confer a victim-status upon Israel. That works, *so long as the Metropolitan police conspires to conceal vitally-relevant evidence which we, the bewildered public, have a right to expect.* Why would they want to do that?

The UK 'peace movement' has greatly supported the two innocent Lebanese citizens - even though it will normally not go anywhere near the 'false-flag terror' concept. It will never endorse anything like the statement, which I heard David Shayler make, about how 'Israel blew up its own embassy,' in 1994, even though that is the logical implication of the innocence of the two Lebanese, and the tremendous conspiracy we have witnessed at the very highest levels of the British Judicial system to prevent the truth from coming out.

The 'evil empire' of Communism had collapsed in 1991, and the US/UK military were facing a difficult future without an enemy in sight. Good God, some people were even expecting peace! The system required that a new enemy come into existence. Real terror is needed for construction of the demonised enemy image, *i.e., blood has to be shed.* The Israeli Embassy bombing of 1992 in Buenos Aires had killed a lot of people, and was followed by another worse such event there in 1994. The 1992 event had key features in common with London two years later: it was alleged that a car had driven up to the embassy and then blown up, whereas scores of witnesses testified that no car had been seen and that the blast came from inside the Embassy. (These witnesses were dismissed as 'anti-Semitic.')

The syntax of the London bombing is commensurate with that on the other side of the world two years earlier: why was it so important for the British government to jail two innocent patsies for twelve years, and conceal the relevant evidence? Answer: the acceptance of this event as described by Israel, implied an acceptance of a grammar of terrorism, that linked it to the events in Buenos Aires. A new, worldwide Enemy was being gestated. Allowing this event to be exposed for what it was - by allowing the evidence to unfold - would have aborted this newly-emerging 'Phantom Menace.'

The 1992 Argentina event involved the complete demolition of the Israeli Embassy. *Who would want to do such a thing?* That has implications for the UK Government's interpretation of the Kensington Embassy bombing. Or, if that shocks you too much, let's put it another way: now that the two Lebanese patsies are out of jail - *the case is over*. Nobody wants to 'solve' the crime - that is the last thing any UK civil rights or anti-war movement wants! There seems to have been only one person in the UK who understood this case.

In 2000 *The Independent* came to accept that 'SHAYLER WAS RIGHT OVER BOMB AT ISRAELI EMBASSY:

> The Crown Prosecution Service was forced by the Court of Appeal yesterday to admit that the former MI5 officer, David Shayler, was right in saying that the security services were warned before the 1994 car bombing of the Israeli embassy in London that the building was being targeted by a terrorist organisation. The terrorist group was unconnected with the two young Palestinians eventually convicted of the bombing...[Shayler] also referred to suspicions that the Israeli secret service, Mossad, carried out the bombing to provoke the UK into tightening its security. (27 October 2000)

In all the time David Shayler was with us in London's 9/11 'Truth' movement, he never mentioned his key role in this case, as if there were something so dire he didn't want to mention it. Other aspects of his life working with MI5 he would talk about quite freely. He has become a bit of a figure of fun since 2007, when he realised that he was the Messiah - I refrain from entering into details - as well as his habit of cross-dressing. Many have surmised that he needed some change of identity to take himself out of Mossad's cross-hairs. He and his ex-partner, Annie, both told me of attempts on their life, mainly (I recall) by his car brakes suddenly failing. At least he's still alive.

Comparing the two London false-flag terror bombings 11 years apart, in 1994 and 2005, in both cases the Government behaved as if the evidence was a state secret. Ordinary people could not be allowed access to it.

'By way of deception shall you wage war' is Mossad's Motto. Let's be honest: *state-fabricated terror without Israeli-Mossad involvement would be like Hamlet without the prince.*

General Comments

* The failure of street CCTV to work for the car-recognition on the day plus data missing for a previous 'dry run' - these things have notable similarities to the 7/7 case, as well as 9/11 and the Madrid bombings.

* The two patsies had no credible means of creating the powerful explosion which took place: many false-flag terror events have this most peculiar characteristic.

* No details are given of the explosives used, or where the bombs were assembled: this remains totally vague. Here is a deep similarity with the 7/7 case and also with the Bali bomb of 2002, where the experts continually changed their minds about what it had been. It had to be a high-powered military explosive, which reduced the car to a charred remain: 'with such high-performance explosives, that not a trace was left behind, leaving no clue as to what kind of explosive was used' - one could say the same for whatever blew up the three train coaches on 7/7.

* The patsies have nothing to gain from the event; on the contrary, everything they have worked for by way of educational aid to Palestine is terminated.

* The building is strangely empty when it goes bang, again reminiscent of certain false-flag terror events: When the Pentagon was struck on 9/11, the plane or missile chose that specific part of the building empty of military personnel - only civilian staff got hit. When a bomb went off in Istanbul in 2003 in the British Embassy (synchronized with Bush and Blair meeting in London), it was empty of personnel, save for one ambassador who was supposed to have left by then.

* Both 9/11 and 7/7 had the characteristic of Mossad foreknowledge: Benjamin Netanyahu received an advanced warning prior to 7/7, and there was debate about whether Scotland Yard or Mossad had been the source of this. Other analysts claimed that Mossad had had a couple of days' foreknowledge. For 9/11, the Israeli Odigo text-messaging firm adjacent to the Twin Towers, had knowledge at least a couple of hours before, its parent company back in Israel being located close to Mossad headquarters. No other intel agency (e.g., the CIA) showed such foreknowledge.

* Continual withholding of centrally-relevant evidence: here we could compare, for example, the immediate concealment of the exploded tube carriages after 7/7, so that no journalist, member of the public or court hearing could have access to them; and their secret destruction a year later.

* An unheard-of group alleged to claim responsibility: in this instance it was the 'Jaffa Unit' or 'Jaffa Team' of the 'Palestinian Resistance,' never heard of before or since - perhaps comparable to 'Al-Qaeda in Europe' which allegedly claimed credit for 7/7, posted on a server having connections with the Bush family - which has also never been heard of since.

3
Bali Gets Nuked
2002

At 11 pm on 12th October, 2002, the Sari club in Jakarta was ripped apart. Some hours before the bombing took place, the US had withdrawn all its administrative staff and diplomats from Indonesia, citing a 'security threat'. The British government also received the same warning, but this wasn't passed on to any relevant authority or to the hundreds of people who were casually making their way to a beach party.

No group stepped forward to take public responsibility. Immediately after the bombing, the FBI, the Australian Secret Service and British secret police swooped in to the bomb site and took charge of the investigation. Both the Indonesian authorities and the Balinese police were indignant but powerless to intervene. The first people on the scene almost immediately were the FBI, despite it being a 17-hour journey from the USA. Australian police arrived within 24 hours. The actual bombers may have escaped from Jakarta airport that night, as flight logs were found to be missing from air traffic control that day and the night of the 12th and for no other night.

The Bali bomb of 2002 was a success, because it drew the Australians, who had shown reluctance, into supporting the Iraq war - which appears to have been its aim. There could be a deeper purpose here involved, in that Bali had an intact and quite spiritual culture, such that *its people were not generally living in fear.* The New World Order does not like that. Maybe the Balinese needed to be taught a lesson. The discerning Canadian scholar, Michael Chossudovsky, found that:

> like September 11th, the Kuta [Bali] bombing was probably either an American (CIA) or an Israeli (Mossad) operation (or perhaps a combined CIA/Mossad operation) …Three days before the Bali bombings of October 1st, the Australian press published several reports pointing to an imminent terrorist attack. These reports were based on statements of the Director of the Australian Strategic Policy Institute, Mr Aldo Borgu … The October 1st Bali bombing occurred barely a few days after the holding of a special meeting of The Council of Australian Governments in Canberra, during which the State premiers agreed to the adoption of far-reaching anti-terrorist measures.

It is the anti-terror chiefs who *enable* the event to happen. Australia, 13th October, 2005:

> Last night, the biggest fraud in the history of Australia was disclosed to the Australian people on TV. The former President of Indonesia (who is widely known in Indonesia as the only honest Indonesian politician there) directly stated in no uncertain terms that the Indonesian police

and/or military had perpetrated the infamous Bali bombing in which over 200 people were killed…about half of them Australians. To remind you, this is the blind former President who is honest and religious and beyond the possibility of being corrupted… In a one-hour documentary/research/investigative program on SBS-TV Date-Line program last night, all the fabricated cover-up story about 'terrorist Moslem Organisations' in Indonesia fell apart. They do not exist! They were all created by Indonesian Military Intelligence! …. The Indonesian Generals are corrupt, they boasted on TV that they got 50 million dollars from the Americans, in order to 'fight terrorism'. In reality, they created 'terrorism' and pocketed the money.[25]

This Australian TV programme endorsed the view advocated by the late, great Joe Vialls, who had resided in Australia:

It was late on Wednesday, 15 November, just one day before the special Hindu cleansing ceremony of the Bali bombsite in Kuta Beach, that the local Indonesian police chief thoughtfully paraded "prime suspect" Amrozi in front of the assembled media pack. The fact that Amrozi was clearly disoriented, rambling, as high as a kite on drugs and separated from western journalists by a thick glass wall, was apparently not a problem for our sacred guardians of the truth.

Despite the obvious audio impediments and complete lack of direct access, Australian and Singaporean media outlets were nonetheless able to "accurately" interpret Amrozi's muffled and garbled mixture of Javanese and Indonesian to mean that he confessed to killing nearly 300 people at Kuta Beach, with a minivan full of potassium chlorate detergent stolen from Java.

Not only that, but as Amrozi peered hopefully through a thick psychedelic haze to wave cheerfully at the television cameras, we were further asked to believe he claimed to enjoy killing people, wanted to kill some more, and in particular wanted to kill lots and lots of Americans. So thick was the psychedelic fog surrounding him, Amrozi completely forgot that the punishment for "confessing" to such crimes in Indonesia is death by firing squad.

Needless to say, the entire media event was contrived rubbish, but it served the purpose for which it was mounted, i.e., to drive increased levels of Australian hatred against Amrozi, and through him against all Muslims across south east Asia.

The Bali bomb left a huge crater in the road, which IRA bombs planted in cars had never done, as Vialls pointed out. A whole lot of concrete around it was just vaporised, leaving twisted steel up to 50 feet away. That is a recurrent theme in New World Order events: special devices from "the necro-technocrats".

A Mushroom Cloud

There were two explosions in the immediate vicinity. The first was small and may not have harmed anyone. It was some sort of political gesture. Let's hear the view of Amrozi, a motorcycle mechanic from east Java, whose wife and neighbours have testified and can prove that he never left his home island. He was convicted for the crime on 9 November, 2008:

> I was responsible for the bombing at the US Consulate [which killed or injured no one] and I'm proud of it, but most of the people were killed by an Israeli micro-nuke that was targeted at the Sari Club at the same moment. You know, to make Islam look bad.
>
> -   from the late Joe Vialls' website

One would indeed like to have heard a bit more on this matter from the late Mr Amrozi. Let's hope the people of Bali remember these words of Amrozi - after he paid with his life as an innocent sacrifice. Amrozi was a 'patsy' - i.e., one who is set up in a situation, for which he is assigned the blame. Shortly thereafter, a fake Al-Qaeda web-message was claiming responsibility.

An excellent ten-part video, "The Truth about the Bali bombings", describes how the bomb was nuclear. The blast area was half a kilometre and the Sari club

was levelled in seconds. At first, people thought it was an earthquake. Experts surmise that the blast was probably from a small tactical-nuclear warhead in the vicinity of 0.01 kilotons (i.e., equivalent to ten tons of TNT).

The Bali blast vaporised all concrete nearby, and a lot of people seem to have just disappeared, with a huge crater formed in the road, etc. Two bangs were heard in close proximity, one a fairly small one which the patsies may have detonated, while the other was a micro-nuke.

ber

A mushroom cloud unfolded brown in the night sky above Bali, having a white core to it. A micro-nuke made with pure plutonium-239 and requires enough to achieve critical mass, but only a small portion goes fissile so it remains a relatively small blast.[100] The electro-magnetic pulse effect knocked out electricity in the area, which is a signature of nuclear explosion; no conventional explosive can do that. Within ten miles or so, electrical systems blinked out. Investigators estimated that its blast pressure ratio was between 10-100, while, for the sale of comparison, that of potassium nitrate and aluminium was around 2 while that of 'C4' is around 4^2.

Discussions of these matters are found on videos about the Bali bombings more than on websites, and are quite absent from the printed page. The key features of the nuclear blast included:

* An EMP electro-magnetic pulse that knocks out electricity in the region;

* A mushroom cloud in the sky;

* A very high pressure wave measured in pounds per square inch;

* Alpha-radiation from the residual plutonium;

* a crater in the road, which conventional explosives packed into a car will never cause;

* Descriptions like, 'The place [Sari club] was packed, and it went up within a millisecond', of that an instantaneous effect;

* Victims were walking around with skin burns and skin peeling off - compare Hiroshima;

* Many in the crowded vicinity simply vanished, with no trace remaining; and,

* Concrete from nearby buildings had vaporised, leaving twisted steel.

* Most of the fissile isotopes produced would soon have been washed away by the heavy monsoon rains, the Sari club being just 200 yards from the beach. It does seem a shame that no radiology department went back there and checked it out. After the blast, the area was not cordoned off; on the contrary people were allowed to walk all over it - presumably to dissipate the radioactive waste.

Local journalist, Robert Finnigan, senior journalist for the *Jakarta Post*, started interviewing people and took soil samples. After putting the question to a US official, 'Will you verify yes or no to any US involvement in this bombing?', he had his visa revoked within 24 hours and found himself being followed and instructed to leave the country right way - despite being married to a Balinese wife. He described how an Israeli officer followed him. Another *Jakarta Post* journalist helping him was likewise given 24 hours to hand over all his material.

On 6th November, a month after the blast, Joe Vialls' claim about a micro-nuke was published in a Javanese newspaper, then on 9th November, Intelligence services in London used the British Home Office to issue a dire warning that "al Qaeda might be planning to attack the west with a dirty radiological weapon". That story travelled around the world but was soon after withdrawn as if it were a mere error by David Blunkett, the UK Minister of Home Affairs. That was, Joe Vialls surmised, a backup contingency plan, just in case someone detected the alpha-radiation.

State-fabricated terror events display a contrast between the high-powered explosive that were used and the home-made explosive used by the 'lone nut' in the story. The experts appeared hardly able to say what the explosive had been. The Bali-bomb story had its alleged explosives continually changing, starting off with stories about 'C4' - 'Plastic explosive clue in Bali bombing' - in which respect it is similar to the London 7/7 story. It even ended up with a narrative about potassium chlorate:[101] its final version appeared after Amrozi and two others were convicted and shot for having perpetrated the event. The Empire *knew in advance* that *all* the world's media could be induced to mistake a fertilizer truck bomb for a nuke - and somebody, somewhere must enjoy that sort of power.

Witness Reports

Witnesses testified to seeing '... that big giant mushroom from the smoke...' - 'when I looked up into the sky, I found it to be a bright red ball with pure white smoke arising from it in mushroom form.' 'Sari's went up in a millisecond...' 'You just saw a blinding light and your ears felt like they were exploding. Outside it was awful, like something you'd see out of Vietnam.' After the blast, 'The flood of people came running down the street screaming and tipping water over each other... There were completely burned bodies with flesh burned through to the bone, lying in the Bali hospital. Burns surgery experts testified they had never seen anything like this' (quotes from video reports).

An Australian army explosives expert 30 meters away observed how the power had cut out: 'All the power went out. And then probably two seconds later there was this huge flash and I was covered in glass and it just started. It was like hell on earth.... It was bigger than anything I've ever blown up in my time, and I've done a bit.' It damaged as many as 47 buildings in the vicinity, and trashed over 120 cars. Cars several blocks away were ignited by a 'white hot flash,' totally pulverised, semi-volatilised by the heat.[102]

The Australia tourist Rachel Hughes said she and a friend had just arrived in Kuta when the blast occurred. Standing in the foyer of the Bounty Hotel, 'people were just walking in, blood dripping off them, burns to their face, skin coming off them.' She told Australia's Seven Network: "Severe burns and skin coming off the bones is a symptom of exposure to a nuclear blast... I felt my hotel shake violently and ran to look out of the window. In the distance, I could see a large white mushroom cloud, and knew I wasn't looking at an ordinary attack."

Balinese villagers buried empty coffins, to honour the 'vanished' victims: 'We know that we will never be able to find any parts of their physical bodies, but this ceremony will help their families to live in peace.' Local villagers understood that this blast had vaporised quite a few people. To quote Joe Vialls again: 'Every survivor standing in its direct line of sight received terrible flash burns .. dozens of full-size victims had vanished suddenly without trace.'[103]

There were quotes such as, "Everything has gone, the whole street..."[104] Would part-time chicken farmers have been able to make such a device? Australia's top Federal police officer Mick Kelty thought so and announced on the 21st October that Amrozi's bomb had been made of fertilizer and fuel. He and two others were executed for the crime of exploding a potassium chlorate bomb. *The world's media could not tell the difference between a nuclear blast and a detonation of potassium chlorate.* Yes, that is the world we live in! This shows the confidence which the Masters of War have, in perpetrating these events.

The event was designed to *create terror and promote war.* Let's hear Indonesia's former President Wahid Abdurrahman (in an October 2005 interview on Australia's SBS TV):

> W.A.: Amrozi was involved in the lighter bomb. That's a problem always. Even though I agree that he should be given a stiff punishment, but it doesn't mean that he is involved. No, no, no.
> REPORTER: So you believe that the Bali bombers had no idea that there was a second bomb?
> W.A.: Yeah, precisely.
> REPORTER: And who would you suggest planted the second bomb?
> W.A.: Well, it looks like the police.
> REPORTER: The police?
> W.A.: Or the armed forces, I don't know.

A report from The Elie Wiesel 'Foundation for Humanity' (I'll here refrain from comment...) six months before the event happened, indicated that Indonesia was due to 'benefit' from a US National-Security campaign.[105] America's President was 'reviewing strategies for the next stage of the War on Terror' and Indonesia was lucky to be that 'next stage'. The *Wikipedia* section on Amrozi has not a word to say about the chemical or nuclear nature of the blast - wherein lies the conclusive proof of his innocence. For shame!

Let's give the last word to Joe Vialls, commenting on Amrozi's conviction:

> It was perhaps on this date that we finally slipped seamlessly into a post-Orwellian media world, where those who control the present ignore the

past, and don't give a damn about the future. As if bewitched, journalists worldwide jumped on the Thought Police band wagon, telling us to believe that an imaginary terrorist organisation had motivated a motorcycle mechanic in Java to kill nearly 300 people in Bali, using only a van full of potassium chlorate detergent.

Bali's President Megawati was instructed to denounce Islamic terror, which she courageously refused to do so, instead denouncing the US as "a superpower that forced the rest of the world to go along with it... We see how ambition to conquer other nations has led to a situation where there is no more peace unless the whole world is complying with the will of the one with the power and strength." After those wise words, did Bali need to be taught a lesson, with a second Bali bombing in October, 2005?

4

The Madrid Train Bombings
2004

NATO War-Game Goes Live

NATO was holding its yearly anti-terror exercise from March 4th-10th entitled 'CMX-2004,' themed as 'designed to practice crisis management procedures, including civil-military cooperation, working in national capitals.' The armies of nineteen nations collaborated in an exercise which war-gamed 'a widespread pattern of terrorist attacks.' The next day, the *very thing* happened in real life. NATO put out this statement:

> The terrorist atrocities in Madrid, which occurred the day after CMX 04 finished, were a deadly reminder about just how realistic such a scenario could be in the present security climate. It perhaps also served as a reminder of the importance of such scenario work for NATO's contingency planning and policy development'.[106]

Peter Power, are you listening? *When the event rehearsed actually happens, it is used as an argument for enhancing the funding of the 'anti-terror' agencies.* In this specific exercise, 'co-ordination between civil and military aspects of the crisis management procedures reportedly went well.' In other words, an unhealthy liaison between domestic police and the military 'Defence' establishment was developed - as required indeed, for false-flag terror to work. NATO then declared that the whole thing was 'classified' so that not a whisper of what happened over that week-long exercise went out to the press.

We will see how, a few months before the London bombings, there was a large-scale terror-drill both on the streets and in government offices of London - all details of which became strictly classified.

The Unseen Enemy

Ten bombs went off in Madrid, on 11 March, 2004, during rush-hour, on four subway trains, after which the Basque group, ETA, issued a statement at 10.30 denying involvement. Then, at 10.50, a white van was discovered with seven detonators, a tape in Arabic, and a Koran. The tape was found to consist of a chant of a Koran sura. This was three days before the elections, and Spain's Prime Minister Aznar then picked up the phone and told a daily paper that ETA had done it: the ETA was his arch-enemy, the Basque separatist movement, which had a history of bombs (but never on so large a scale) and political assassinations. He had not then heard about the white van story. Later, his government appeared unsure who to blame and Aznar urged everyone to go on the anti-terror march -

which 11 million did. His government fell because of this wrong, unsupportable accusation.[107,108]

An 'unexploded bomb' mysteriously appears in a nearby police station in the small hours of the next morning, having a cellphone as detonator, which belonged to some Moroccan Arab. Also on that day, the London-based Arab newspaper *Al-Quds Al-Arabi* said it had received an e-mail from an Al-Qaeda group, taking the credit and declaring that it was retribution for Spain's role in the Iraq war. On Saturday, 13th March, the day before the election, three Muslims were arrested as perpetrators. Then on the 14th an Arab videotape was found in a trashcan with someone claiming to be a spokesman for Al-Qaeda in Europe taking credit for the deed. This fourfold Muslim-implicating sequence of events sounds planted and contrived, reminding one of the trail of Korans, etc., found after 9/11, left in hired cars and baggage of the 'hijackers.'

After unexpectedly losing the election, the Aznar government secretly paid thousands of pounds to have *all computer records erased and all documents shredded,* especially around the 11th March but more generally over the previous eight years. That is suspicious behaviour! Zapatero, as Spain's incoming Prime Minister, swiftly committed himself to the hypothesis of Islamic guilt. With his propensity to wear a Palestinian scarf, one might have expected some slight hesitation on this matter - but no! He pledged cross-party support for an international 'War on Terror' and used that as his reason for not prosecuting Aznar for such outrageous conduct. Thus, when the great trial began three years later, its outcome was fore-ordained: *Muslims had to be guilty.*

The Muslims accused were suspended in a huge glass case in the trial-room through the five months of this rather theatrical trial. The indictment itself, for Spain's worst terror attack, was over 100,000 pages long. Halfway through it, in May of 2007, 14 of the defendants went on a week-long hunger strike, objecting to the presumption of guilt which they felt was being thrust upon them by the media. Condemning the bombings, they declared they had "lost faith" in the Spanish judicial system. After coming off their hunger strike, they issued a plea that their trial be 'extracted from the political arena.' Some hope!

The Court's judgement involved a hitherto-unsuspected group of Al-Qaeda terrorists from Morocco. It ascertained, in October 2007, that: 'The March 11 suspects - both dead and alive - were mostly young Muslim men from a hodgepodge of different backgrounds who allegedly acted out of allegiance to Al-Qaeda to avenge the presence of Spanish troops in Iraq and Afghanistan, although Spanish investigators say they did so without a direct order or financing from Osama bin Laden's terror network.'[109] Someone ought to have told the judge that Osama bin Laden had died six years earlier. That judgement was hardly compatible with the disclosure made by the Spanish newspaper *El Mundo* six weeks after the event, that:

24 of the 29 alleged perpetrators were informers and/or controlled by the Spanish Police, Civil Guard and C.N.I. (*National Centre of Intelligence*), before the attacks. (24.4.06)

All of the prosecuted appealed, protesting their innocence.

That court explained the cause of deaths:

The blasts, from 10 backpacks filled with dynamite and nails, killed 191 people and wounded more than 1,800.[110]

An unexploded '13th bomb' contained nuts and bolts mixed together with its explosive, where clues from this rucksack pointed towards the now-jailed Muslims.

Three months after that Court judgement, the medical forensic expert who oversaw the post-mortem work, Carmen Baladia, spoke out in an interview on *Libertad Digital* (with researcher Louis del Pino, 30 Jan, 2008), affirming that nuts and bolts of this kind had *not* been found in the 191 bodies.[111] This obviously put a question-mark beside the grounds on which the Muslims had been prosecuted.

For comparison, the London bombing story of July 7th featured images of 'nail-bomb' explosives which appeared on the US ABC news (27.7.05) as allegedly found by police at the Luton station car-park. This never became a part of any main narrative, presumably because no such nails were found in autopsy reports. Or again, in the Brussels mock-terror event of 2016 (Chapter 13), stories of nail-bombs were put about, but no trace of damage by flying nails was ever shown.

Asturian Dynamite

Major features of the story had to be ignored or downplayed by the Spanish Court:

• No CCTV captured images were found of 'bombers' with rucksacks at any railway station in Madrid - shades of the London bombings, where this allegedly-key evidence was missing.

• The story was of Muslim suicide bombers carrying rucksacks, but not one witness reported seeing Muslims with rucksacks in the Alcala de Henares railway station.

- The man accused of supplying the high explosive was in possession of the private telephone number of the head of Spain's Civil Guard bomb squad, Señor Suárez Trashorras. The number was written on a piece of paper found in the possession of his wife, Carmen Toro (*The Times*, 21 June 2004). Two other men implicated in the bombings had already been identified as police informers.[112]

- Of the two police informants arrested as plotters, Mr Rafa Zhueri had worked for years as a police informant for a unit of the Spanish Civil Guard: 'I informed the Civil Guard that the Asturian offered me dynamite' was a provocative headline.[113]

- Spanish police forensic experts concluded that the bombs were made from the highly restricted Spanish-made dynamite variant called Goma-2 Eco. This type of high explosive, manufactured for industrial use (chiefly mining) by Unión Española de Explosivos, is a gelatinous, nitroglycerin-based explosive widely used within Spain and exported abroad. They estimated that these Madrid attacks had been perpetrated by means of an estimated 120 kg of stolen Goma-2 Eco. This Spanish explosive was subject to tough and effective security measures that had successfully prevented ETA terrorists from getting their hands on any of it for over 20 years. The police informer who procured this explosive evidently did so despite the stringent security measures that had kept ETA from doing the same. No Moroccan al-Qaeda group could ever have gained access to this nor carried such a hefty amount onto trains in the morning rush-hour without being noticed.

- This highly-restricted military-grade explosive used was comparable to that of the earlier 'Gladio' operations. No fires broke out at any of the ten blast sites, a fingerprint of the military-grade explosive used. (The more 'home-made' an explosive, the more likely it is to produce fires and combustion)

- Detonations were synchronized to within a single minute, 7.38 - 7.39 am on the four trains, just as in London, but one hour earlier.

- The alleged perpetrators were reported by the Spanish police as having committed suicide together on 3rd April - thereby rescuing the Spanish tourist industry, as Joe Vialls pointed out (see below). The remains of two 'terrorists' were subsequently found in a nearby swimming pool with bags of the requisite explosive tied around their bodies, while a third was hiding behind a mattress when killed. The bodies were buried without autopsy.

- Bombs may have been placed under the floorboards in at least some cases, as four trains were on 'first service' out of the night railyards after overnight servicing and cleaning. Three of the trains had come straight out of the Alcala de Henares night rail depot, which Joe Vialls reported.[114]

•   A 'Kabbalistic' numerology was found by the judge in the passage of 911 days between September 11th (9-11) and March 11th (3-11).[115]

The Joe Vialls' version remains an important narrative for the Madrid bombings:

> Only a few hours later in what appeared to be a chilling and apparently stupid rerun of 9-11, police officers were tipped off by media about a suspicious white van parked near Alcala de Henares railway station, which was then found to contain a handful of detonators, and several Muslim religious tracts on a cassette tape. The names of the five Moroccan 'terror suspects' were provided to the western media by American and Israeli intelligence agencies, thus creating the illusion that Spain would never be safe until these fictional terrorists were caught.

> By doing this, America and Israel were ensuring that international fear would destroy Spain's huge tourist industry, which has already suffered tens of thousands of summer holiday cancellations since the bomb attacks in Madrid. The subliminal message to the new incoming Spanish Labour Government was therefore obvious: "Leave your troops in Iraq or we will … destroy what is left of your massive tourist industry." It must be said that the Spanish Spec Ops solution to this massive national threat was ingenious. By faking the explosive 'suicides' of the five imaginary 'terrorists' named by America and Israel, Spain completely neutered this contrived threat, because no tourist on earth is going to be frightened of 'terrorists' who have already died very publicly on international television!

The front wall of the apartment block, in a Madrid suburb, was blown out with light frame demolition charges, after which police reportedly found 200 detonators of the type used in the railway attacks. The number of blown-to-bits plotters is given as five, six, or seven, in different reports. (*Wikipedia* cites four.[5])

The 13th Bomb and Islamic Guilt

We have seen how, hours after the atrocity, a 'dummy' rucksack turned up at 02.40 am in a police station. The so-called 13th or 'Vallecas' bomb contained *different* explosive material from that used in the ten bombs that exploded. Supposedly, it had been brought in from the nearby train station of El Pozo along with other bits and pieces. However, there turned out to be a major problem with that story: the bomb disposal squad of the local police had earlier combed through the remains at that railway station right after the blast, at about 10 am, checking for any unexploded bombs. They had found none, especially not a heavy one weighting 24 pounds, as the '13th bomb' did.[116]

Bristling with nuts, bolts and screws, this would-be bomb had a 'SIM' card in its detonator that led directly to a group of Muslims, just in time to alter the course of the Spanish election. The rucksack was shown by X-ray exam to be unexplodable, because its detonator-wires were not connected. Despite this, it had a cellphone supposed to induce detonation, which had on it the fingerprints of Jamal Zougam, alleged ringleader and now in jail (with a 40,000-year jail sentence)! The phone in this backpack was one of very few types on the market that required a SIM card to operate the alarm. *El Mundo* asked the pertinent question:

> Why would terrorists who owned a cellphone shop and are deemed to be very technically proficient, deliberately choose to use a device that would lead the police to their door?'[117]

Madrid gave a vitally-needed affirmation to the 'war on terror' announced on September 11th, two and a half years earlier, bringing the theme of Muslim suicide-terrorists over to Europe, and thereby assisting to validate and explain NATO's continued existence. There are some deep similarities with the July 7th story, and a translation into English of some of the work of Luis Del Pino (e.g., his *Los Enigmas del 11-M*-the Spanish name for the event) would be a help in this direction. For example, both cases have enduring uncertainty and ambiguity over the explosives used, with experts initially agreeing that it was the hard-to-obtain military grade C3 or C4. The clearly-fabricated '13th bomb' invites comparison with those allegedly found in Luton car-park after the July 7th event, where the US-released images of 26th July, 2005, bristled with nails and shrapnel, when there was no hint from post-mortems of any London July 7th bodies that they were embedded with them.

Ch. 5.
The London Bombings
2005

The Inquest

In Britain's High Court of Justice, an "Inquest" was held over five months, which ended in May, 2011 concerning the terrible explosions and carnage that had taken place in London on July 7th, 2005, with Lady Justice Hallett presiding. Remarkably, the UK never managed to have an enquiry into the event concerning what had happened and who was guilty. The Inquest did not ever doubt the official story that four young men from Dewsbury, Leeds, were 'suicide bombers' who had perpetrated the crime: Mohammed Siddique Khan (31 years), Shehzad Tanweer (22 years), Germaine Lindsay (20 years), and Hasib Hussein (19 years).

My book, *Terror on the Tube, Behind the Veil of 7/7: An Investigation,* contested this thesis and argued for Islamic innocence. I believe it was the only book doing this, and it's fair to say that little notice was taken of it: *the people of London did not want to hear its message.* Here we shall presuppose its basic narrative of the event, and focus upon the Inquest's evaluation thereof. Readers who wish to brush up on this epic tale may wish to view the video, "7/7 *Ripple Effect",* by 'Muad' Dib (John Anthony Hill). The authorities made the point of having the author of this video *in jail* for the duration of this Inquest on a rather absurd charge - no doubt because it exposes the charges as fraudulent.[118]

Five years after the dreadful event, there appeared a *judgement* from Britain's High Court, after it had heard 'evidence' for five months. We learned that:

- The 7/7 killings were 'unlawful.' Uh-huh.
- Nobody was to blame, except the wicked Four who are dead.
- A public enquiry into 7/7 would not be a good idea.
- There is no need for an Inquest into the Four alleged perpetrators.
- No 'conspiracy' would have been possible.

We recall the proper purpose of an inquest: it is meant to come to a judgement concerning *cause of death.* In the very strange circumstances of the 7/7 Inquest, Lady Justice Hallett could not do this, because *no post-mortems had been performed* upon the 52 dead bodies.

Instead, she produced a rather long judgement proceeding from the unproven assumption that the four suspects were guilty of the crime. She chose elements of the evidence presented to fit in with this question-begging assumption. *Criminal guilt is not the business of an Inquest.* It should be the business of a criminal court instead, where adversarial lawyers representing two opposing viewpoints grill witnesses, enabling one of their competing narratives to gain an ascendancy.

As in any murder trial, the Inquest should have first considered whether any of the four owned a weapon capable of perpetrating the crime -*that they possessed the means to carry it out.* Can it be shown that any of them had a 'bomb'? I believe that it cannot. Even if they had bought 30% peroxide from a hydroponics shop, then what? If there is no murder weapon, there is no criminal guilt.

To ascertain guilt, the Inquest should have had to show that the Four were up in King's Cross station that morning by 8.30 am at the latest. But the weight of evidence is massively against that being the case.

The Inquest should have shown that credible CCTV evidence existed of the Four in London on that morning. They have surely failed in this respect - and have produced no such credible evidence. One reason for holding a public enquiry would be to ascertain why the most CCTV-rich environment on Planet Earth could not produce one single credible CCTV image of the Four in London on the morning of 7/7.

A proper Inquest should have asked if the pattern of damage of the coaches - in the shape of the holes in the floor & the distribution of dead bodies & the sitting positions of persons who had legs and feet blown off - were at all concentric, around alleged positions of the rucksacks? I believe we have seen abundant evidence that this was not the case and that fatalities were spread in a more elongated shape along the central axes of the carriages. In the case of the Edgware Road blast, the carriage had three big holes in the floor, one some fifteen feet from the other two, and lifted clean off the rails! Does anyone suppose a rucksack on the floor could do that?

Has not the suicide-bomber hypothesis been conclusively refuted by such factual and scientific evidence? In a normal court of law, it is such physical evidence that would carry the greater weight.

While the Inquest heard from literally hundreds of witnesses, it could not find one single credible witness who saw any of the Four on the train coaches or on the number 30 bus. Yes, it produced Mr Danny Biddle ('I saw Khan') and Lisa French on the 30 bus; but I suggest any psychologist would conclude that these witnesses were not reliable: Mr Biddle's testimony has flipped about like a flag on a pole, while Ms French only acquired her 'memory' of seeing Hasib Hussein some years after the event. Both had been put, I suggest, under enormous pressure to produce their 'eyewitness' evidence.

Instead of attempting to dismiss 'conspiracy theories' on its last day, the Inquest should have started off with certain facts that would surely act as starting points for an entirely different conspiracy theory:

> 1) The fact that three coaches (and maybe also the 30 bus) were kept hidden, then destroyed after the first year of the Met's investigation ('Operation Theseus'): this was the primary evidence from the scene of the crime.

2) The fact that no post-mortems were conducted on any victims.

3) The fact that so much of the CCTV, that must have existed of the day of the Four, cannot be shown.

Answering the question, 'Is an Inquest into the deaths of the Four necessary?', Lady Justice Hallett states, "I can find no cause whatsoever to resume the inquests into the deaths of the four men. None of the families have sought to argue that any of these inquests should be resumed." One is puzzled by that silence - given that members of two of the families appealed to be allowed to give evidence at the Inquest but were refused.

The reliable website 'Official confusion' states that at least some of the bodies of the Four were handed back to the families intact. We want to hear the view of the families as to whether or not this is the case. Was the cause of death a bullet through the back of the head or from a rucksack blowing up?

Lady Justice Hallett commented on the 'unthinkable' conspiracy theory:

> To argue or find to the contrary [i.e., that Khan, Tanweer, Hussein, and Lindsay were not the bombers] would be irrational. It would be to ignore a huge body of evidence from a vast array of sources. Had there been a conspiracy falsely to implicate any of the four in the murder plot, as some have suggested, it would have been of such massive proportions as to be simply unthinkable in a democratic country. It would have involved hundreds of ordinary people, members of the bombers' families, their friends, their fellow terrorists, independent experts, scientists, as well as various police forces and the Security Service [MI5]. It would have cost millions of pounds to fabricate the forensic evidence. Independent barristers and solicitors who have had access to the source material (for example, the CCTV footage) during the criminal trials and these proceedings would have had to be involved. Just to state the proposition is to reveal its absurdity.

The issuing of this verdict immediately followed the alleged shooting of Osama bin Laden (May 1st) when he'd actually *already been dead for ten years.* It made front page headlines everywhere, with no peep of protest from the British media. Does not this rather undermine the claim that no large number of people can be involved in a 'conspiracy?' Let's here quote from Michael Ruppert's 600-page masterpiece, *Crossing the Rubicon,* about who did 9/11. How many might have had foreknowledge of the event? 'The number of people with complete foreknowledge of the attacks of September 11th would likely not exceed two dozen.' (p.3)

Globally, the only national TV station (that I could see) to cast doubt upon the official story of bin Laden was the Iranian *PressTV.* Every Bin Laden video and tape since 2001 has been faked - and not a single British media outlet can allow itself to contemplate this possibility: it would mean the whole 'War on Terror' had been totally bogus.

Magic Numbers, Synchronized Detonations

A major sequence of false-flag terror events has set the tone for the new millennium: 9/11 in 2001, the Bali bomb in 2002, Madrid in 2004, 7/7 in 2005, and then the Mumbai bombs in 2006 (There was an Istanbul blast in an empty British embassy in 2003, but this is comparatively unimportant).

None of these were what they appeared to be and all in some degree have number-symbolism in their timings. Thus, add one to each term of the 9/11 date, and you'll get 12.10.2002, the date of the Bali bomb. Like 7/7, 9/11 was also a fourfold event, with three fairly-close together and a fourth an hour later. The first plane impact on 9/11 was at a quarter to nine, not so different from the 7/7 timings. Four planes ostensibly crashed on 9/11 and four trains were bombed in Madrid (11/3 - 911 days after 9/11) and then again four trains in London on 7/7.

In Madrid, the prosecutor Olga Sánchez saw that 911-day interval as evidence of 'un factor cabalistico.' All the blast times on the four trains in Madrid were within three minutes of each other.

The close synchrony of the Madrid bombs was evidence for remote detonation - and therefore no 'suicide bombers' were alleged.

A year after the London 7/7 event, in India at the Mumbai railway station, the bombs went off on the 11th of July - 11/7. Quoting CNN news, 'No group has claimed responsibility for the blasts, which came in a span of 11 minutes.' Seven trains were bombed over a period of eleven minutes. Somebody seems to be playing number-games here, and is this a clue as to who is doing it? That discerning publisher John Leonard has taken the view that, 'Their little numerology game helps these psychopaths enjoy their work and laugh at us mere mortals.'

On 7/7 in London, how likely is it that three young men, who were in the agony of terminating their own lives and being far apart from each other, would choose or be able to ignite their bombs at the very same moments? One of the first experts on the scene was Vincent Cannistro, former head of the CIA's counter-terrorism centre, and he told *The Guardian* that the police had discovered 'mechanical timing devices' at the bomb scenes. Likewise, ABC News initially reported, 'Officials now believe that all the bombs on subway cars were detonated by timing devices' (8th July). The original story, with military-grade explosives, timing devices and synchronous detonations, mysteriously vanished once the suicide-bomber story appeared - but it made a lot more sense.

Two days after July 7th, we were informed that the three Underground blasts had been synchronous, with the first, at Aldwych, going off at 8.49 am. When I composed the J7 timeline (as in Ch. 4 of *Terror on the Tube*), I inserted that time, because there was general agreement on it. The Westbound Circle Line train number 216 had left King's Cross at 8.42, and was blown up seven minutes later.

The 7/7 Inquest added precision to this timing - as Hugo Keith stated on the first day:

> The Circle Line, the westbound inner rail section, tripped at 08.49.00, that is to say, the inner rail - not the outer rail where the explosion occurred, but the inner rail - but it can only have been tripped by force of the explosion on the other rail. So we can say with confidence that the explosion at Aldgate occurred at that moment, 08.49.00.

The Piccadilly Line westbound section tripped between Holloway Road and Russell Square at 08.49.48 and, two seconds later, the indicators in the control room that indicated that the track had current in it were also extinguished.

The Circle Line went off westbound between Baker Street and Bouverie Place, incorporating the section of the track where the explosion on the westbound Circle Line occurred, but no absolute time can be computed for that explosion because there is a variant of plus or minus 30 seconds or so in the process by which the printout in the control room prints out the time stamp of the moment of the trip. But the time was somewhere around 08.49.43. (Oct 11 pm 15:1-5)

Wikipedia puts the blasts one minute later at 8.50 am, which was the initially-reported time, and added: 'Three bombs on the London Underground exploded within fifty seconds of each other'.

Atomic Time

The Inquest heard about how this admirable second-by-second precision was obtained, calibrating the very moments of catastrophe using atomic time:

> Using Lextranet - the Metro's data system - the times have been amended through the good offices of Transport for London to reflect a more accurate Atomic time rather than a time that the system recorded. Just after 08.49, just before 10 to 9, the Metropolitan Line controller called the eastern power desk at the London Underground power control room to report that all the lights at Aldgate had gone off and that the station was in sheer darkness. (Oct 11 pm 71: 9-16)

At that key moment, much of East London tube power went down. We surely ought to accept that the authorities know when this happened. They seem proud of using atomic-clock time, thereby adjusting a few seconds here and there - let's accept this.

Hugo Keith did NOT surmise that this moment might have been chosen within a second to make the link to 9/11 he merely said, "For some unknown reason - perhaps to cause maximum devastation in the morning rush hour - it seems that the bombers intended to explode all four bombs at the same time, namely, 49 minutes past the hour"; but he added that the bus bomb went off one hour after the others.

Whatever one's view of Mr Keith (he's been described as 'a state-sponsored legal hatchet man') - I suggest it is unlikely he would have wanted to adjust or prefer data to get a 7/7 - 9/11 tie up. We note that such 'magic numbers' seem to be Cabbalistic, rather than an Islamic phenomenon.

The electrical event at 11 minutes to 9: electrocution of Aldgate victims, plus total power blackout of East London line.

An astonishing Inquest session on 18th October returned to this subject:

> The whole of the East London Line lost power, which affected nine stations in total from Shoreditch to New Cross." The East London Line can be seen there [Hugo Keith explained]. "This was due to the temporary loss of the following power assets." He then reads out a number of different power assets which I won't trouble my Ladyship with. "There was a complete cessation of traction current and signal supplies to the entire East London Line which caused all trains to stall with only battery-powered lighting. There was also a cessation of all lifts and 16 escalator supplies in the affected stations on the East London Line and emergency lighting only was available. (Oct.18th pm 4:8-18)

But, just before the blast:

> [Damage to a feeder cable] caused the 11-kilovolt electrical feeder to trip at Moorgate substation at 08.48.40. This in turn caused the 22-kilovolt coupling transformers, which supply the Mansell Street distribution network, to trip at 08.49.02. This caused widespread power disruption to a significant area of the London Underground network. (18th, 3:15-21).

That indicated an electrical blowout just before the bomb went off. We are reminded of the experience of persons in the Aldgate coach which blew up, of being electrically frazzled during and just prior to the event.

The circle-line tube station at Moorgate is West of Aldgate, and there was a bit of a mystery as to how a big power-cable at Moorgate had fused. At 08.50, the London Underground Network Control Centre in Broadway in Victoria received a call to say that there had been a loss of traction current at Moorgate (Oct 18, 18: 23-25).

On the 18th Mr Keith reiterated *the exact blast times to within a second*: "In summary, the times recorded by the power control room are 08.49 in respect of Aldgate East, 08.49.43 in respect of Edgware Road and 08.49.52 in respect of King's Cross/Russell Square." (18th am 8:7-14)

I suggest we are seeing reliable evidence here, most of which emerged immediately after the 7/7 events. These details did not (in contrast with much of the CCCTV and mobile phone 'evidence') emerge tortuously and unconvincingly years after the event, thereby magically supporting the final version of a repeatedly-changed Official Narrative.

We see here the very fingerprint of False-Flag terror (11 minutes to 9) ... the carefully recorded and almost synchronous, remotely-triggered explosions ... major electrical events both inside and outside of the devastated Aldgate carriage ... an initial diagnosis of the use of military-grade explosive and remote timing devices ... every last detail contradicting the possibility of 'suicide bombers' as responsible for this crime.

Practice Makes Perfect

Most of us who have been paying attention have known for some time that there were two 'drill-type' events associated with the 7/7 London bombings:

- The first was the *Panorama* program of May 2004, during which one above ground and three underground explosions take place over a short space of time during the morning rush hour.

- The second was the famous 'drill' revealed by Peter Power on the day of 7/7 itself, when he said that drills were taking place in the same three stations and at the same time as the bombs actually went off.

For many, including this author, these were coincidences beyond all reason. However, it was revealed to the 7/7 Inquest that there had been at least two other separate drills in London prior to 7/7 that used as their template the same three underground bombs scenario.

We now have a group of public services practicing FOUR TIMES for the exact circumstances that prevailed on the terrible morning itself.

Does it not eventually become reasonable to suppose that those that organised ALL THESE VERY SIMILAR DRILLS also organised THE IDENTICAL EVENT ITSELF?

The media, unsurprisingly, failed to report these staggering circumstances. All the anomalous evidence in this Inquest pointed in the direction of 7/7 being a classic 'false-flag' state-sponsored attack. The evidence that supports the official narrative is dubious and much of the evidence nailing the new (twice-altered) timeline has not been seen before this Inquest. Here is a detailed run-down of the drills:

The Panorama Program

BBC's *Panorama* ran what looked like a management training exercise on screen fourteen months before 7/7. Present around the studio table were various leaders of government, public and police services, including the Conservative ex-minister Michael Portillo and Peter Power, head of Visor Consultants.

The crisis scenario there described featured three blasts on the central London underground, around 8.20 am, and one above ground an hour later.

This program made the then-fictional events seem like real news: 'The headlines at 9 o'clock. In the past hour there have been three major explosions on the London underground'. It added, 'The Home Secretary has said the attacks bear the hallmarks of Al-Qaeda,' (A year later on the day of 7/7 we heard Jack Straw intoning the same phrase, 'The attacks bear the hallmarks of al-Qaeda.')

Panorama also used the memorable phrase, 'The fictional day of terror unfolds through the immediacy of rolling news bringing the catastrophic attack into our living rooms,' adding that the event was 'Set in the future - but only just.' Here one can only quote Webster Tarpley:

> No terrorist attack would be complete without the advance airing of a scenario docudrama to provide the population with a conceptual scheme to help them understand the coming events in the sense intended by the oligarchy.' (*Synthetic Terror*, 2008, p. 408)

The Contemporaneous 7/7 Drill

On 7/7 itself, Peter Power conducted a terror drill that shadowed the cataclysm as it happened - over the same three tube stations at more-or-less the same time. On the afternoon of 7/7 he was interviewed on Radio 5's "Drivetime" program:

> Power: ...at half-past nine this morning we were actually running an exercise for, er, over, a company of over a thousand people in London based on simultaneous bombs going off precisely at the railway stations where it happened this morning, so I still have the hairs on the back of my neck standing upright!

Atlantic Blue

The massive, totally-secret Atlantic Blue exercise was held over 5-8 April, 2005. All echelons of government participated in this international terror-drill. It featured walking wounded being taken into hospitals, etc., and, as usual, it is difficult to ascertain how far this was happening on the pavement, etc., versus being on a video screen. Two thousand Met police were involved, plus 14 different government departments, the NHS, etc. It was themed to have terrorist attacks upon UK transport networks coinciding with a major international summit. Visor Consultants were involved in coordination with the US Department of Homeland Security.

It was managed from Hendon, the same place that 'Gold Command' police acted from once 7/7 started to happen (and it thus had a connection with the Northern line of the London Underground). Total secrecy was imposed upon the British media. *The Observer,* remarkably, was able to publish a brief outline of what had happened in the UK's Atlantic Blue exercise - *from Washington sources!* It revealed that this had been the biggest transatlantic counter-terrorism exercise since 9/11 and that it included bombs placed on buses and explosives on the London underground.

After July 7th, *The Independent* would carry out an hour-by-hour analysis of the catastrophe, and made the following comment on what had happened at 9.10 am:

By an extraordinary coincidence, all the experts who formulate such plans are together in a meeting at the headquarters of the London Ambulance Service - and they are discussing an exercise they ran three months ago that involved simulating four terrorist bombs going off at once across London.

What a surprise to have top London Ambulance Service experts gathered together on the morning of 7/7, reminiscing about a game-simulation in which they had been involved three months earlier - *Atlantic Blue!* We would like to be told exactly when the four mock-bombs went off during the Atlantic Blue terror-game.

London's mayor Ken Livingstone was over in Singapore on the day of 7/7 - to celebrate Britain's being awarded the Olympic Games for 2012, the day before - and in giving his evidence to the July 7th Review Committee he recalled the Atlantic Blue exercise a few months earlier:

> I said from Singapore that we had actually done an exercise of multiple bomb attacks on the Underground as one of the exercises...

That is almost the only British statement about Atlantic Blue! America and Canada also participated in the event, which overall was called 'Global Shield.' The US exercise was called TOPOFF3. (alluding to Top Officers, and it being the 3rd such event) The latter had an intriguing 'Red Team' which generated the 'enemy' simulation.

Operation Hanover

London's police hold a little-known yearly terror-drill practice, called Operation Hanover, which in 2005 happened to be held on 1-2 July. Its game-plan had just three 'simultaneous' bomb attacks on three underground stations. The police have been reticent about discussing this astounding precursor event, mere days before 7/7, only revealing it in 2009:

> The Metropolitan Police Service told the Committee that they had, in the past, run exercises with scenarios similar to what actually happened on 7 July 2005. Since 2003, they have run an annual exercise known as Operation HANOVER which develops different scenarios for attacks on London and rehearses how the Metropolitan Police Service would respond. By coincidence, their 2005 exercise, run by the Security Co-ordinator's office in the Anti-Terrorist Branch, took place just a few days before the attacks - on 1-2 July. The office-based scenario for this exercise was simultaneous bomb attacks on three London Underground trains at Embankment, Waterloo, and St James's Park stations. Once again, the scenario is quite similar to what actually took place, and the fact that it took place so close to the actual attacks is an interesting coincidence.

One would like to have the time of day for that Operation Hanover simultaneous-bomb game-simulation.

I posted as article up about this in October 2011, since when the web-link to the Met's account of the Operation Hanover has vanished. A reference to the above paragraph remains in the J7 submission to the 7/7 Inquest - scroll down to 'Hanover Series.'[119]

The series of impossible coincidences we have here reviewed point to the startling fact that these terror-drill rehearsals actually comprise *the unfolding elaboration of the 7/7 event itself.*

What Really Happened

The perfect crime had been planned. It would make history, and be the British answer to 9/11. After years of planning, it was ready to go! No one would ever guess...

It was part of the sequence of terror-events which have arced across our world in the New Millennium, extinguishing the bright hopes of the new century: 9/11 in New York, the Bali bomb of 2002, the Istanbul bomb of 2003, Madrid railway station in 2004, and then London in 2005, followed by the Mumbai train blasts of 2006. They have served to define the new Enemy - the *phantom menace* - and to ratify the Empire.

Two things went wrong for the July 7th event. Both came out of the blue, and were totally unexpected - almost, one could say, acts of God. Firstly, the train selected (Luton to London) was cancelled for 7.40 am, and the other trains that morning were severely delayed - so that the Four just could not get to London in time. Secondly, Mohammed Khan's beloved young wife suddenly started having pregnancy complications and, by July 5th, it was clear that Khan had to pull out.

The 'handler' of the Four faced a tricky moment of having to persuade the other three - the two young men in Leeds, Tanweer, and Hussein, plus Lindsay in Aylesbury - to carry on with their agreed participation in the terror-drill without Khan. Khan had been the boss and ringleader amongst them, and he was older. My book found no evidence that Khan had participated in the events of 7/7: no one ever saw him after he took his wife to the hospital for that checkup on the 5th.

People in what is loosely called the 'truth movement' had been puzzled by the absence of any credible CCTV - or human witnesses - testifying that the Four had been in London on that morning. The police kept announcing that they had lots of CCTV, but why could they not show it? *Why were the only bits of CCTV they released suspicious and tampered-with?* If the problem was that the four had arrived too late, surely the police could have adjusted the timestamps?

I was ridiculed on the BBC's "Conspiracy Files 7/7" program (June 2009), for being sceptical that the Four had arrived in London on that morning. No doubt I deserved it - *because I was wrong!* Much CCTV of Hasib Hussein pottering around King's Cross station was shown at the Inquest on October 13th and fortunately I was there. The public were never shown that untampered-with CCTV footage. At last, I became finally convinced of two things: firstly, that he really had been there, wandering around in a rather lost manner for 25 minutes; and secondly, that the police had no CCTV of him there before 5 or 6 minutes to nine, after the bombs had gone off: after which he abruptly appeared on their CCTV screens.

Maybe we will never know what happened to the 18-year old Hasib Hussein. All we can say is that the three places we are told he went - the MacDonald's over the road, the 91 bus, the 30 bus - all mysteriously had their CCTV switched off, or the film went missing.

The Inquest heard what I and fellow-researcher Kevin Boyle felt was quite credible testimony, from a guard at King's Cross, who had seen Germaine Lindsey and spoken to him - and I noticed how careful the Inquest was to avoid defining the time when this happened. It has to have been sometime before the bombs went off at ten to nine.

The *Ripple Effect* video proposed the story of the young men arriving too late and then fleeing to Canary Wharf - quite an easy journey for them: they just had to get back onto the same Thameslink line they had just come from, and they would be there in a few stops. It had clearly been reported that two 'suicide bombers' were shot by the police at Canary Wharf at 10.30 am - which appeared on at least two UK news broadcasts at 11 am that morning before being officially denied. That event has to be a crucial clue as to what happened that morning.

The British philosopher Professor Rory Ridley-Duff (at Sheffield University) compared the BBC's "Conspiracy Files" account with that of the *Ripple Effect*, he had to conclude that the latter had a higher 'truth value.' He found the Canary Wharf story to be central, *after locating no less than 17 news reports about it!* Those accounts were of *two* young men being shot dead - not *three*. I posted this story on my website and was startled by how many posts then appeared from people confirming the story.

The police could never show all of their reams of CCTV, which it had declared would be shown. Why not? *The Ripple Effect* narrative could never explain this. I suggest that only three lads were ever in those photos, whereas *a fourfold story had to be imposed upon the British public, with four explosions*. In the crush of rush-hour, lots of others were milling around in the background. Adjusting timestamps was too risky because of the unpredictable way in which other commuters in the pictures would be liable to come forward. That's why the only CCTV we have been shown is of dubious origin, with the only images of the Four on that morning artfully contrived to have no one else around.

I once asked Muad'Dib (composer of the *Ripple Effect*), why did he believe Khan was travelling down with Hasib Hussein and Tanweer that morning? He alluded to photos released at the Woodall Service Station on the M1, just before 5 o'clock in the morning. "Could one not see a glimpse of Khan in the car?", he replied. I never managed to see him. There was one other person visible in the front of the car, identifiable as Hasib Hussein. The forecourt manager of the

Service Station testified at the Inquest, after taking a solemn oath, that he had seen only one other person in the car, besides Tanweer (Oct 13th pm 55:5-6).

For Tanweer at Woodall Services station on July 7th, note his white trousers which had apparently changed to dark by the time they arrived at Luton station.

That Woodall forecourt scene is important, I suggest, as being the only CCTV sequence for that day which does not appear to have been tampered with apart from the sequence at King's Cross of Hasib Hussein solo. Even though it was only released three years later, it seems genuine enough to me. We see a smartly-dressed Tanweer filling up with petrol then entering the shop, and the Inquest duly produced the bill: twenty pounds for petrol and ten pounds for crisps and sweets - which does not sound much like a suicide bomber (Oct 13th pm, 54:12-15).

Let's quote a summary by Andrew MacGregor:

Mohammed Khan and his 'co-conspirators' had been hired to take part in a drill by Visor Consultants. They had no idea that they were being set up to be 'suicide-bombers'. When Mohammed Khan informed his 'minder' that he was pulling out because of his wife's condition, Mohammed Khan sealed his own death warrant. Suicide bombers never survive, even if they change their minds.

So Mohammed Khan disappears on the 5th July 2005.

Thus ended the life of the gentleman 'Sid' Khan, the Anglicized Muslim - aide to deprived children in a special school, known for assisting local police in peacemaking between teenage gangs. We recall that, when his wife saw him on the 'suicide bomber' video, her immediate words were, "That's not my husband".

Message from the Perps?

For five years, we had been told that I.D. of Khan was found at three different locations: the Edgware Road, Tavistock Square, and Aldgate Station blast scenes. This was more a sign of his absence from London that morning than it was of his presence. It seemed comparable in its meaning or rather lack of meaning to the bizarre Khan image shown at Luton at 7.22.

He is meant to be the figure in the background in this alleged image of the Four. It is inadequate merely to describe this as a bad or blurred image: it is so bad - with his legs faded away and two lots or railings passing in front of him that should be behind - that it looks like a coded message from the perps indicating his absence from Luton, rather than his presence. A close-up of his 'head' is also shown.

The Four alleged perps at Luton Thameslink station on July 7ᵗʰ at 7.22 am, with close-up of Khan's face.

But, if so, people did not get the message; and so the Inquest added a fourth location where Khan's ID was located: Russell Square, the Piccadilly line blast. His mobile phone was located there by the blasted carriage - complete with the (faked) text-message sent from it that morning!

So we have Her Majesty's Inquest gravely listening to the four different sites where ID of Khan was located: *all four of the blast sites.* Nobody laughs, nor does a single newspaper journalist express doubt.

7/7: Made in Israel

For years I have kept clear of this subject. My book, *Terror on the Tube,* about the London bombings assigned only a very minimal role to Israeli agents, by way of manipulating the surveillance and security companies (ICTS, Verint Systems, etc.), operating on the London Underground, which are Israeli-owned. It did allude to Netanyahu's apparent foreknowledge of the event, but drew no conclusions from it.

However, things have now changed, with a former Mossad agent more or less admitting, in a slip of the tongue, that they did it, in 2014:[120] while discussing an explosive maybe used in the London bombings, Mr Juval Aviv said: "It's easy to put a truck bomb as we did… as happened in London." All comments below that video accepted that he had made an admission of Mossad perpetrating the London Bombings.

Mr Aviv was the Mossad counter-terror agent described by George Jonas in his novel, *Vengeance: The True Story of an Israeli Counter-Terrorist Team*

(1984) and the central character in the Spielberg film about this. He even has a book, *Staying Safe*.

The Australian ex-policeman Andrew MacGregor had a theory which I had always refused to go along with. "You can't prove it," I would say. (Several articles of his are posted on my *Terrrorontthetube.com* website.) This is what he wrote:

> I would like to quote from Efraim Halevi, a former head of Mossad in an article that was printed in *The Jerusalem Post* on the 7th July 2005. This article was headed, 'Rules of conflict for a world war:'

> "The multiple, simultaneous explosions that took place yesterday on the London transportation system were the work of perpetrators who had an operational capacity of considerable scope. They have come a long way since the two attacks of the year 1998 against the American Embassies in Nairobi and Dar-Es-Salaam, and the aircraft actions of September 11, 2001."

> Like the rabbit that hops out of the top hat before the magician is ready for his stunt, the truth has been exposed. This article was written prior to the actual bombing that took place in London, and thus, Efraim Halevi had to have been one of the planners for this 'Terrorist' event.

> The Jerusalem Post describes Efraim Halevi as: "The writer, who heads the Centre for Strategic and Policy Studies at the Hebrew University in Jerusalem, is a former head of the Mossad. (© 1995-2005, The Jerusalem Post 07/07/05)"

> In simple words, The London bombing was a 'planned' terrorist attack by a group of people including Efraim Halevi, of the 'Centre for Strategic and Policy Studies' at the 'Hebrew University' in Jerusalem.

The article by Efraim Halevi went up at 4 pm onto the *Jerusalem Post* website which is 2 pm in London. Strangely entitled, 'Rules of Conflict for a World War', it is a deeply meditated piece, and it knows far too much, e.g., that the explosions were simultaneous - a fact which only became evident some days later. (Scotland Yard initially averred that the explosions had been 45 minutes apart.) For some years, I wrestled with the question, does that precognition of the event imply that 'Israel did it'? *Yes - I now believe that there is no avoiding the logic.*

Halevi's article surely has to have been written well before July 7th. His phrase '… that took place yesterday' shows it was written with the expectation of being put into a newspaper for the next day - that could not happen if it were being written to go up onto a website at once. (Note well: Some web-versions of this influential article have removed the word 'yesterday.')

And who are 'they' who Halevi says have 'come a long way'? 'They' have to be the Mossad team (as Andrew MacGregor observes) and those two 1998 operations were the ones that successfully created the new demonised enemy image of Islam. The two attacks were blamed on Osama bin Laden, who had previously been used by the Americans to wage war against the Russians in Afghanistan. It was from these two attacks that Americans came to know Osama bin Laden as 'Public Enemy No. 1.'

That newly-demonised enemy image was then used successfully for the 9/11 event and so Halevi saw these 1998 events as a beginning. He alluded admiringly to the 'perpetrators who had an operational capacity of considerable scope' - as if congratulating the Mossad team responsible. But how could he know that the event showed "careful planning, intelligence gathering, and a sophisticated choice of timing as well as near-perfect execution"? Monitoring the terror-event that morning, he would have seen the delayed trains Luton to King's Cross causing the patsies to turn up too late at King's cross which nearly wrecked the whole plan - how could they take the blame if they weren't there? His phrase 'near-perfect' implies that he knew what the plan was.

Halevi had recently joined the Advisory Board of the UK company, Quest, described as 'The professional Intelligence company' and a "risk mitigation" organisation. It specialised in 'Technical surveillance operations, mobile, foot and static surveillance, close reconnaissance and covert and overt photography.'

Ephraim Halevi and Peter Power are two UK citizens who need to be questioned under oath over the crime of 7/7. Peter Power made some comment about his customer that day being an Israeli firm, and it may have been these clients who selected the three stations Power was using for his terror-drill - which so mysteriously synchronized with the actual events. Peter Power said on the afternoon of July 7th 'We planned this for a company and for obvious reasons I don't want to reveal their name' and then later on in this context he alluded to 'Jewish businessmen.'

Those conducting this war, Halevi explained, had to be able to "carry the combat into whatever territory the perpetrators and their temporal and spiritual leaders are inhabiting", i.e., they have to have the capacity to sneak into other countries, which the Mossad is able to do.

For both 9/11 and 7/7, only Israeli intelligence appears to have known when those events were going to happen.[121] The CIA and FBI knew in a general sort of way that something was going to happen. US politicians had been warned to stay clear of the London Underground some months earlier,[122] just as they had been warned to stay clear of American Airlines for a week or two prior to 9/11. Did the British Intelligence know when the 7/7 event was going to happen? If so, there is no sign of it.

Although he later denied it, Benjamin Netanyahu made clear that he had had prior warning, while he was in his hotel in Russell Square, before proceeding on to the TASE conference (Tel Aviv Economic Summit) at Liverpool Street where he was due to give a keynote speech. He wanted to draw attention to himself, being an egoistic character, which his announcement of foreknowledge certainly achieved - but, at a cost of rather letting the cat out of the bag regarding who had planned the event.

'Within hours of the explosions, Israeli Army Radio was reporting that, "Scotland Yard had intelligence warnings of the attacks a short time before they occurred." This report, repeated by *IsraelNN.com*, added that "The Israeli Embassy in London was notified in advance, resulting in the foreign minister Binyamin Netanyahu remaining in his hotel room...' (Webster Tarpley, *Synthetic Terror*, p. 461) Tarpley always takes the mistaken view that Israel was a mere passive spectator. As a damage limitation exercise, to account for Netanyahu's foreknowledge, immediate Israeli news statements tried to pin 'blame' on Scotland Yard for telling Netanyahu in advance - which it denied - but why would it want to do that? It makes no sense. The Israelis had foreknowledge.

Terror Planning in Israel

Let's return to Andrew McGregor, with his antipodean insights:

> With Halevi we have 'the Centre for Strategic and Policy Studies at the Hebrew University'. So what else comes from the Hebrew University of Jerusalem? We get this!
>
> In 2005, the Nobel Prize in Economic Science was awarded to Israeli mathematician and game theory specialist Robert J. Aumann, co-founder of the Centre for Rationality at Hebrew University. (See *http://intifada-palestine.com/2009/08/20/how-israel-wages-game-theory-warfare/*) This site explains the situation as such: 'Israeli strategists rely on game theory models to ensure the intended response to staged provocations and manipulated crises. The waging of war "by way of deception" is now a mathematical discipline.' This site also explains how Israel uses this developed strategy as: *Such "probabilistic" war planning enables Tel Aviv to deploy serial provocations and well-timed crises as a force multiplier to project Israeli influence worldwide.*

Is there is a possible link between Halevi's "The Centre for Strategic and Policy Studies" at the Hebrew University and Robert J. Aumann's "Centre for Rationality" at Hebrew University? Efraim Halevi's statement that: "There was careful planning, intelligence gathering, and a sophisticated choice of timing as well as near-perfect execution" certainly suggests there is a connection between these two bodies and the series of 'Terrorist' attacks from 1998 up to the 7th July 2005 and most probably thereafter.

So what we actually have from Efraim Halevi is a statement that demonstrates the actual hierarchy of the planners of such 'terrorist' attacks as 9/11. The highest tiers of these players are the Zionists who control their various fields, such as media, military, government bureaucracies, and of course the politicians. The second tier consists of the various politicians and other 'leaders' who have accepted their bribes and must now dance to the

Zionist's tune. The third tier consists of the various bureaucratic and military chiefs who are embedded within these plots.[123]

Do these two Hebrew University departments, the Centre for Strategic and Policy Studies (Halevi) and the Centre for Rationality (Aumann), really co-plot the terror events? The evidence we have reviewed suggests that they do.

Game Theory

Thus, MacGregor is arguing that Aumann's theories being used at the Hebrew University along with the views of Halevi would have provided a good planning group for that event. It was Halevi's comments about the 'planners' coming a long way from the earlier bombings' that gave him the clue - Aumann's involvement would have been vital for those events, possibly why he was given the Nobel Prize.

Let's quote from an article in the prestigious *US Foreign Policy* journal by Jeff Gates clearly explaining how game theory has been developed and used in Aumann's Centre of Rationality (where 'the mark' signifies the target of the attack):[124]

> With a well-modelled provocation, the anticipated reaction can even become a powerful weapon in the Israeli arsenal.

> For instance, a skilled game theorist could foresee that, in response to a 9/11-type mass murder, "the mark" (the U.S.) would deploy its military to avenge that attack. With phony intelligence fixed around a pre-set goal, a game theory algorithm could anticipate that those forces might well be redirected to invade Iraq - not to avenge 9/11 but to pursue the expansionist goals of Greater Israel...To displace facts with credible fiction requires a period of "preparing the minds" so that the mark will believe a pre-staged storyline.

> Israeli game theorists operate not from the Centre for Morality or the Centre for Justice but from the Centre for Rationality. As modelled by Zionist war planners, game theory is devoid of all values except one: the ability to anticipate - within an acceptable range of probabilities - how "the mark" will react when provoked.

Brilliant stuff - no doubt, worth Robert Aumann's Nobel Prize. There were many similarities between the Madrid and London bombings, not least between the sophisticated explosives that may have been used and the primitive backpack bombs, which the 'terrorists' had allegedly constructed. To quote Richard Cottrell, 'Taken altogether, the extraordinary sum of the over-lapping similarities in Madrid and London point strongly to an experienced organisational hand - which we appear to have uncovered - moving in the world of synthetic terror.'[125]

6
The Heathrow Liquid Bomb Hoax
2006

"Put simply, this was intended to be mass murder on an unimaginable scale," said Deputy Commissioner Paul Stephenson from the Metropolitan Police. Nothing had actually happened, no bomb had been taken on board a plane - no one had *even made one*. So what was all the fuss about? Why all the plane cancellations at Heathrow, costing hundreds of millions in delays and lost flights, and why can't we take toothpaste in hand luggage anymore? Britain's new anti-terror legislation, where you don't actually have to do anything to get arrested, had swung into action. Britain's Prime Minister Tony Blair, on holiday during these events in Barbados at Sir Cliff Richard's luxury villa, decided to stay there.

The COBRA meeting began at 9.30 pm on the 9th August, 2006, in the high-tech bunker deep below the Cabinet Office. The police raids began at midnight, with 24 suspects arrested: British-born Muslims, some of Pakistani descent, from London, Birmingham, and High Wycombe. It was an overnight operation, and their finances were frozen. Those detained included a soccer fan, cricket players, a taxi driver, an accountant and his nursery teacher wife who was expecting a baby within a few weeks, a security guard with a three-week old baby, a pizza worker, a tyre businessman and a science student.[126] British police found tins of baked beans, peanut butter, some low concentration hydrogen peroxide and a sugar solution (i.e., the latter were possibly bleach or disinfectant and a cup of tea) at the suspects' homes. These apparently normal, peaceable, well-adjusted people had all been consumed with an irresistible urge to kill themselves and were prepared to kill hundreds of others, we were told.[127] These arrests appeared to be the result of a long-standing investigation coordinated between the US, British and Pakistani governments.

On Thursday morning, thousands of holidaymakers began arriving at airports to discover total disruption and the biggest terror alert since 7/7. It was alleged that multiple commercial aircraft were intended to be targeted, maybe for the 16th August, and that their fiendish plot aimed to destroy as many as ten aircraft in mid-flight from the United Kingdom to the United States, using explosives brought on board in their hand luggage! News media reported that planned targets included American Airlines, British Airways, Continental Airlines, and United Airlines flights from London Heathrow and London Gatwick airports to Chicago, Illinois; Los Angeles, California; Miami, Florida; Orlando, Florida; Boston, Massachusetts; Newark, New Jersey; New York City; San Francisco, California; Cleveland, Ohio; and Washington, D.C. The BBC's security correspondent Gordon Corera said the plot involved a series of simultaneous attacks, targeting three planes each time. The plotters planned to use Lucozade bottles (or so *The New York Times* reported) to contain certain 'liquid explosives'. They were going to use peroxide-based explosives, the media seemed to agree, probably the dreaded triacetone triperoxide (TATP).

These arrests were *followed by* the search for evidence, as the *Financial Times* explained: "The police set about the mammoth task of gathering evidence of the alleged terrorist bomb plot yesterday" (August 12, 2006). This was an odd reversal of normal investigatory procedures, commented the French 'Voltairenet' (of Thierry Meyssan), in which arrests were only supposed to happen *after* the gathering of evidence.[128] On what basis had the arrests been made? The British government, backed by Washington (or vice versa), averred that the Pakistani government's arrest of two British-Pakistanis provided *"critical evidence"* in uncovering the plot and identifying the alleged terrorist. The Pakistani intelligence services (ISI) are notorious for use of torture in extracting 'confessions.' In this case, their evidence was based on a supposed encounter between a relative of one of the suspects and an Al-Qaeda operative on the Afghan border. The Al-Qaeda agent supposedly provided the relative and thus the accused with the bomb-making information and operative instructions. But, transmission of bomb-making information hardly required a trip half-way around the world, least of all to a frontier under military siege by US-led forces on one side and the Pakistani military on the other. Were the Al-Qaeda agents in the mountains of Afghanistan supposed to have some detailed knowledge of Heathrow airport?

Prime Minister Tony Blair had alerted George Bush to the investigation on Sunday, 6th August, 2006, before flying out with his family to Barbados on the 8th. Bush and Blair had discussed the matter prior to the police arrests. On 9th August, hours before the arrests, the Home Secretary John Reid gave a major speech to Demos (a British think-tank) hinting at a new round of anti-terror legislation, claiming that the country was facing 'probably the most sustained period of severe threat since the end of the Second World War.'

And he decried those who "don't get it," i.e., who failed to comprehend that democratic liberties had to be surrendered to the state. He blamed them for the fact that "we remain unable to adapt our institutions and legal orthodoxy as fast as we need to," making it clear that the required "adaptation" meant the gutting of traditional democratic rights:

Sometimes we may have to modify some of our own freedoms in the short term in order to prevent their misuse and abuse by those who oppose our fundamental values and would destroy all of our freedoms in the modern world.

On the next day, 10th August, George Bush commented, upon his arrival in Wisconsin: "The recent arrests that our fellow citizens are now learning about are a stark reminder that this nation is at war with Islamic fascists who will use any means to destroy those of us who love freedom, to hurt our nation."[129] Israel was brutally assaulting Lebanon as Bush slipped in that key phrase 'Islamic fascists.' Israel's July invasion led to the killing of over 1,000 people, the creation of more than a million refugees who were forced to flee their homes, and the contamination of large swathes of the countryside with lethal land-mines.

The US Homeland Security Secretary Michael Chertoff on August 10th described the (non-) event as an attack which *had the potential to kill hundreds of thousands of people.* Inevitably, he added that 'it certainly has some of the hallmarks of an al Qaeda plot,' and agreed with his interviewer that, 'this plot was the biggest terrorist threat since the attacks of September 11, 2001'. A senior congressional source claimed that the plotters planned to mix 'a sports drink with a peroxide-based paste to make an explosive cocktail that could be triggered by an MP3 player or cell phone.' Uh-huh. Meanwhile, Israeli warplanes bombed the heart of Beirut.

Seventeen of the suspects were charged with conspiracy to murder and commit acts of terrorism *or failing to disclose* information about acts of terrorism. Little did this (alleged) 'group' know that an undercover British agent had infiltrated them. On 28 August, 2006, the NYT reported that seven martyrdom tapes made by six suspects were recovered. Gigabytes of information had been confiscated from homes of dozens of suspects. Hundreds of computers and mobile phones were taken. But, that still wouldn't give the police any connection between the persons arrested who hadn't bought air tickets or made bombs, and a terror plot that never happened over the skies of America. The suspected ringleader Rashid Rauf in Pakistan almost certainly had 'extraordinary rendition' applied to him, i.e., been tortured, to 'confess.'

Heathrow Airport was closed down, then hand luggage was forbidden; later, liquids were forbidden in hand luggage (e.g., milk and toothpaste). The first day of delays cost the airlines over £175 million. Huge queues of passengers waited to check-in and get through the strengthened security procedures. On Sunday, 13th August, 30% of flights out of Heathrow were cancelled to reduce pressure on the screeners. British Airlines reported that 10,000 items of baggage belonging to their passengers had gone missing while Ryanair called on the British government to employ police and military reservists to speed up the full-body searches that had become mandatory. By August 12th, the owner and operator of London Heathrow ordered all airlines using the airport to make a 30 percent reduction in departing passenger flights. Carolyn Evans, head of flight safety at the British Airline Pilots Association, said that "the procedures put in place are not sustainable long term, and unless the passengers are treated more reasonably we will not have an industry left." In November 2006, BA claimed that the increased security measures since August had cost it £100 million.[130]

Amidst the madness, a word of sense was spoken by former UK Ambassador to Uzbekistan, Craig Murray:

> Many [of those arrested] did not even have passports, which given the efficiency of the UK Passport Agency would mean they couldn't be a plane bomber for quite some time ... In the absence of bombs and airline

tickets, and in many cases passports, it could be pretty difficult to convince a jury beyond reasonable doubt that individuals intended to go through with suicide bombings, whatever rash stuff they may have bragged in Internet chat rooms....

Then an interrogation in Pakistan revealed the details of this amazing plot to blow up multiple planes ... Of course, the interrogators of the Pakistani dictator have their ways of making people sing like canaries. As I witnessed in Uzbekistan, you can get the most extraordinary information this way. The trouble is it always tends to give the interrogators all they might want, and more, in a desperate effort to stop or avert torture. What it doesn't give is the truth.[131]

Another British voice of sanity was that of political scientist Nafeez Ahmed., who expressed the view that:

The British and American governments, for all intents and purposes, invented a terror threat in August 2006, to trigger a climate of fear and paranoia convenient for the legitimization of a political agenda of intensifying social control at home, and escalating military repression in the Middle East.

He gave several talks together with munitions expert Lt. Colonel Wylde on the topic.[132] Apart from these, the entire British media believed the story. It was a dream-hallucination from start to finish, with no semblance of rational evidence to link together those arrested and an alleged plot which never happened. According to Lt-Col (Ret.) Nigel Wylde, a former senior British Army Intelligence Officer with decades of anti-terror and explosives experience, the whole plot was a 'fiction' and the explosives in question could not possibly have been produced on the plane.[133] 'So who came up with the idea that a bomb could be made on board? Not Al Qaeda for sure. It would not work. Bin Laden is interested in success, not deterrence by failure,' Wylde explained. He suggested that the plot was an invention of the UK security services in order to justify profitable and wide-ranging new security measures that threaten to permanently curtail civil liberties and to suspend sections of the United Kingdom's Human Rights Act of 1998. Wylde added that, if there was a conspiracy, 'it did not involve manufacturing the explosives in the loo,' as this simply 'could not have worked.' The process would be quickly and easily detected. The fumes of the chemicals in the toilet 'would be smelt by anybody in the area.' They would also inevitably 'cause the alarms in the toilet and in the air change system in the aircraft to be triggered.'

Key information was supposed to have been obtained from Pakistan, but what did Pakistan have to do with it? There's no need to go to Pakistan to learn that mixing acetone, sulphuric acid and peroxide won't make a bomb, especially not in an aircraft toilet - that's only in the Hollywood movies. Those three chemicals would form a nasty mixture which would stink very badly, but they would require a freezing cabinet and a fume cupboard for the reaction to work, i.e., produce

TATP - adding a drop of sulphuric acid at a time, taking several hours, then a day for the TATP to separate out. Also, what about the detonators? Without a detonator, it's not a bomb.

Had the alleged ringleader, 25-year old Rashid Rauf (born in Birmingham) invented the plot under torture in Pakistan, as Craig Murray suggested? Rauf attended a court hearing in Rawalpindi, on 22nd December, 2006:

> Head bowed and covered by a black shawl and Muslim prayer cap, the Briton named as a 'key suspect' in the alleged terror plot to blow up transatlantic airliners was escorted to a court in Pakistan yesterday... Yesterday Rauf, from Birmingham, protested his innocence of any involvement in a plot. Handcuffed and flanked by 12 armed police officers, he claimed he had been framed by the authorities. 'I have done nothing wrong but I have been framed, I am not optimistic that I will be cleared... everything against me is based on lies.'[134]

Despite his prosecutors alleging that Rauf was in possession of a number of bottles of hydrogen peroxide, the court dropped the charges, ruling that this case 'did not fall into the category of terrorism.'

An article by chemist Thomas Greene in Washington explained how the 'binary liquid munitions' story had come out of movies rather than a chemistry textbook:

> So the fabled binary liquid explosive - that is, the sudden mixing of hydrogen peroxide and acetone with sulphuric acid to create a plane-killing explosion, is out of the question. Meanwhile, making TATP ahead of time carries a risk that the mission will fail due to premature detonation, although it is the only plausible approach. Certainly, if we can imagine a group of jihadists smuggling the necessary chemicals and equipment on board, and cooking up TATP in the lavatory, then we've passed from the realm of action blockbusters to that of situation comedy.[135]

The bomb plot hoax has caused enormous losses not only to the airlines, but also to business people, oil companies, duty-free shops, tourist agencies, resorts and hotels, not to speak of the tremendous inconvenience and health related problems of millions of stranded and stressed-out travellers. So what was the point of it? What was its *purpose*? We've already quoted Nafeez Ahmed, and let's now hear a pertinent judgement from France's Voltaire Network:

> Clearly the decision to cook up the phony bomb plot was not motivated by economic interests, but domestic political reasons. The Blair administration, already highly unpopular for supporting Bush's wars in Iraq and Afghanistan, was under attack for his unconditional support for Israel's invasion of Lebanon, his refusal to call for an immediate ceasefire and his unstinting support for Bush's servility to US Zionist lobbies. Even

within the Labour party over a hundred backbenchers were speaking out against his policies ...

The criminal frame-up of young Muslim-South Asian British citizens by the British security officials was specifically designed to cover up for the failed Anglo-American invasion of Iraq and the Anglo-American backing for Israel's destructive but failed invasion of Lebanon. Blair's *"liquid bombers"* plot sacrificed a multiplicity of British capitalist interests in order to retain political office and stave off an unceremonious early exit from power. The costs of failed militarism are borne by citizens and businesses.[136]

The liquid bomb story was soon ridiculed into obscurity, after which British Deputy Assistant Commissioner Peter Clarke merely claimed that *"bomb making equipment including chemicals and electric components had been found."*[137] Also, the Clark team claimed that they found 'martyr videotapes' in the homes of those arrested, without clarifying the fact that the videos were not made by the suspects but only viewed by them. In mid-December, the police announced that they were calling off the search at a strip of woodland where bomb-making equipment had allegedly been hidden, as none of the authorities were prepared to continue funding the operation. On May 20th, 2007 the arrested alleged plotters entered their plea of 'not guilty,' and their trial took place in 2008.

How did it begin? Some days before the arrests, on Sunday, 6th August, American Airlines flight 109 from London Heathrow to Boston boarded a family of five; after the plane left, Heathrow authorities determined that the father appeared on a British suspect list drawn up after the 7/7 London transit attacks. The pilot was instructed to fly to Boston but refused, fearing for the safety of his passengers and crew, and quickly returned to Heathrow without informing the passengers. Once on the ground, it was discovered that the male had in his carry-on baggage the combination of liquid explosive and an electronic device that was now being hyped by the British and American media. That sounds a quite unlikely combination: featuring on an alleged 'July 7th suspect' list and carrying binary liquid explosives; no wonder no one has released the name of this person. As Alex Jones' Prison Planet article concluded, 'The Israeli attack on Lebanon created a rift within Blair's Cabinet ... As a result, a suspect passenger was permitted to board an American aircraft at Heathrow with a liquid bomb to lay the groundwork for the media and travel hysteria five days later.'[138]

The police responsible need to brush up on chemistry concerning what can go bang in a bomb, for example, in the 'Crevice' trial, the mere possession of bags of a *fertiliser,* ammonium nitrate was enough to put Muslims in jail, whereas fertiliser-grade ammonium nitrate is made so that it will not detonate very readily.[139] In the July 7th, July 21st, and the Heathrow liquid bomb story, TATP was featured, whereas in real life no 'terrorist' has used it for a bomb-maybe because it is too unstable and needs to be stored below 10° C.

In April 2008, the Heathrow liquid-bomb trial began at Woolwich Crown Court, with eight men accused. One of them, 27-year old Abdulla Ahmed Ali, denied any intention of boarding planes - 'We did not even think about boarding a plane' - and insisted that a device was merely intended as a demonstration of protest against Britain's foreign policy. "This whole thing has been blown up out of proportion. I'm not going to admit to something I didn't do and never intended to do." He maintained that the plastic bottle and battery explosive device he attempted to make was never intended to harm. "That's the truth," he said. "I've done something which is an offence, I'm putting my hand up to that." He claimed the charges against him had been "exaggerated", with the media being used "to ruthless effect".[140]

It would appear that Britons are prepared to pay a heavy price for their daily dose of fear, their tingle of terror, and that politicians now have to cater for this need, which has somehow spilled over from horror and action movies. No politician trying to claim that the British did not have an enemy, or did not need an enemy, could possibly hope to get elected. This writer would suggest that wolves should be re-introduced into selected woodlands. Possibly hearing the howling of wolves at night might satisfy the atavistic need for fear, and would obviate the continual need to have innocent Muslims banged up in jail on phantom terror allegations.

The Fictional 'Ricin Plot'

These phantom terror events remind one of the 'Ricin plot,' where a flat in Wood Green was raided on 5th January, 2003, by the police. They found some castor beans plus a few other ingredients. Ricin, a poison, *can be extracted* from castor beans. News reports alleging that 'traces' of ricin had been found in the flat were soon contradicted by top British experts at Porton Down - despite which, like an undead zombie, the story refused to lie down. Why not? Britain's Master of Deception Tony Blair held forth with one of his 'be afraid' speeches, on January 7th, 2003:

> The arrests which were made show this danger is present and real with us now. Its potential is huge.

'Terror on the Doorstep,' as a *Sunday Times* headline proclaimed, was ideal material for the new, pointless war into which the Prime Minister was dragging Britain. A hapless Algerian 'mastermind' was arrested, who was, of course, named Mohammed - the name of the Prophet is almost mandatory for these 'masterminds', e.g., Mohammed Atta (9/11), Mohammed Khan (7/7), and this disturbed loner was thrown in jail for *writing out a recipe* for making ricin.

The *purpose* of the Ricin Plot appeared a month later, when US Secretary of State Colin Powell brandished a phial of what was allegedly ricin before the United Nations on 6th February, alleging that the London 'terror cell' was part of a global network originating in Iraq. It appeared as part of his case for military intervention in Iraq.

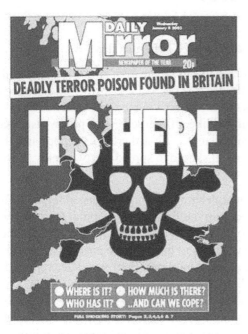

Figures: *Daily Mirror* front page plus Colin Powell showing 'ricin' at the UN, February 2003

Two years later this vacuous 'threat' could still be resurrected as a reason for Britons surrendering their democratic freedoms: Ian Blair, police superintendent, declared on the 'Breakfast with Frost' program 17.4.05 that the 'Ricin plot' demonstrated the need for new anti-terror laws; later on (5.10.05), Met police assistant Andy Hayman was citing the Ricin plot as showing the need for 90-day detentions without trial.[141] Did anyone ever apologise for all this outright mendacity, frightening the British people, dragging them into illegal war and arresting the innocent?

7

Constructed Terror on Christmas Day 2009

Who would want to cause terror on Christmas day?

Twenty minutes before a Northwest Airlines flight from Amsterdam landed at Detroit, on Christmas day, some kind of firework was set off: 'A passenger on board has reportedly set off fireworks as it was arriving in the US city of Detroit,' quoting from an early report: "It sounded like a firecracker in a pillowcase," said Peter Smith, a traveller from the Netherlands. "First there was a pop, and then (there) was smoke." Flames were seen: "It started to spread pretty quickly. It went up the wall, all the way to ceiling."

That was the experience. A photograph shows unsinged seats, along with fire-extinguishers and a bit of white powder on the floor. I suggest that the plane was never in danger. We were shown no photos of seats burnt by fire on that flight 273 to Detroit[142] and what people saw seems to have been a sparkler-type effect. The 23-year old 'terrorist' (Umar Farouk Abdulmutallab) was later reported to have had sixty grams of PETN (a military explosive) strapped to his crotch, which 'failed' to blow up - I do not recommend believing that bit! His trousers may have burnt and he spent a day or so in hospital being treated for burns had he had that small amount of PETN positioned on a seat and cushioned underneath him, and *if* he could have made it explode, using a detonator - which he did not have - then such an explosion would *not* have caused significant damage to the plane. Strapped against the wall, maybe - but hardly with him sitting on it.

Air Travel without a Passport

A Mr Kurt Haskell of Newport, Michigan and his partner were sitting near their boarding gate in Amsterdam's Schiphol Airport, when they saw Mutallab approach the gate with an unidentified South-Asian man. Mutallab was poorly dressed, but his friend was dressed in an expensive suit. The suited man asked ticket agents whether Mutallab could board without a passport. "The guy said, 'He's from Sudan and we do this all the time.'" (Mutallab is Nigerian). The ticket agent referred Mutallab and his companion to her manager down the hall, and Haskell didn't see Mutallab again until after he allegedly tried to detonate an explosive on the plane.

We now hand over the story to Ian Crane[143] ...

> Public reaction to the Christmas Day attempt by Umar Farouk Abdulmutallab to blow Northwest Airlines flight 273 all over Detroit, by allegedly igniting explosive strapped to his nuts, can be gauged by the willingness with which travellers will now accept the four hour check-in time for flights to the US and the quiet acceptance with which they subject themselves to increasingly invasive body searches. The

campaign to make air travel a nightmare experience, for all but the political elite, continues to be ramped up. The US Transport Security Administration has just issued the following directive to all airlines flying to US destinations:

Passengers are also required to remain seated during the last hour of flights, and cannot access carry-on baggage or have blankets, pillows, or other personal belongings on their lap during this time. Aircraft phones, Internet service, TV programming and global positioning systems are to be disabled prior to boarding and during all phases of flight. Flight crews are also prohibited from making any announcements to passengers about the flight path or the plane's position over cities or landmarks.

Not only is Umar Farouk Abdulmutallab permitted on to the plane without a passport, he is accompanied by a 'smartly dressed man' who smoothes the way for him. Call it a hunch but I'd say it's a fair bet that the 'Indian looking gentleman' was on the payroll of the Mossad/CIA/NSA/MI6 globalist terror organisation. The CCTV cameras that cover the Schiphol Airport complex should provide all the evidence necessary to identify and apprehend Umar's smartly attired escort, but I doubt any of us will fall off our chairs in shock when it is announced that there was a system failure at the precise times that the scruffy student and his dapper chaperone were making their way to the gate.

Neither will anyone be surprised to learn that the Company responsible for security at Schiphol is none other than ICTS, the same company that was responsible for the security at all the airports from where the planes allegedly departed on 9/11 and was responsible for the security camera network on the London Underground on 7/7. Clearly ICTS is regarded as a 'safe pair of hands' by the perpetrators of these Hollywood style events but that should be of no real surprise to anyone who has conducted even the most cursory research into this organisation. If ICTS is new to you, here's a few selected links to bring you up to speed:

http://www.rense.com/general68/dutch.htm

http://whatreallyhappened.com/WRHARTICLES/ICTS.html

Conveniently for the Nobel Peace Prize winning President of the USA, Umar Farouk Abdulmutallab commenced his journey in Yemen. That provided the necessary excuse to bomb the crap out of another oil producing country in the name of 'Freedom & Democracy'.[144] Yemen is strategically essential to controlling the entrance to the Red Sea (effectively the southern end of the Suez Canal) but perhaps even more importantly, it provides access to the southern Rub Al-Khalil or Empty Quarter of Saudi Arabia. Surely, you only need one guess as to what lies

beneath the largest expanse of sand dunes on the planet?... The people who live in this part of the world live simple lives and are incredibly generous with their hospitality but by a quirk of the geo-strategic importance of this generally unspoilt landscape, it's about to become another military base as the globalists go about the business of securing Full Spectrum Dominance. The perpetrators of these collective atrocities are confident in their belief that the vast majority of humanity remain ignorant and disinterested in the pernicious globalist agenda ....
(31.12.09)

That overview gives us about as much sense as this story is ever going to make! Next we move over to the US expert on 'synthetic terror', Webster Tarpley. Tarpley is always reliable as long as you don't want to hear about Israeli/Mossad involvement. (www. Tarpley.net). Umar he described as 'a protected patsy or puppet deliberately used by the US intelligence community for a Christmas Day provocation designed to facilitate US meddling in the civil war in Yemen', and as 'a set-up provocation controlled by US intelligence,' adding: 'Banker's son Umar Farouk had been denied an entrance visa to Great Britain, and had been denounced to the US Embassy in Lagos, Nigeria, as a possible terrorist by his own father in mid-November.

His one-way ticket to Detroit was bought in Ghana for cash, and he reportedly entered Nigeria illegally. In Amsterdam, he was assisted at the Northwest Airlines gate by a "well-dressed Indian" who explained that Umar Farouk had no passport. He did have PETN, the same substance supposedly used by the mentally impaired shoe bomber Richard Reid in his abortive attack of eight years ago. In spite of all this, Umar Farouk's US entry visa was never revoked, he never made it onto the no-fly list, and he was never thoroughly searched. These egregious lapses in normal procedure show that Umar Farouk was part of an orchestration sponsored by the CIA, which has now yielded four solid days of media hysteria.

Obama has formulated his new version of the Axis of Evil, composed of Afghanistan-Pakistan, Somalia, and Yemen... The new CIA-promoted synthetic entity is "Al Qaeda on the Arabian Peninsula or AQAP, a gaggle of US patsies, dupes, and fanatics which is claiming credit for the Umar Farouk incident. The US hopes to further dominate the exit from the Red Sea and the Suez Canal, while also easing pressure on the battered US dollar by jacking up the price of oil in an atmosphere of tension on the Arabian peninsula.'

Tarpley has well described the motive for the act as: 'the desire of a rogue network inside the US government to unleash a new wave of Islamophobic hysteria to rehabilitate the discredited "global war on terror" strategy in a new and more sophisticated form, while imposing a new round of outrageous and degrading search procedures at airports (such as the full body scanners peddled by the venal Michael Chertoff) to soften up the American people for heightened totalitarian control and political repression.' That's about it. Tarpley is here envisioning a rogue network that is responsible. As to how Mutallab was gotten onto the plane despite a pile of documented terror-links (mainly over 2008-9, after he had left his London College UCL): 'Only the active complicity of treasonous moles can explain Mutallab's miraculous immunity to all surveillance and screening despite all these factors of suspicion.'

Several strands wove into this fake-terror event. Once the young man became news we are never allowed to hear him speak - as in, e.g., 'No, of course, I didn't try to blow my balls up.' That is always the case with patsies (i.e., set-up victims) - *you never get to hear their view.* A question you might here like to ask is, 'How come a former president of University College London's Islamic Society with a millionaire uncle would want to perform so clueless an act?' - You won't hear that answered! Why would a young, wealthy Nigerian want to commit suicide over the plight of Afghanistan - if that was supposed to be his motive? Abdulmutallab (if that was him) boards Flight 253 in Amsterdam with only a carry-on bag for his international flight. After the event, he was strangely vacant and calm, offering no resistance when floored as a flight attendant sprayed a fire extinguisher and a passenger jumped on him: "He didn't fight back at all," Kurt Haskell recalled. Witnesses also reported a man standing ten rows behind Abdulmutallab who used his camcorder to film the whole incident starting before it began - no one has heard of him since, or found out who he was.

Second Suspect Detained

Kurt Haskell recalled that after landing there was another suspect handcuffed at the airport - this emerged on the Alex Jones show of 1st January. The FBI has changed its tune several times in explaining this. Haskell says the detained passengers were told this man was identified by a bomb-sniffing dog as having explosives in his luggage. He recalled the following FBI announcement: "We have those we believe are responsible for this in custody, we will now be doing interviews with each of you and then you are free to go. "Appearing on The Alex Jones Show yesterday, Haskell related how after being allowed to disembark from the plane by officials, passengers were detained in customs with their carry-on luggage for six hours while they waited to be interrogated by the FBI. Bomb sniffing dogs then detected a possible explosive device in the luggage of an Indian man around 30 years old before the man was arrested and led away to an interrogation room. The probability that there was a bomb in the man's luggage was all but confirmed when the FBI moved the passengers to another location. "You're being moved," the FBI told them, "it is not safe here. I'm sure you all saw what happened and can read between the lines and why you're being moved." The identity of the second man has not been discussed by authorities or the media and Haskell's description of his own interview with the FBI suggests that the feds are deliberately trying to bury the notion that the bomber had one or more accomplices.

A week later, Amsterdam security admitted that the terrorist did not have to "Go through normal passport checking procedures" and Haskell has challenged them to define what they mean by that. Had they scanned his passport's barcode, a lot of damning information would have come up. Dutch police have admitted that they have reviewed the video of the "sharp dressed man" that he alluded to - but this has not been released anywhere. He has appealed to them: 'Release the video!' Let's have a quote from him on his sense of trauma in the aftermath: 'Today is the second worst day of my life after 12-25-09. Today is the day that I realised that my own country is lying to me and all of my fellow Americans.' The world has benefitted from the integrity of Kurt Haskell and his wife Lori, and let us hope they do not have to pay too high a price for their testimony.

It turns out that the Detroit Christmas bomber was deliberately allowed to keep his US entry visa as the result of a national security override issued by an as yet unknown US intelligence or law-enforcement agency with the goal of blocking the State Department's planned revocation of that visa (Hearings held on January 27 before the House Homeland Security Committee). Commented Tarpley, 'What we see here is a classic example of the use of a national security override on the part of subversive moles who are performing their most basic responsibility of protecting a patsy by preventing him from being arrested or otherwise interfered with until that patsy can perform his assigned task and produce the desired incident, with the goal of inducing an intensive political response in the form of a wave of public hysteria... We do not need body scanners at airports. We need mole detectors installed ... The urgent necessity is now to find out precisely who issued a critical override that allowed Mutallab to keep his visa and board his flight to Detroit.'

The smartly-dressed Indian man who accompanied Umar at the Amsterdam airport is suspected by Asian intelligence services of being an agent of India's Research and Analysis Wing (RAW). His influence convinced airline and airport security personnel that Mutallab was a bona-fide Sudanese refugee. This event is being viewed as a false flag operation carried out by the intelligence tripartite grouping of the CIA, Mossad, and RAW, according to Asian intelligence sources who closely monitor the activities of these three agencies in India and Southeast Asia.

Binary Munitions

On Friday, January 8th Umar Fizzlepants (as he is being called) was in court in Detroit, pleading not guilty. The court was told that he had 'tried to destroy the plane carrying nearly 300 people by injecting chemicals into a package of explosives concealed in his underwear.' What chemicals might those have been? So-called 'binary munitions' involve an alleged deadly explosive made by mixing two harmless chemicals together. Major fake terror trials have hinged upon this concept, notably the Heathrow 'liquid bomb' hoax. The chemicals involved always have to remain unspecified - because you can't actually do it! Promoting such a story means relying upon the cluelessness and servility of the media - always a safe bet. The Hollywood films use binary munitions, so you will believe it, won't you?

The Defence should have put the question, What was the liquid in the syringe that would have caused the PETN to explode? No liquid will do that, because it needs to have a detonator. PETN is a high explosive, not easy to detonate, and it will only burn slowly if ignited. This story involves sixty grams of PETN being found (possibly with some TATP according to the Wikipedia account). Let's hope they are not allowed to change this - these fake-terror stories tend to vacillate over what chemistry was involved.

No image of the accused was seen and pictures of the court case had his face blurred out. Surely this was not the same person who had been at UCL for three years? 'There were no pictures of Umar taken inside the courtroom or anywhere outside it for that matter. So right now, all we have is the "good word" of those helpful FBI and CIA types as far as Umar's identity is concerned. Oh well, we do have that one picture of him on the plane where they blurred out his face… for some reason.' (Scott Creighton)

Fake Jihad Videos

"Jihadist websites" produced a picture of Mutallab with what they claimed was the flag of the media arm of the "al-Qaeda in the Arabian Peninsula" and a message claiming Mutallab as one of their own: "We tell the American people that since you support the leaders who kill our women and children … we have come to slaughter you (and) will strike you with no previous (warning), our vengeance is near," the statement said.

To make a comparison, on July 7th 2005, a message from the equally unheard-of 'Al Qaeda in Europe' was posted on a Houston notice board having connections to the Bush family - and has never been heard of since.

This Christmas-surprise story licensed attacks against the tiny nation of Yemen. 'We're reminded that 'yes, Yemen has oil and natural gas reserves worth stealing' noted one commentator. Its villages began to be strafed with unmanned drones a few weeks *before* this event - personally ordered by President Obama: he placed the order for US air strikes in Yemen on 17 December 2009 which killed scores of civilians, including women and children.

He re-defined the 'Axis of Evil' on December 16th to include Yemen. Both Pakistan and the Yemen were now being broadcast as foci of 'Al-Qaeda.' Let's quote Tarpley on this weighty issue: 'As a result of Mutallab's handiwork, Obama has now declared a new Axis of Evil composed of Afghanistan-Pakistan, Somalia, and Yemen. Yemen was thus catapulted to the centre of international attention by an Anglo-American propaganda blitzkrieg of monumental proportions.' Iran has strangely dropped off the list! Local officials and witnesses in the area of Mahsad, the site of the heaviest US bombardment in Yemen, put the number of those killed at more than 60 and said the dead were mostly civilians. They denied that the target was an al Qaeda stronghold.

As Chossudovsky ('Global Research') observed, 'Yemen, like Afghanistan and Iraq before it, is being targeted … because of its strategic location, bordering

Saudi Arabia, the number-one oil exporter, and the vital Bab al-Mandab strait, through which three million barrels of oil pass daily.'

Deadly X-ray Exposure

On the same day as the Detroit trial, January 8th, President Obama announced one billion dollars for airport X-ray full-body scanners to be implemented: 'We are at war' he helpfully explained. Around thirty percent of UK deaths are due to cancer (and, over one in three Britons will get cancer) which will not be helped by these radiation machines.

The most lucrative growth industry of our times is the "terror" business, churning out police state technology, and it isn't unduly perturbed about civilian radiation impact. Suddenly, very expensive and invasive full-body scans at airports were being called for, that will enable Israeli security firms to ogle naked images of men, women, and children at airports, using cancer-inducing X-ray scanners. Alarming headlines appeared, such as:

Full-Body Scanners To Fry Travelers with Radiation

Strip Search All 18-28 Year Old Muslim Men at Airports

As of 2012 these X-ray airport scanners have been banned by the European Union on health grounds (One in eight UK women are liable to get breast cancer, a higher rate than elsewhere in Europe, which is much affected by X-ray scanners), but they are still permitted in the US.

One could view this incident as a follow-on to the Heathrow liquid bomb hoax, where some Muslims were arrested for allegedly having the intention of blowing up planes over America. It had a similar crackpot chemistry, but in that case nothing actually happened - some young men may have bragged of what they might do in Internet chat rooms, but it was hard to see anything else. At least Umar got onto a plane. Both of these constructed fake-terror events entailed a vast inconvenience to passengers.

A BBC film on this topic omitted just about everything we have here considered (How safe are our skies? Detroit flight 253, March 9th, 2010). But, even the BBC could not get any film of Mutallab - not in Amsterdam, nor on the plane, or in Detroit.

UCL President

This young man had apparently been President of University College London's Islamic Society 2006-7, when he lived in a £4 million pounds apartment in Central London, although only a student: his father was one of the richest men in Nigeria as manager of a bank. The UCL Union has put out a statement confirming that the young man arrested is that same person. I went back to UCL (my old College) and spoke over an Islamic lunch to members of the Islamic Society: they reckoned that they did not have anyone who recalls him from three years ago, or even had any photos of him as having been their president (which seemed rather strange). I urged them to post a more cautious statement on their site, noting that no images of his face appear either from the plane photos or from the Detroit trial (nor, for that matter, Amsterdam airport). The young man must have had considerable ability to become President in his second year as an undergraduate (he studied mechanical engineering). I believe there is not a single photo up on the web of him at UCL. The luxury flat he lived in was registered to a US company. One may reflect on the initial statement which UCL put out on this subject: 'But the College said it wasn't certain the student was the same person who was on the plane.'

The UCL Islamic Society declined to do any of this. Soon after, the police requested all of the College's files on its Muslim students - surely a fitting reward for such timidity. Identity theft must here have taken place.

8
False-Flag Terror in Norway?
2011

77 Dead on 22/7

Was Anders Breivik a Zionist who massacred the children in response to Norway's anti-Israel stance? Or, did he do it for the reason he stated, namely that too many Muslims were flooding into Norway? The media have taken the latter view.

Norway's Labour party had passed resolutions on this matter just a day or two before. The day before the event, "Norway's Foreign Minister was met with claims that Norway must recognize a Palestinian state when he visited the Labour Youth League summer camp: The Palestinians must have their own state, the occupation must end, the wall must be demolished and it must happen now, said the Foreign Minister to cheers from the audience." As Breivik and his fellow operative made their way onto the beautiful, heart-shaped Utøya Island at five o'clock, the teenage Labour Youth activists "were chanting for BDS (Boycott, Divestment and Sanctions) against Israel."

Breivik published a long manifesto on the web, where the *Jerusalem Post* found that in 1,500 pages he mentioned Israel 359 times and "Jews" 324 times. Condemning Muslims, Marxism. and multiculturalism, he espoused what the newspaper describes as "far-right Zionism." For example:

> So let us fight together with Israel, with our Zionist brothers against all anti-Zionists, against all cultural Marxists/multiculturalists.

There is a deep ambiguity here. Did he act, as stated in his 'Declaration,' because of the threat of an ever-growing Islamic population, that he estimated will soon swamp traditional Norwegian culture, by somewhere about 2060? On this view, he feels friendly towards Jews primarily because he is anti-Muslim. This view implies that he did the massacre and let off the bomb(s) in Oslo all by himself. Or was he 'manipulated' and was the act primarily against the state of Norway, for its anti-Israel stance? On the latter view, he did not act alone.

Timeline

c. 2-3 pm: Teenage Labour Youth activists on Utøya island have a banner saying, 'Boycott Israel,' and are chanting for 'BDS' (Boycott, Divestment and Sanctions) against Israel.

2:20: Breivic e-mails an Israeli friend.

2:59: Police end their terror-drill rehearsal in the island, involving 'a mobile terrorist attack in which one or more perpetrators' aim to shoot as many people as possible and then shoot the police when they arrive.

3:19: Mr Andreas Olsen sees a lone policeman, in uniform and equipped with a gun, helmet and visor (on a warm summer day) walking quite slowly away from the government offices. He noticed the police badge on his uniform. He got into a civilian silver-grey van at Hammersborg square.

3:25: An explosion goes off near the offices of the Prime Minister & other governmental buildings in Oslo.

3:35: Police helicopter pilots start offering to return to work and get airborne, but are told to wait.

4:45: Anders Breivik is seen wearing a police uniform, arriving at a lake some 40 kilometres northwest of Oslo. He gets on a ferry to the island of Utøya.

4:50: Young people on Utøya island gathered together to hear shocking news about the Oslo bomb.

4:57: The ferryman is alerted that 'a policeman' wants to take the ferry over to Utøya, a journey which takes 1-2 minutes.

5:00: Breivik arrives at Utøya, where he asks the young people present to gather around him for information. He starts firing at them.

5:02: Local police learn about the shooting from phone calls, and three minutes later the police in Oslo are informed.

5:15: At a camp site, Breivik and a colleague go systematically from tent to tent, shooting whoever he finds there.

5:27: Norwegian police *claim* they received the first notification of the massacre on the island.

5:38: Local police ask Oslo police for assistance. A Delta-group is dispatched from Oslo to Utøya.

5:42: A mother receives text message from her 'Julie': "Mummy, tell the police they must be quick. People are dying here!"

5:45: Survivors begin to reach the shore after swimming the 600 meters from the island.

5:52: Local police car arrives at the shore of the lake, but the officers have to wait for a suitable craft before they can cross over to Utøya.

6:01: Breivik calls 112 (emergency telephone number) to surrender, hangs up, and continues to kill.

6:09: The police group arrive at the lake, but have no boat.

6:19: The boat that is finally provided is too small for the amount of personnel and equipment, and nearly sinks during the crossing.

6:25: The police group arrive on Utøya and go ashore. A TV news helicopter filmed them, i.e., it arrived before they did.

6:26: Breivik calls 112 again to surrender and hangs up.

6:34: Breivik still with some unused bullets does not resist arrest, as he is called by name by the police.

6:45: Supporters of the 'Global Jihad terror group' claim responsibility for the attack.

6:55: First army helicopter gets up into the air.

7:00: Police have three or four helicopters in the air after Breivik is arrested.

9:16: Police helicopter arrives at Utøya island, hours after the massacre.

A Lone Nut?

The media averred that a single 'lone nut' did all the damage: he blew up two government buildings in central Oslo - leaving 'debris over half a kilometre' - then rushed over to an island 90 kilometres away, mysteriously acquiring a police uniform, and single-handedly shot down seventy people. Some Rambo indeed! But eyewitnesses saw at least two terrorists on their shooting spree at the Utøya summer youth camp outside of Oslo.

The shootings were coming from "two different places on the island at the same time," according to several eyewitnesses, in the Norwegian newspaper *Verdens Gang*. The second was described as 180 centimetres tall, dark-haired man with Nordic appearance and "a pistol in his right hand and a rifle on his back." One witness described how these two 'always made sure that their victims were dead.' When it was over, Breivik quietly allowed his own capture - like Mark Chapman or David Hinckley before him. His Facebook page was changed, *while he was in custody,* with a 'Christian' theme being added in. The police took an inordinately long time to arrive on the island, over 90 minutes - and then immediately knew Breivik's name: he surrendered and came quietly when they called his name.

Initially the story broke as Islamic terror, but when it turned out that AB was blond and blue-eyed, he was suddenly no longer a 'terrorist' but instead a far-right 'lunatic' and 'mad-man.'

The date of 22nd July has two important 'echoes': firstly, the blowing up of the King David hotel in Palestine, killing 91 Britons, on 22 July 1946 - organised by Menachim Begin (who subsequently gained a Nobel Peace prize and became Israeli Prime Minister); and secondly, it has been designated as the 'International day of action against Israeli aggression.'

Breivik's last email an hour before was to a Jewish friend in an Israeli Kibbutz. Was the bombing a swift reaction to the Norwegian campaign to boycott Israel? A view of the event by US commentator Wayne Madsen begins, 'Israel's most secret and tried-and-true weapon is the "false flag" terrorist attack.' That's true enough, but does it apply here? He shrewdly concluded:

> Mossad is a master at false-flag terrorist attacks designed to alter perceptions and punish opponents of Israeli policy. The fingerprints of Israeli intelligence are all over the 9/11 attacks on the United States, the

3/22 train bombings in Madrid, the 7/7 transit bombings in London, and, now, the 7/22 attacks in Norway... While the Israeli-influenced corporate media has droned on and on about the dangers of Islamist terrorism, it is now obvious that the major threat to public safety comes from the State of Israel, a rogue nation that does not hesitate to murder the innocent to achieve its sordid political aims.

Israel had accused the Norwegian government of funding and encouraging blatant anti-Israel incitement: being maybe the premier organiser of Palestinian statehood. According to reports received by the Foreign Ministry in Jerusalem, the Trondheim Municipality was funding a trip to New York for students taking part in the "Gaza Monologues" play, which "deals with the suffering of children in Gaza as a result of the Israeli occupation." The play, written by a Palestinian from Gaza, was presented at the United Nations headquarters. It joined an exhibition by a Norwegian artists displayed in Damascus, Beirut, and Amman, with the help of Norway's Embassies in Syria, Lebanon, and Jordan. The exhibition shows killed Palestinian babies next to Israel Defence Forces helmets, which are reminiscent of Nazi soldiers' helmets, and an Israeli flag drenched in blood. Thus Norway took such constructive action against the terrorist state that is modern Israel - for which it must expect to pay a price.

Likewise Webster Tarpley took the view that it was in fact, false-flag terror:

It is reported that, although the world media are attempting to focus on Anders Behring Breivik as a lone assassin in the tradition of Lee Harvey Oswald, many eyewitnesses agree that a second shooter was active in the massacre at the Utøya summer youth camp outside of Oslo. It has also come to light that a special police unit had conducted drills or exercises near the opera house in downtown Oslo which involved the detonation of bombs during 2010 - exactly what caused the bloodshed a few hundred meters away this Friday. Further research reveals that United States intelligence agencies had been conducting a large-scale program of recruiting retired Norwegian police officers with the alleged purpose of conducting surveillance inside the country. This program, known as SIMAS Surveillance Detection Units, provided a perfect vehicle for the penetration and subversion of the Norwegian police by NATO.

If indeed 'subversion' of Norwegian police took place, that would explain the 'stand-down' of twenty search-and-rescue 'counter-terrorism' helicopters nearby - rather reminiscent of 9/11 - so that instead the police drove out to the island and eventually found a leaky boat, claiming not to have had an 'operative helicopter' available. Whereas a media helicopter was out there *before the police arrived*. Distraught parents, getting messages from their children as they were being shot, were bewildered that they could not get the local police to act.

No Bomb Crater

The huge blast at the government buildings in central Oslo was heard by people at least 7km away, causing extensive damage to a complex of government buildings housing the prime minister's office and the ministries of finance, justice and petroleum. The US website *Veterans Today* received reports from sources in Oslo indicating that the bomb was no car bomb, and that, had conventional explosives been used, e.g., "fertilizer slurry" explosive, it would have required enough to have filled a rail car. It was an explosion estimated to resemble that of the Marine Barracks in Beirut in 1983, which killed over 200, or the Oklahoma City bombing.

Black helicopters were swarming around Oslo shortly *before* the bomb went off. What is supposed to be the epicentre of the Oslo 22/7 blast was a main road, however no one could see any wrecked car, or a crater.[145] People started to write into Norwegian newspapers, pointing this out, and then on the 28th, six days later, an image of a huge crater was released - in a very different location. This was very close to the main government building, more or less inside it. CCTV that would resolve this matter is being withheld.... we've heard that one a few times before.

A few minutes after the blast, the first TV team to arrive were intercepted by a group of three military police, with MP on their shoulders, and told to go away.

Video sequences have shown no hint of a car or van that blew up. We've been shown the white van driving around and parking in the corner where it supposedly exploded - that is all. It is important to appreciate that pictures of that white van appeared only five days *after* the bombing.[146] Thus the authorities are claiming to have key CCTV footage, but can't release it - just as with the London bombings. One should not endorse the media and government calls for more surveillance in response to the event. Mossad and MI6 agents have been invited by the Norwegian government, to come along and help solve the matter - which is like putting a shark in charge of the swimming-pool.

If the story had really happened as we've been told, it should be possible to obtain traces of the aluminium powder which Breivik ground up, together with fertilizer on his farm. His manifesto describes the hard work he had to do to grind it up - but we have never had any suggestion of this, or that anyone could get a bang out of it. It should be identical with traces of the explosive found around the government offices near where the van supposedly blew up. Here the story becomes similar to the 2005 London bombings, where the explosive allegedly used is just vaguely alluded to with no forensic analysis.

The Terror Drill

As usual, a 'terror drill' shadowed the event: "Oslo police were conducting a bombing exercise at a location near the Oslo Opera House just 48 hours before a terrorist blast hit a government building in the Norwegian capital. According to the translated version of an *Afternpost* report 'Anti-terror police fired explosive charges at a training centre in Oslo, two hundred meters from the Opera, but forgot to notify the public.'"

Another source reported that, only hours before Breivik was shooting youths in Utøya, a special police unit was practicing an almost identical situation. On the same day there was 'a terror drill that was almost the same as the one that would later take place on Utoya'. It had received confirmation from a central police source (who did not want to be quoted by name) about this, happening at 3 pm on the time of the attacks. Police had barely finished their training before what they had trained for became reality.'[147]

'Captain America' opened on 22nd July and around the world generally on the same day 22nd of July, and concerned an attack upon Norway. By comparison, the UK horror film 'The Descent' about people trapped underground and dying had to be delayed from its scheduled launch date 8.7.05, because of people trapped underground and dying on the London July 7th incident. We are reminded of Webster Tarpley's dictum, published fourteen years earlier:

> No terrorist attack would be complete without the advance airing of a scenario docudrama to provide the population with a conceptual scheme to help them understand the coming events in the sense intended by the oligarchy. (*Synthetic Terror,* p.408).

The Norwegian investigator Torstein Viddal[148] obtained the terms of reference for Norway's 'inquiry' into the event, and found: 'it is clearly stated there is only one perpetrator - 'the perpetrator' - and that the Commission shall not determine legal responsibility or other judicial responsibility concerning the events, and neither judge the police and the prosecutor's own investigation of the attacks' - i.e., it was banned from asking any important questions about the event. That is in itself evidence for the thesis, that it was an inside job.

Norway's post-war history gives it no context for evaluating the re–cent assault upon its government and its political youth. The Breivik attack needs to be evaluated in the context of the several major 'false-flag terror' events of this new cen–tury, mainly 9/11 in America and 7/7 in London.

Let's summarize some of the main anomalies:

1. Doubt over Car Bomb

The massive damage caused to several government buildings was not produced by Anders Breivik's ammonium-nitrate bomb - if that ever existed. Fires were burning mainly at the 6th floor of the government building near its roof helipad. The next day, people started writing into newspapers about how they could not see any bomb crater or remains of a car in the road where AB's VW van had supposedly been parked[149] - then, a crater magically 'appeared' days later, a distance from the original alleged bomb site; along with a bit of old car engine.

Figure: Van shown as parked underneath SMK Ministry of Justice building

Figure: Blast Site as shown on Swedish TV

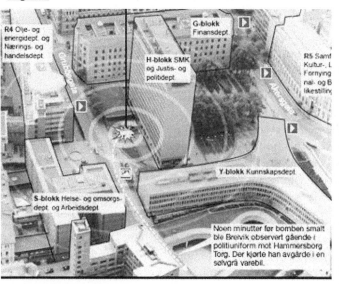

An early diagram indicated the position of the alleged parked VW car that exploded. It was supposed to have been near the road between the main Government buildings. The above Figure appeared in the Wikipedia article about the Norway bombing, for a few weeks. It was then removed because, once the alleged CCTV images were released (on 16 September) a rather different new van-blast position appeared, now *under* the main government building, quite a way from the road. Shortly before this 'van CCTV' was released, an old fountain near to the earlier-assumed blast position, a helpful reference-point, was removed.

The new van blast position is hardly compatible with the damage to the front of the H-block SMK building, surely caused by something quite a way in front of it, rather than directly underneath it; nor with very severe shattering of the Energy-Department building, about 80 yards away, mainly to its upper storeys which were burning (see figure): no car bomb in such a position could have caused such damage.

Has anyone shown that a bomb consisting of aluminium powder and ammonium nitrate, exploded there? Or credible physical remains of that VW, e.g. remains of its number-plate? Will any witness testify to having seen that white VW van in town that afternoon? It would appear not, instead they have only shown a chunk of some metal engine on the ground, which could have come from anywhere.

If the official story puts the white van adjacent to or even inside the Government's building, then embedded remains of that white van - with traces of fused aluminium explosive - will have been found inside that building. When Norway's 22-July Commission came to inspect the crater, they were not allowed inside the building, allegedly because of the 'asbestos' danger (8.9.11, report by 'VG News'). One presumes they would find the whole area reconstructed.

Norway's Prime minister Jens Stoltenberg happened to feel unwell and stayed at home that day, so was absent from his heavily-damaged office building. In 2014 he was promoted to being NATO's Secretary-General.

2. A Very Strange Crater

<u>Figure:</u> Department of Energy: note helipad on top

A hole appeared of almost three square metres just beside the entrance doors of the government building, where later the white van was shown to be parked. What made this clean, white hole, first reported on 28th July? The walls of tunnels below it - under the surface crater - all appeared as *white.* Why should that be? As a crater-hole, it was too clear-cut and bright, lacking burns or soot and the usual raggedness. A ban on publishing photographs of it hardly improved public confidence. This ban on taking and/or publishing high quality photos of the crater reminds us of the US ban on photographers at Ground Zero after 9/11.

A fertilizer bomb would hardly leave a white, clean surface after the blasts, nor would it cut cleanly through solid steel/iron tubes - as here appears - or knock out and break windows over a radius of 2 km in downtown Oslo.

The pictured VW remains, from a single photo credited anonymously, by 'Foto: Tipser,' stops short of showing the crater, a meter away: but this person must surely have photographed it? The only photo of the 'crater' is a still image from Johan Christian Tandberg's mobile phone video. The Tipser and the Vitnet (tipper & witness) appear to be the same anonymous person. This anonymous tipster and photographer - and 'expert' analyst - appears as a suspiciously well-informed type who rushes out to shape the official story.

Figure: A fragment of engine on the ground: had it come from the white VW?

3. Terror-Drill and Fake 'Breivik' Images

A terror 'drill' supposedly makes the country safer by preparing for possible catastrophe. But alas such drills can also be a cover for 'anti-terror squads' who make the atrocity happen. Only a few disloyal renegade elements concealed within them are needed.

Figures: this Star-Wars type figure is meant to be Breivik, walking away from the Government offices

Anders Breivik (AB) is alleged to have dressed himself as a lone police-man, in uniform and equipped with a gun, helmet and visor, to have got out of a badly-parked white VW van primed to explode, next to where the Prime Minister works in Oslo, strolled over into the car-park, then entered another civilian car - a few minutes before the bomb blew up. Who can seriously believe that a huge van could be parked right under the Prime Minister's office, without permission, and then a 'man in black' could get out of it, with a gun, and walk away - with no one taking any notice, without witnesses? He would have been viewed on CCTV cameras, as well as by other policemen in that area, and accosted: would not the police have wanted to checkout a lone, unscheduled policeman with a visor, helmet and gun?

And, who gave him all that police equipment?

Had Breivik planned this alone, he would have *expected* to be accosted by police after thus strolling across a high-security area, looking like a policeman but doing something no policeman could ever do - walk with a gun between two civilian cars. He could only plan such a thing, had he been somehow assured that it would be OK. His high-powered gun was stored in the grey car he walked over to, so any police check of that car would have terminated his whole plan.

False-flag terror is perpetrated with a terror-drill that shadows the real event, with the terror drill echoing what happens shortly after. Several of these were ongoing in the days prior to this event: in one of which, a lone assassin is going on a killing spree and has to be apprehended - ON THE SAME DAY, mere hours earlier. The 'man in black' with visor, gun etc. walking past government offices was spotted just fifteen minutes after that terror-drill had finished - at 3 pm, and we surmise that this was the actor playing the part of the 'lone assassin.'

We've basically been given two different Breiviks - the guy on the left appeared in the courtroom, with a broader face and blonder hair, while that on the right was in earlier images. The image on the right is to some extent photoshopped.[150] As regards its military appearance, we remind ourselves that this is a market-gardening draft-dodger, having no known military experience.

The 500-page book 'Story of a Massacre and its Aftermath' about Anders Breivik,[151] which has received glowing media reviews, makes no mention of any such government terror-drill which so closely shadowed the 'real' thing.

<u>Figures</u>: Are these two faces of Anders Breivik the same person? The hair-partings are different. Note suggestions of image adjustment.

4. The Vanishing Taxi

Five days after the event, *The Independent* described how Anders Breivik had hailed a cab to drive him from Oslo town centre - dressed all in black, and with a large gun slung over his shoulder!

> He then hailed a silver-coloured taxi which drove him, by now dressed in a stolen police uniform, and his assortment of weapons to Utøya island where 600 adolescent members of the Norwegian Labour party were enjoying a summer camp for the nation's "most promising future politicians".

> The taxi driver recalled this week: "There was nothing suspicious about him at all. He seemed just like any easy-going cop. He told me he was just going to check the security on the island because of the bomb blast in Oslo that we were hearing about on the car radio."

> The taxi driver hailed the Utøya island ferry boat to come and pick Breivik up. The ferryman willingly obliged. Breivik, with an automatic rifle slung over his arm in a case, was also carrying a large black plastic suitcase full of his other weapons. The ferryman remembers lugging the case up the jetty. "I was a bit surprised how heavy it was," he said in an interview yesterday. (27.7.11)

Where had the large black plastic suitcase full of other weapons come from? The released pictures of the Man In Black, walking down the Oslo street, shows him merely holding a hand-gun. The bomb blast went off at 15: 22 (Wiki timeline) some four minutes after he allegedly got into the car/taxi.

Nothing suspicious here - just a man dressed all in black, with a large gun slung over his arm, and the taxi driver hears about the government buildings blowing up a few minutes into the drive!

A witness is here cited and quoted, a taxi-driver. Indeed we have two witnesses, because the ferryman would recall being hailed by the taxi-driver. The latter then vanishes, he fades out of the story, as does his taxi, and instead later versions of the story have Breivik getting into his own car and driving it over to the island. On this later version, his bag full of guns and his automatic rifle are in that car which he has parked, he is not carrying them. We may presume that the earlier story just imploded owing to its inherent absurdity.

This change of story casts doubt on Breivik having been in the Oslo town centre and travelling to the island that morning. Had he done so, there would surely be but one narrative.

5. Fabricated CCTV

Two months after, the world was finally shown a few strange images allegedly of Breivik in Oslo, but none of the explosion: reminding us of the London bombings of 2005, where the authorities had great difficulty in producing any credible CCTV images of the alleged bombers for that day, it took them several years to do so. *Five weeks* after the event the police released a couple of images of the 'Man in Black,' looking like some extra from a Star-Wars opera. I suggest he is not Anders Breivik. This figure appears far more blurred than anything else in the image.

6. Normal Protocols Ignored

Norwegians face the same haunting question as Americans found themselves having to ask after 9/11: how was it possible, that all standard operating procedures had somehow been set aside on that day? It appears that everything the national emergency response unit had worked on for years was brushed aside on the day when terror struck Norway.

Mr Viddal has posed some key questions to the authorities: at what time, if at all, were the roads out of Oslo closed after the blast and why was air traffic not suspended that day - a normal response to a terror attack? Can the police show that they did anything at all in response to the Oslo city bombing? What caused the paralysis, whereby their helicopters arrived at Utøya island only *two hours after* a news helicopter went there - to film the police arrival by boat? For at least two hours no one closed borders, airports, subways, or roads out of Oslo, nor did anyone alert helicopter pilots for almost four hours, with offers of help being turned down - all amounting to a virtual stand-down order.

7. Police Delay

It takes about one minute to get over to Utøya Island on a rubber dinghy.

While appreciating that July is the holiday season, the unbelievable delay in police response - such that the two or more perpetrators (Anders Breivik probably with an unknown accomplice, as reported in the Norwegian newspaper VG) enjoyed AN HOUR AND A HALF killing spree with no interruption - suggests something other than mere bungling incompetence.

It is reported that police helicopter pilots were phoning in for duty to the central police station at around 3.40 pm, but were told NOT to come. That does not square either with the huge blast next to government ministries, or with the news of the killing spree of which the police were multiply informed from 5.02 pm onwards. Why was helicopter assistance from the Armed Forces nearly as slow as the police?

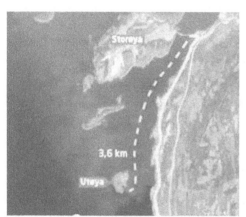

Figure: Police detour

Frantic parents and children started phoning the police from 5.02 pm onwards, and it is therefore unacceptable to state that the police were first informed of the event at 5.27 pm, as widely reported. There was a tragi-comic episode of the police drifting in a leaky rubber boat while children were being exterminated - videos of this seem to have been removed from the web. The huge detour taken by these 'police' is here

shown - what on earth were they playing at?

Some months later, Norway's biggest newspaper *Aftenposten* had these comments about the terror-drill that had - as usual - synchronized with the real thing:

> Only hours before Breivic began shooting youths in Utoya, a special police unit was practicing an almost identical situation. For days in advance and also the same Friday on which the attack occurred, a special emergency police unit was engaged in a terror drill, which was almost the same as the one that would later take place on Utoya. Aftenposten receives confirmation from central sources, a central police source that the exercise ended at 3 pm, the same Friday as the attacks. Police had barely finished their training before what they had trained for became reality. 'It was very close to what happened' said a central police source, who did not want to be quoted by name. (18.10.11)

Peter Power are you listening? There is an exact synchrony here, and moreover we are puzzled by the allusion to Utøya island, where there were no security police - were there?

Earlier, Aftenposten had carried the story on 25 August that "All of the officers from the anti-terror unit that took part at the bomb site, and later went out to Utøya, had been training on the exact same scenario earlier the same day and in the days preceding." This tells us that the 'police' team that dithered around getting to the island, *was the same as had been participating earlier that day in the anti-terror drill.* These would not have been normal police officers.

8. The 'Delta Team'

Somebody rang up the political gathering on Utøya island at around 4.50 pm, telling them to gather around, because a policeman was coming. The plan would not have succeeded without that phone call, because it caused the youngsters to gather together, and made them trust him. Survivor Adrian Pracon recalled how the young folk "gathered together to hear shocking news about the Oslo bomb... they were very, very happy to hear that one policeman is on his way to supervise us and to help us." Who phoned the children to say that "one policeman was on his way?" Breivik needed *someone* to prepare the ground for him by psychologically rendering his quarry Defenceless.

Breivik kept calling the police, and asked to be put through to 'Delta's operations leader. ' How did he, Breivik, know that the head of the Delta police unit was the one which was, in fact, assigned to capture him? At his trial, police officials released the transcripts at the request of his lawyer. This showed that he had made *between eight and ten phone calls* to the police, specifically the anti-terrorism unit, while on his killing spree. His earliest phone call was at one minute to six, when he said he was willing to surrender: "A Norwegian-speaking man says that he will surrender to police," is recorded in the police log:

> Breivik to Commander. Organised in the anti-communist resistance movement against Islamization. The operation is completed and will surrender to the Delta.

That was at twenty-six minutes past six - one minute after the police team had arrived on the island. The Internet connection had gone down at the local police station, while a couple of black helicopters hovered over the island. One minute after the massacre was over, he was arrested by the Delta squad. He was somehow confident that the army helicopters would not be used. The first police officer who stepped ashore recognized him immediately and called out his name, and at once he put down his gun (see Timeline).

Delta Force is an American concept, being the US Army's elite counter terrorism unit, with many rumours of it being involved in 'black ops'.

The role-duality between those involved in their terror drill and the actual assassins on that island was well expressed by Gordon Duff: 'Breivik played out his routine to police, alternately shooting, calling and talking to police, then assuring those hiding he was a police officer there to help them, killing them and then calling police again for another chat.'[152]

9. Destruction of Crucial Evidence

The police performed a 'controlled explosion' at AB's 'bomb factory' in his farm, on Tuesday 26th, thereby destroying the main forensic evidence in relation to how his alleged bomb had been constructed. Police have a duty to collect evidence relevant to a crime - not to destroy it. No one will ever know whether the bomb which went off in town was made in AB's farmhouse because police have destroyed the evidence.[153] (In the London bombings of 2005, there were similar patterns of police behaviour)

10. US Intelligence Penetration

Traitors are here involved, i.e., people not loyal to Norway. A traitor is the very worst enemy of the State. The 'patsy' AB may not be aware of this, and believe that it is all happening for the reasons given in his Manifesto. As to the motive, Tarpley commented:

> A motive for the attack is also present: as part of its attempt to mount an independent foreign policy, including the imminent diplomatic recognition of a Palestinian state as part of a general rapprochement with the Arab world, Norway was leading the smaller NATO states in dropping out of the imperialist aggressor coalition currently bombing Libya. Norway was scheduled to stop all bombing and other sorties against the Gaddafi forces as of August 1 at the latest.

Norwegian security analysts need to study this Tarpley critique. It continues:

> In early November 2010, the Oslo television channel TV2 exposed the existence of an extensive network of paid assets and informants of US intelligence recruited from the ranks of retired police and other officials.... The official name for the type of espionage cell which the United States was creating in Norway is Surveillance Detection Unit (SDU). The SDUs in turn operate within the framework of the Security Incident Management Analysis System (SIMAS). SIMAS is known to be used for spying and surveillance by US Embassies not just in the Nordic bloc of Norway, Denmark, and Sweden, but worldwide. The terror events also raise the question of whether SIMAS has an operational dimension. Could this apparatus represent a modern version of the Cold War stay-behind networks set up in all NATO countries and best-known under the name of the Italian branch, Gladio?... A memo written in 2008 shows how the US felt that Norway was not awake to the possibility of a potential terrorist attack. The cable reads: "We repeatedly press Norwegian authorities to take terrorism seriously. We will seek to build on this momentum to fight the still-prevalent feeling that terrorism happens elsewhere, not in peaceful Norway.

That language indicates an intention in certain quarters to give Norway a terror-event, to assist it in 'taking terrorism seriously' and perhaps to underline the dangers of opposing the imperial US/UK/Israeli will. For comparison, we earlier quoted a US document of 2002 some months before the Bali bomb, as to how Indonesia needed to be assisted in taking the terrorism threat more seriously.

The 22-July Commission should have asked Johan Fredriksen, Chief of Staff at Oslo Police Department, concerning his helicopter stand-down order: why did no Army helicopter get airborne until 6.55, three hours after Norway's biggest-ever terror attack? (from Rygge airport) To ask Anders Snortheimsmoen, Delta Force Commander, also located at the Operations Centre in Oslo, why did he put out a request for support from faraway Trondheim airport - which he claims to have done at 15.37 pm - but did not request support from the much nearer Rygge airport until an hour later? (There are some deep analogies here with the 9/11 event). Can he comment upon the army helicopter finally arriving at Utøya island at 7.15 pm, or the police helicopters only arriving two hours after that, at 9.16 pm? To ask the Chief of Security at the Ministries Jon Ivar Mehus, who had all the CCTV needed, but failed to alert guards or police: how come he told NRK

reporters on August 11th that an unknown parked car outside government HQ was not a 'potential terror threat'? These people need to be grilled in public so the people of Norway, especially the families of the dead, get to hear the evidence.

Norway would have become perceived by Israel as an enemy, on account of its criticisms and calls for trade boycott, etc. of Israel. Can anyone believe that a nation clearly opposing and provoking Israel should allow a whole island of youngsters calling for anti-Israel measures, with not a single security-guard to protect them - even over the 22/7 date, an anniversary of the blowing up of the British King David Hotel in Jerusalem by Zionists in 1946?

Can an open inquiry be held, into these issues, or will the pretext of 'National security' be used to control the information and, hence, the outcome? If the latter, a spiritual darkness must descend upon Norway, as a bond of trust is broken: a defining moment for Norway's police, its government, and the proud and decent people they supposedly serve.

Here is a sensible blogger commenting on what will never happen and the answers we'll never get:

> The connection between Zionism and the Norway mass murder appears to me vastly stretched. Apart from some rantings by the murderer, there is no hard evidence of any links between him and Israel or Zionist organisations. As in any case of murder, the focus should remain - at least at the outset - on forensic evidence, direct witness testimonies, and a thorough and transparent investigation of When, Where, What, Who and How. Possible motives can help focus an investigation, but cannot supplant it. Here are some relevant questions for which I still await an answer:
>
> * Could a non-skilled person construct - without harm to himself - such a powerful bomb as was used in Oslo? And design the remote-control

necessary for such an operation? Are there precedents that prove that this is easily within reach of an amateur?

* What is known about the murderer moving the bomb into place, obtaining (or buying) a vehicle, placing the bomb at the right site, changing his uniform, driving to Utøya, where did he hid his ammunition and weapon while on the ferry, how did he manage to kill so many people, one after the other?

* Why did it take the police 90 minutes to arrive at Utøya, when it is told that people are being murdered? That's far longer than an ambulance or a firefighter team would take. Is it some kind of severe negligence by the police, or something more sinister? If negligence, aren't we entitled to know WHOSE negligence?

I therefore recommend that a public inquiry into the circumstances of Utøya be held, with truly independent commissioners, including representatives of the victims. Since 9/11 there is no reason to trust any state agency to investigate such crimes. Western governments, due to their cover-up of 9/11 have forfeited the trust of the populations".

-emmett23sier.

Hear, hear! However it is of the very essence of SFT that the state does not want any such Enquiry, because it is aware of having been corrupted, of having betrayed the trust of its citizens. Instead it legislated for large sums to be paid to 'victim-families' of around eight hundred thousand pounds per family, to keep them quiet.

Anders Breivik was a character well known to the police and secret service prior to the bombing and the massacre. At the court hearing, it was noted 'his brief public appearances in court conveyed the impression of an individual transfixed in some entrancing dream. One of his closest friends wondered if he was drugged or brainwashed, finding his appearance eerie and quite untypical.'[154] In the event, he was judged to be sane. He began telling the court how he had committed the acts as part of a group, but did not here make much progress.

He complained about the luxury three-room 'prison' flat assigned to him, complete with a gym, objecting - as noted by world syndicated reports - about its standard of decoration, about his coffee being cold and how he has not got the latest version of Playstation. He can look forward to being released by his mid-50s - the reward for a pro-Zion terrorist?

As a general comment on this incoherent tale, one can hardly improve on that by Richard Cottrell in his opus *Gladio*: 'The security drill that paralleled Breivik's effort, his talk of other partners in crime, the long-winded and rambling elegy, his strange access to rather fabulous sums of money coming from such an unpromising background, suggest a manufactured personality in the pattern of so many stooges and patsies that we have studied on these pages.'[155]

The Woolwich Terror Hoax
2013

A short walk from the Woolwich DLR station in south London took one to an incredibly moving tribute scene, a huge mass of flowers, national flags and various gifts - and this was wall to wall, stretching some thirty yards down the road, on both sides - for a 'Fuselier Guard' whose death became known on 22nd May, 2013: Drummer Lee Rigby. Deep are the passions aroused by this death, which have echoed around our world. Had one ever seen so many Union Jacks a-fluttering in the breeze - here in competition with the simple Red Cross of the St George's flag? There were all sorts of moving tribute messages to the deceased, pinned on the wall, together with *open bottles of beer* left for the deceased to partake of - and this was all solid, right down both sides of Artillery road and around the corners!

I was trying to remember, during the Falklands War, or the marriage of Lady Di and Charles, had one then seen *so many* national flags?

And yet, we are here dealing with a constructed terror event, an illusion where nothing was what it appeared to be. Actors act their parts, a crushed-up car is placed onto the pavement and a rubber dummy as 'the body' is thrown into the road with no drop of blood in sight: the primal War-on-Terror theme was powerfully reinforced by this mirage, as 'the Phantom Menace' struck again.

We here go through the sequence of apparent events, examining a series of what I have called *Absolute Physical Impossibilities*. In picturing this, you might find the video I did with two members of the Kent Freedom Movement a few days after the event helpful, in getting a 3-D picture of the road where it happened.[156]

A car ends up on the pavement of a busy street under some trees. Because of the way it is facing it would have had to veer over from the other side of the road, having just emerged from a traffic-lights crossing, somehow waiting for a brief gap in the traffic to cross over - and bump up onto a good 4" pavement, then somehow drive along until, whump! It hit DLR (Drummer Lee Rigby). He was walking away from them just by a traffic sign held up by two posts, wearing a 'Help for Heroes' T-shirt.

First Absolute Physical Impossibility This alleged event could have been synchronised only by an overhead helicopter, to see DLR walking along, see the gap in the traffic, see the lights changing, and then give the car its instructions. There was no such helicopter.

On the story we are given, there is no way the car driver could have identified DLR, given the brief second or so between possibly seeing him and deciding to drive across the road. And yet the whole point of the story, is that 'terrorists' killed a British soldier.

Had such a car been coming towards him bumping up onto on the pavement, an army lad would have been trained to sense it behind him, and he only needed to spring forward a yard or so to the other side of the big traffic sign, to have been safe. At the point where you might expect the car to have crossed over the road there is a lamp post, ten yards or so from the afore-mentioned traffic sign, so the car would have had to skirt round that lamp post - but then further down is a railing, near the traffic lights. We're talking about Artillery Road, Greenwich where this whole drama was constructed. Skid-marks on the pavement, coming from the tyres (see below, 2nd picture) - or possibly trails of car oil - point towards that lamp-post, not shown in this image. It could not have happened!

Second Absolute Physical Impossibility The car had its whole front crumpled up, as if it had hit something substantial, inches from the poles of the traffic sign right in front - yet those poles were untouched, with no scratch from any bump. That has to be a stage setup. The poles were soon covered choc-a-bloc with flowers, messages, etc., but fortunately Morris Herman ('Morris108') visited the scene and reported this central fact.[157]

We are then supposed to believe that two 'evil terrorists' emerged unharmed from the car, one brandishing a meat cleaver and the other a gun - but why slam the front of the car into something if you have a gun you are intending to use?

On a busy city street, we are supposed to believe that no one took any photos of this extraordinary sequence of events?

Third Absolute Physical Impossibility: with DLR lying knocked over from the car bump, one killer starts chopping his head off, causing death, but - there is no blood. Eight pints of red blood should have spurted out onto the pavement.

The picture above shows two undamaged posts that hold up a traffic sign - which the car supposedly bumped into. There is evidently no blood on pavement. One can also see the lamp-past alluded to (with 'Signal Timings' on it) and behind it one can just see the railings: the car would have had to mount the pavement between these two. There was no blood on the pavement, shown by close-up photos of the scene, however 'blood' did appear from an overhead police-helicopter photo. The latter has to be fake.

Quoting here Jim Stone:

> When the helicopter flies over, you can see blood where they supposedly dragged their victim from under the bushes to the road. That blood is NOT THERE in the videos shot before the helicopter arrived, and ALL video is AFTER they drag their supposed victim into the road. That´s one obvious set-up team blooper. In Hollywood, that's what is called a continuity error. (May 24th)

The air photo supposedly shows a trail of blood as the body was dragged out into the road. Murderers usually try to hide themselves after committing the act, but these didn't.

The *Daily Mirror* video (part 2, v30 seconds) shows various people standing around while the body is heaved out into the road.[158] The road was evidently sealed off in advance, before 2.20 pm on 22 May, that being the only way something could have been dragged into the middle of a busy London road. All this time there has not been a single photo taken by a civilian passing by.

Fourth absolute physical impossibility The corpse supposedly lies in the middle of the road for twenty minutes. The two perps (or rather, patsies) hang around waiting for the police to arrive. What were they waiting for?

In this second image, again, not a drop of blood is seen! Here we clearly see the traffic sign which the car supposedly bumped into. Casual conversations are here meant to be going on, after a soldier has been hacked to death: clearly no one expects the Fuselier guard to come storming out of the nearby barracks. In no photos can the head or lack of head be seen. The t-shirt appears pulled up to cover over the head.

The army does not arrive, though this is right outside their barracks. DLR was supposedly coming from the Tower of London back to his barracks, so he would have had to carry ID to get in. But, the evening paper said merely that he was believed to be a soldier. Then the identifying was done by his teeth? This is an impossible storyline. We express this as -

Fifth Absolute Physical Impossibility: If DLR was returning to his barracks, he would have to have had some physical ID. Then he would have been identified and the army barracks told. They would have stormed out. If the army did not come out, after half an hour, it basically means that DLR did not die there - he was already dead.

We see a large white lorry at one end of the road (away from the traffic lights) and a bus containing schoolchildren at the other end, and the road is blocked off for traffic. All the normal traffic on this busy road has been blocked off. The bus has been parked opposite the lamp-post alluded to above although there is no bus-stop there.

The Rant

The two alleged killers were Michael Adebowale (22) and Michael Adebolajo (28).[159]

The 'rant' by Michael Adebolajo is the most famous image of the whole constructed sequence: the photo-shopped blood on his hands, the lady-with-shopping walking by, his MI5 programming. This was presumably shot well before whatever happened at Woolwich on May 22nd: to quote the perceptive 'September Clues:' 'they probably just filmed the guy as they would an interview, TV show or scene from a movie, on the corner of a regular street, somewhere in London. Onlookers and passers-by don't see anything out of the ordinary, just a guy giving an interview on a street corner. Blood on his hands added in post-production.'[160]

Sixth Absolute Physical Impossibility: The carelessly-photoshopped 'blood' moves around Mr Adebolajo's hands, fades away and returns, at one point gets stuck onto the trees behind him. People noticed the extra red-glowing kerb-lines as his red, red hands move about, also the blurred red coming off his hands and sticking onto the trees behind him!

There are two different camera angles, implying that two persons were standing a few feet in front of M.A. as he ranted at them, filming him. Watch the video as the old lady walks by with her shopping trolley, unperturbed: what did she see? I suggest she saw no red colour on his hands, nor was there any corpse in the road. And why did they not re-film it, after she had ruined the whole effect, turning it into a joke? I suggest that M.A. has to have been programmed by MI5 to rant in this manner, which he did very effectively, however it might not have been easy to get him to 'do it again.' We see no red stain on his clothes after hacking someone's head off.

For a change, here is an earlier image of Michael Adebolajo, together with his beautiful girlfriend Justine, who works as a hairdresser/beautician. This may remind us that a real human being existed, behind the terror-image. His ex-girlfriend, Justine Rigden, testified to how he had been 'lovely' and just a 'normal boy' - 'He had a group of friends from Hackney. They weren't "wrong-uns", they were OK, and he used to do a bit of MC-ing, rapping. Nobody can believe it. He was just this normal, regular boy' (*Mail Online* 23.5.13). His school friends testified to how he had lived a Western lifestyle, growing up in Essex as a Christian with hard-working Nigerian immigrant parents. Such comments could remind us of what bewildered friends of the alleged four London bombers had recalled about them. Notice how confused you are feeling now: there is an *incoherence* between the demonised hate-image you've been given, and what traces we may find of the real human being, whose identity has been erased by the state.

<u>Figures</u>: Michael Adebolajo plus his girlfriend Justine - in happier days

On May 25th, a long-time friend of M.A. Came into the BBC Newsnight studio, to tell how he believed M.A. had been tortured and raped by MI5 agents while he was in Kenya (*The Guardian,* 25.3.13). The security police turned up during the interview, and arrested him (under the Terrorism Act) as he came out![161] We gathered that his brother worked for MI6 for years.[162]

Bad Actors Arrive

Twenty minutes after the 'event' some police lookalikes arrive, but not in real police cars[163] and are soon firing blanks around the place. One of them is wearing white, trainer-type shoes (5.30 mins) - which police don't, in case you need reminding. Their arrival is the cue for 'the terrorists' to start running towards the police car. Surely, these have to be programmed characters. They do not threaten to attack, despite which the police open fire. Note the unlikely way in which a 'bad actor' waves his legs about, after supposedly having been shot and lying on the ground (7.20 mins) Compare this with the dummy-type human figure dragged into the road by several people (Part 2, 45 seconds). The Inquest would not comment upon the cause of death. The one and only thing we needed to know from that Inquest was, how long had the corpse been dead? When the court case began of the 22-year old suspect, the cause of death was reported as being from 'multiple injuries.' If he died from having his head hacked off, why would the inquest not confirm it?

Figure: police easily carry bag containing rubber dummy

When it's all over, 'The police remove a body bag from the scene:' this image shows a yellow body bag rather too small, or the body would be folded up if it had fitted into there, and judging by how the two men are carrying it, it does not seem to weigh much.[164] That bag did not appear to have the weight of a human body, reinforcing the impression from the *Mirror* footage (above) that some sort of dummy was put into the road, which is why it didn't bleed. That's why no pictures show its head, because it was not DLR. Whenever DLR died - if indeed he ever existed - rigor mortis might by then have set in, so it was not convenient to use his dead body.

In a normal murder scene one would expect to see the body lifted onto a stretcher and put carefully into an ambulance -- not crumpled up into a 3-foot body bag. The men carrying it do not look like police.

The two suspects in this case will remain forever silent -- never do we get to hear their view of what happened.

Mr Peter Eyre is a Middle East consultant, geopolitical analyst, investigative journalist and anti-war activist, let's hear his view concerning 'The gruesome scene of a decapitated actor with no police or paramedics at the scene and no blood':

> The offenders are shot by armed police who are in attendance in the background, but the murder scene has not been secured!

> Many awakened to this amazing Shakespearean play that has unfolded in Woolwich, London where all the actors were so bad they would not even qualify for an interview as an extra in some third rate movie!

Eyre asked if police had "dragged the (victim's) body around the corner?" [Because of the way the 'crime scene' moved around the junction, from one road to the other]

> The BBC stated a man wearing a Help the Hero's T Shirt was hit by a car, then attacked and killed with a machete or sword by the car's occupants. So much vivid violence and yet still no blood at the scene! Why? Because the actors had not had time to splash it around before they filmed the scene.

> It was however added later as the picture (in his article) shows! The blood is only on the pavement and not on the road. Do you think they attempted to copy the Boston Bombing, but somehow did not get it right?

Eyre suggested that the 'blood' on a signpost was tomato ketchup. If MI5 wants to do any more of these mock-up horror stories, maybe they should employ Quentin Tarantino to improve the authenticity.

An Incoherent Tale

Could the police really turn up and shoot the two perpetrators at close range with eight shots -- and miss? Neither were killed! The police turn up twenty minutes after the event, even though armed police are stationed less than a mile from the incident at Plumstead police Station. Lewisham Police Station is less than three miles away and is lauded as the largest in Western Europe. Since when do crazed killers with blood on their hands just hang around, waiting for the police to turn up?

Initial reports had the two killed, but soon we learnt that they were still alive in hospital. *The Daily Telegraph,* reporting on the event the day after, pointed out that nothing in the story made sense.[165] Had the two Africans been driving, hit the Army fellow, then got out of their car, and hacked his dead off? If so, that would hardly result in such a crumpled-up car. And where was the head? Then during an interview, as the 'killer' was speaking, "I noticed a lady in a blue dress, and pulling a trolley, just casually walking past the man with meat cleaver and the blood soaked hands. It was like she was just out doing a bit of shopping."

Did two men gruesomely behead a random stranger in broad daylight, with everyone around quite calm and the only blood to be seen on the perpetrator's hand and knife? There is no blood on the victim's clothes nor blood on the street. Supposedly very crude cuts had been made, with "gruesome hacking'. Then, who walks around and gives an interview with a meat cleaver, as if they want to be seen on as many cameras as possible after committing a horrific murder? After the "horrendous" attack, the two men in their 20s stood around, waving knives and a gun, and asked people to take pictures of them "as if they wanted to be on TV".(BBC news, 23 May)

Nurse Amanda Donnelly gets off a bus and kneels down to feel the pulse of the beheaded Army man lying in the middle of the road. "When it became apparent Drummer Lee Rigby was beyond their help, they shielded his body from further desecration by his savage attackers….Kneeling at his side, she cradled him gently, seemingly unfazed by his horrific wounds." (*Mail Online,* 23 May) The corpse had no head, no blood was pumping out of his neck, and she felt his pulse? The Mail adds, untruthfully, "A pool of blood lay where Drummer Rigby was attacked".

After 20 minutes, it seems to have been the SO19 who turned up - not the ordinary police. The 'Special Operations' cadre are elite army killers.[166]

Here is a comment by a local policeman: "I asked the on-site police officer in our school: I bet your briefing this morning at the station was an intense one." Officer: "I was expecting exactly that, but it was just too odd. I asked why there's no briefing, believing we'd be told which streets to be in and what to look out for, but no. Nothing. It was as if it hadn't happened." In fact, the Skipper said, "It didn't happen." He told me he didn't recognise any of the officers on his own patch at the scene either nor any of the members of the public, despite always seeing the same people.'[167]

The police put up their tent around the scene of the crime, covering the headless torso. They moved it about thirty yards from where it had been set up round the corner, as air-photos showed.

Lee Rigby is surely dead - if he ever existed - however: "A post-mortem into the death of Drummer Lee Rigby has formally identified him but failed to confirm the cause of death, Scotland Yard said." You can't corrupt everyone, and the doctors have not endorsed the idea that he died as stated.

Pseudo-Islamic Hate Message

The alleged killers are identified as Muslim, with the usual war-of-civilisation hate-message, according to an ITV News video:

> We swear by Almighty Allah, we will never stop fighting you until you leave us alone. The only reasons we killed this man is because Muslims are dying daily. This British soldier is an eye for an eye, a tooth for a tooth. We apologize that woman had to see this today, but in our lands our women have to see the same. You people will never be safe. Remove your government. They don't care about you.

The story as reported by Sky News and the BBC was full of anti-Islamic propaganda, with the perps yelling the usual "Allahu Akbar" just before the beheading (although nobody seems to have heard it). The people have to be told who to hate - presumably the aim of the exercise. This was all rather similar to the messages posthumously-attributed to two of the alleged London bombers.

M15 and COBRA

It turned out that MI5 had asked Woolwich murder suspect Michael Adebolajo if he wanted to work for them, about six months before the killing. The childhood friend of M.A., Mr Abu Nusaybah, told BBC Newsnight that his friend had rejected the approach from MI5.[168] but, he had been tortured and somehow programmed by MI5. Then Mr Nusaybah found himself being arrested by the police immediately after giving this interview, *the Guardian* reported! (The police would not say why they were arresting him.)

The Deputy PM at once cancelled his trip to Germany, and the Prime Minister David Cameron returned from France, in order to hold a deep-underground COBRA meeting to discuss possible escalation in terrorist attacks - after just one man had been killed. Suddenly, this terror attack on the streets of London had become global news.

The Prime Minister convened an emergency meeting with top advisors and intelligence officials attending, not usual for a street killing. UK Home Secretary Theresa May called an emergency Civil Contingencies Committee (COBRA) meeting with Cameron chairing it. That included cabinet ministers and high-level security officials, and deals with terrorism and other major crises. COBRA refers to the room where committee members meet - Cabinet Office Briefing Room A, deep below Downing Street. Soon, a 'terrorist alert' was imposed.

The very next day a long policy speech by US President Obama, in which he was trying to get Guantanamo Bay closed and limit drone strikes, (or, that was my impression of it) alluded to 'yesterday's terror attack' in London. The event thus validated the War on Terror premise - presumably its purpose. Soon *Russia Today* was discussing it - the event echoed around the world.

In the immediate wake of the attack the former government anti-terror tsar Lord Carlisle declared that it would be necessary to revive the bill to monitor all e-mails and the Internet. His opposite number on the Labour benches said the same. This was after the 3rd day of 'Islamic' terror (supposedly) in Sweden, a very handy synchrony for the war-of-civilization message. Mosques were attacked all across southern England.

The Old Bailey Trial

The public can sit in the gallery of London's Old Bailey, as I did on Tuesday 2nd December. The purpose of the trial was to reinforce a War-of-Civilization message, with one of the two accused holding a copy of the Koran, to give the impression that the Koran condones such acts, which it does not. I found it to be a gripping experience, with the two accused sitting in a huge glass cage and various testimonies being read out or spoken, to hear what witnesses saw that afternoon in Artillery Place.

Their accounts started off with their seeing a 'crashed car' and the two black men outside the car, plus a dummy-like figure on the pavement, who initially had his back against the wall. They then saw both of these men hack the body with knives, 'frenzied stabbing,' one with a butcher's cleaver. No sound came from the victim, we never heard whether he was alive or dead. A crowd of people gathered round and were filming on their mobile phones (NB We have never seen these pictures).

A Ms Gill Hicks testified to having seen the car as having already crashed into a road sign. That was the initial setup, and I believe that no witness claimed to see it happen. One witness, while stopping to see this horror, noticed a 'line of traffic behind him in the rear-view mirror.' That is what one would expect on this busy road - but my impression was a complete absence of traffic in all pictures of that event. A witness described seeing a lot of blood on the pavement - as one would expect. Again, there was a problem with ground-shot images failing to show any trace thereof.

Mr Gary Perkin described how a brave woman tried to 'comfort' Lee Rigby while he was lying in the road. One would have thought he was beheaded (and therefore thoroughly dead) by then, so this rather strained our credulity. No one questioned Mr Perkin to clear up this obvious anomaly. I believe that no adversarial questioning of witness took place at this trial, a traditional feature of British justice.

The Old Bailey trial saw the goalposts moved drastically since the original story in May - with a *different location* of Lee Rigby's death. Media-amnesia seemed to prevail at this Old Bailey trial, in relation to the original version. Perhaps the video which I and two Kent Freedom Movement colleagues had made at Artillery road highlighting the impossibilities in the story, induced this shift in narrative?

The new story (30th November) has DLR hit *while crossing the road*, adjacent to the Royal Artillery Barracks to which he was returning, after (we were told) a visit to the Tower of London where he was interviewing/recruiting new army employees. (we notice how deep British resonances are being built into this story)

The image shows a view away from the main traffic lights. All along the left-hand side of this image stretches the wall of the Royal Artillery Barracks. Why would he have been crossing over *away* from that? (NB there is an entrance to the army barracks along this wall, not quite visible here.)

And, where is all of the traffic? You can wait for hours on this busy street at noon and you will never see it so empty. Here is an official TfL (Transport for London) Traffic News twitter item released on the day, with the time given in the bottom left-hand corner: 1:07 pm on 22nd of May, and alluding to 'Closures still in place on Artillery Road.' It plainly states that a diversion had been put in place sometime before. Why did no newspaper mention this fact?

One noticed how blurred was the video-sequence of 'DLR' crossing the road released at the trial - the figure in it could be anyone; whereas, in contrast, the CCTV images of the schoolchildren at the scene were bright and crisp (Shades of the 7/7 videos).

Moving the Goalposts

We supposedly see the car after it has just crossed over the traffic lights, driving up a hill. It has managed to filter into the right-hand lane, so is most unlikely to be doing more than 20 mph: not 30 or 40 mph as the court was told.

But, if you believe it was just driving up the hill, straight over the traffic lights, there IS NO WAY the driver could have known DLR would have chosen to be crossing the road (the wrong way) at just this moment. In other words, the event would have had to be unplanned. There is no way the car driver could have waited around anywhere, until DLR was spotted, then revved up and driven out to hit him. This alleged crime was *unplannable,* especially given that the two perpetrators were both in the car.

But, even if that impossible sequence had somehow happened, it leaves DLR lying down in the middle of the road, where he has his head hacked off: 'The defendants chose to mutilate the soldier in the middle of the road, just yards from a primary school, so people could watch, the court was told.' This is a rather drastic change, this site being a good ten-fifteen yards away from where we had earlier been told he had his head hacked off: on the pavement, under some trees, behind a big signpost (which you can see to the far-left in the first image). We were never shown any trace of blood in the road.

A whole lot of 'blood' was shown on the pavement, behind the big signpost, from an overhead air photo you may recall. The trial's locus of the 'beheading' was nowhere near the 'pool of blood - but, was anyone bothered? No British journalist, that's for sure.

Then what happened to the car? After knocking down DLR, did it drive right over him?[1] Recall that the car on the earlier story has to keep going, mount up onto the pavement, veer sharp left then drive along and HIT the large signpost. We are shown oil leaking out as it screeched to a halt - or whatever is supposed to have happened, and one wheel removed somehow from the impact. None of that would have happened just from hitting DLR in the middle of the road.

To quote from the court hearing: 'The video showed a Vauxhall Tigra knocking the soldier down before crashing into a road sign.' Is that supposed to

mean, that the car drove right over DLR in the road, to (inexplicably) mount up onto the pavement then drive along it and crash into a street sign? That could not have happened - not least because of the huge rucksack he was carrying. Whatever was in it would have been all over the road had the car driven over him. To remind you, the original story about why the car mounted up onto the pavement, and hit the road sign, was because DLR was walking along the pavement, and the car, in order to hit him, could not avoid also hitting the road-sign. You might want to check out the rucksack in the original version of the story, which was left under the trees on the pavement.

The *Daily Mail* helpfully resolved this dilemma: ' …flinging him on to the bonnet before it smashed into a sign post.' Do you really want to believe that the car impacted DRL in the middle of the road and did not knock him down, but instead had him flung up on the car bonnet, then the car kept on driving, bumping up onto the pavement and then swerving round (presumably still driving at 30-40 mph?) - all the time keeping DLR balanced on the bonnet, until it hit the sign post?[169] (2)

The story grew madder and more impossible with each new twist. Readers will not need reminding that the sign post in question showed no sign of having been hit. The buckled-up car next to it was just a stage-prop, presumably lifted out from

the big, white lorry parked nearby then put back in again when the day was over.

Figure: DLR at the DLR

An image pro-vided of Drummer Lee Rigby at the Woolwich station of Docklands Light Railway, with rucksack, has a carefully cut-off date-stamp, but we can see it's 2 pm in a May day of 2013. It would have been nice to have had his feet included, just to make sure they were properly on the platform and that his shadow was falling in the right direction. Readers intrigued by this story may wish to travel along the Docklands Light Railway, which is a pleasant, scenic ride, to Woolwich, where they can then stroll up the hill to Artillery place, a traditional heartland of the British army, and there come to more fully apprehend the multiple impossibilities of this story.

Did He Exist?

DLR would have been born as Lee James McClure. His mother Lyn Seville married Philip McClure in September 1986 in Rochdale, Lancashire, and her son is said to have been born in North Manchester hospital on either the 1st or 4th of July, 1987. The hospital would not confirm this when I asked them, they said they could not give such info to private individuals.[170] Lyn Seville did not take the name McClure herself, but she gave it to her son. An online tribute gives his birth as July 1st but a plaque commemorating his life gives July 4th - not the sort of thing one would expect to get wrong.

I couldn't see his birth on ancestry.co.uk so I applied to the Registrar's Office for his birth certificate, informing them of his parents, the hospital, and both dates of birth. Four weeks later my cash was refunded with the reply that they had not been able to find any such birth: "We have searched the indexes for events registered in England and Wales during the years specified (1986-1988). We have been unable to find any entry with the details you provided."

In 2003 on his 16th birthday, Lee got the urge to change his name, or so Lyn Rigby's book avers.[171] By deed-poll he became Lee Rigby instead of McClure. Why would he want to do that, when his Father Phil McClure was still around, and claimed to be getting on OK with Lee? His mother was not then even married to Ian Rigby, they were just together. Has one ever heard of such a thing, adopting the name of someone who *might become* one's stepfather?

His mother Lyn Seville then re-married, to a Mr Ian Rigby in Rochdale, Lancashire in July 2005 (as given in ancestry.co.uk) - but, she did not take his name, she kept her maiden name: only her son took her new husband's name. In most stories a son does not much like the new stepfather, but this one takes his name! This marriage happened in the same district where she had earlier married. In the next year 2006 'Lee Rigby' is said to have joined the army. Don't expect to see any documents saying that.

2007 Marriage solemnized at St. Anne's, Southowram				in the Me
Columns: 1	2	3	4	5
No. When married	Name and surname	Age	Condition	Rank or profession
8th	Lee James Rigby	20	Single	Soldier

The next year in 2007 he married Rebecca Metcalf in St Anne's church, Southowram, near Halifax. I obtained a copy of the wedding certificate and found it not unduly convincing - it lacked both his signature and his father's name: instead it had his stepfather's name, Ian Rigby. So a young man not only wished to change his name to that of his mother's new husband, before their wedding, but also put his stepfather's name onto *his* wedding certificate - when his real father was alive and well? This is a fishy tale.

The obituary in his local newspaper[172] gave the date of this wedding as October, 2007 - whereas the wedding certificate I was sent gave it as 8th of August.

So for both the birth and the wedding we have an ambiguity of dates. It showed the one, standard photo we have all seen, with a head looking as if photoshopped onto a body, suggesting that the paper did not have access to any local images, which it might have preferred.

<u>Figure</u>: the Royal Fusilier Guards, drummer corps

Here's an image of the drummer corps of the Royal Fusiliers in 2008:Names of the drummers are given, and these include two young men next to each other: 'Drummer Lee' and 'Drummer Rigby' in the 3rd row. 'Duplicity is the infallible sign of an intelligence operation' - who was it who said that? Enlarging this photo, it's hard to recognize him anywhere.

The UK national archive 'findmypast.co.uk' does give the weddings of Lyn Seville to Philip McClure in 1986 and then to Ian Rigby in 2005, but it had no record of DLR's marriage to Rebecca Metcalfe, even though its records go up to 2008.

His Mother's biography of her son *omits his wedding,* which seems a strange thing to miss out, nor does it give any hint as to where the couple lived.

Lee Rigby was registered as living in London at 35, Beavers Crescent, Hounslow together with his wife, in the year 2010, according to the yearly volumes of Electoral Register for Hounslow (in the British Library). That is near to Hounslow Cavalry Barracks. But, the public archive 'searchelectoralroll.co.uk.' puts him at that address for four years, from 2010 to

2013, with his wife Rebecca only there for 2010/11. As that is the sole bit of evidence for Lee living anywhere, in the public domain, it seems odd that the biography by Lyn Seville should omit mention of it.

The 2nd Battalion Royal Regiment of Fusiliers had a presence in Hounslow, at one point. Beavers Crescent accommodation is associated with Hounslow Cavalry Barracks and was upgraded in 2011.The Royal Fusiliers had been there from 2008-9 before they moved to Cyprus, too early for the happy couple. An online biography of DLR has him returning to Hounslow barracks in the early party of 2008 from Cyprus. I doubt whether anyone has any evidence for him living at Woolwich barracks.

He's a phantom-like character, where it's hard to find historical evidence of his existence that dates from prior to his death - his signature, or a photo of him in some army regiment, for example.[173,174] Chris Spivey - who has been banned by court order on pain of imprisonment from ever blogging on the subject again - ascertained that there was no Facebook profile of Lee James Rigby anywhere, prior to his death.

In 2006, we are told, he completed his infantry training course at Catterick and was selected to be a member of the Corps of Drums, being posted to 2nd Battalion the Royal Regiment of Fusiliers.

Generally speaking, we're told that DLR joined the Fusiliers to be a drummer. However, Lyn Seville's biography tells us how, once he turned 18 he enlisted for the Army and then she visited him in Cyprus in November 2006. From there he goes out to Jordan in the Middle East - to 'help train the Jordanian army in how to use the latest weapons.' While out there he wins a 'top gun prize' for his shooting skills. She tells us that 'Lee was an exceptional soldier' (P.65) and was top rifleman in his unit (P.66) - which all leaves us wondering, if he was so good at everything, how come he never made it past the rank of private?

We're told that both in Afghanistan and Cyprus, he was a machine-gunner. It seems odd to set up someone trained as an army drummer to handle a machine gun - quite apart from why they would want such on the tranquil island of Cyprus.

On returning to the UK, his 'unit of drummers' performed at prestigious venues: Windsor Castle, Buckingham Palace and the Tower of London. In 2009 he was posted to Afghanistan with the Royal Fusiliers where he served for three months, but had to fly back because he had gallstones. Next he moved with the Battalion to Celle, Germany in 2010 and remained there until the summer of 2012 - which doesn't sound much like he was living in Hounslow. He certainly got around, in a somewhat invisible manner.

Lyn Seville's book does not seem to find anything wrong or shocking about the adultery committed by DLR against his lovely new wife, right after she produced his child. Let's have a bit of chronology here.

In September 2007 he marries Rebecca Metcalf and their son, Jack, is born in September 2010 (but, NB, no record of this in ancestry.co.uk, nor search.findmypast.co.uk/). DLR 'left the marital home' in the summer of 2012 and is 'already separated' from Rebecca when he meets Aimee West in August 2012 (at an Army cadets training camp in Wales). She would 'visit him in Woolwich, where he was stationed at the barracks with his regiment.' It could be a problem having him there in 2012, if the searchelectoralroll.co.uk has him living in Hounslow that year.

In February 2013, he gave Aimee West an engagement ring, she claimed. But as his wife Rebecca never instigated any divorce proceedings, it would surely be impossible for him to have offered an engagement ring to some new girl? This was just over a year after his child had been born, in which case he would be two-timing his wife, and would British army troops really condone such behaviour? The biography by Lyn Seville has Lee's wife Rebecca just fade out of the whole story and instead we get a glowing account of his affair with Aimee, just as if he were some single lad, with no hint that this could be unethical.

We'd appreciate Rebecca Metcalf's testimony over these perplexing issues. Did he impregnate her in the winter of 2009/10, then fly off with his regiment to Celle, Germany, and return in the summer of 2012, when he immediately started having an affair with a younger girl? Why could he not even sign his wedding certificate? Could he have given an engagement ring to anyone when Rebecca had not started divorce proceedings?

On the last night of his life, DLR went out drinking with the lads, so Lyn Rigby tells us, and so hung-over was he at work the next morning - at the Tower of London, where he was working for army recruitment - that his boss took pity on him and let him off early, so he could go to bed. That is the reason why he was crossing Artillery road at 2 pm. Aimee who was on duty out in Afghanistan avers she received a last message from him, a mere twenty minutes before he was murdered:

> Princess, keep smiling for me. I know it's hard and you really want to come home, but just remember I am always there for you and I will always love you no matter what. We are on the home stretch... you will always come first in my life.

Can anyone believe this? His new wife with his one-year old child is living near to him, yet he is pining away for another on the other side of the world? Especially with his wife Rebecca stating after the death: "I love Lee and always will. I am proud to be his wife and he was due to come up this weekend so we could continue our future together as a family. He was a devoted father to our son, Jack, and we will both miss him terribly." (ITV news 24.5.13) This leaves us with, to say the least, an incoherent narrative.

Army budget cuts mean that the 2nd battalion of the Royal Fusiliers was being axed, as announced in 2012. That could have enabled this story to be brewed up, as no one can verify the facts, with the records being disposed of.

This incoherent tale smells like a put-together story and one is therefore disturbed by the huge revenue streams derived from Lee Rigby charity foundations. We'd like to be told just how large these are and who gets them. As with most state-fabricated terror events, at the core of the story is a haunting mystery of real identity.

10
Ukraine: 777 and the Vampire Elite
2014

Now I'm going to test your numerology skills by asking you to think about the magic seven ... Most of you will know that seven is quite a number

speech by Christine Lagarde, President of IMF on 15 January 2014

Numerological Prelude

Russian royalty wiped out (Nicholas II and family)	17 July 1918
TWA flight 800 blown out of sky, US Navy missile[175]	17 July 1996
Maiden flight of Boeing MH-17	17 July 1997
Death of Dr David Kelly	17 July 2003
BRICS bank signed into existence	16 July 2014
NATO-Ukraine 'exercises' Sea Breeze, Rapid Trident	17 July 2014
President Putin flies back from Brazil to Moscow	17 July 2014

A Boeing 777, Flight MH-17, was shot down on 17/7.

On 17 July 2014 over Eastern Ukraine, the remains of a crashed Malaysian Boeing 777 aircraft were reported. Had it exploded into flames at thirty thousand feet, hit by a surface-to-air missile? Or, had Ukrainian fighter jets been shadowing the plane immediately before it was blown out of the sky, and were they responsible? One eyewitness reported on how "[I] saw a spinning plane without a wing with something falling out of it. The plane was shot down," (on RT), adding: "There were explosions in the sky. And apart from the loud sounds of the plane itself, I heard the buzz which fighter jets make." All 283 passengers plus crew were reportedly killed.

Blame was abruptly laid out, before anyone could know who did it - exactly as Blair blamed Muslims for the 7/7 London bombings, or as US authorities for 9/11 on the same day. At once the media were braying in concert: Putin, Putin. *That is the sign of a pre-staged event.*

Oddly enough, the daily 'Malaysian Hospitality' ('MH') MH17 flight from Amsterdam to Kuala Lumpur was registered as cancelled that day:[176] one is here reminded of the 9/11 enigma, when the two allegedly-hijacked American Airline flights were officially recorded as cancelled for that day.[177] Immediately after the downing of MH17, an adviser to the Ukrainian Minister of Internal Affairs Mr Anton Gerashchenko stated categorically that the Malaysia Airlines Boeing 777 MH17: "had been downed by an air Defence missile system Buk." As reported from the Ukraine Interfax News Agency, Anton Gerashchenko "said on Facebook that the plane was flying at an altitude of 33,000 feet "when it was hit by a missile fired from a Buk launcher." That never happened, because to quote Jim Stone: "Buk missiles produce a very noticeable plume, and no one documented any. In the day of cell phone cams, I would say zero documentation of something so noticeable means no missile launch."[178]

<u>Figure</u>: Buk missiles - not used

As the wise US commentator Paul Craig Roberts wrote on that same day July 17th:

'The appearance of a Wash–ington operation is present. All the warmongers were ready on cue. US Vice President Joe Biden declared that the airliner was "blown out of the sky." It was "not an accident." Why would a person without an agenda be so declarative prior to having any information? Clearly, Biden was not implying that it was Kiev that blew the airliner out of the sky. Biden was at work in advance of the evidence blaming Russia. Indeed, the way Washington operates, it will pile on blame until it needs no evidence.

Senator John McCain jumped on the supposition that there were US citizens aboard to call for punitive actions against Russia before the passenger list and the cause of the airliner's fate are known. The "investigation" is being conducted by Washington's puppet regime in Kiev. I think we already know what the conclusion will be.

The probability is high that we are going to have more fabricated evidence, such as the fabricated evidence presented by US Secretary of State Colin Powell to the UN "proving" the existence of the non-existent Iraqi "weapons of mass destruction." Washington has succeeded with so many lies, deceptions and crimes that it believes that it can always succeed again.

At this time as I write, we have no reliable information about the airliner, but the Roman question always pertains: "Who benefits?" There is no conceivable motive for separatists to shoot down an airliner, but

Washington did have a motive-to frame-up Russia-and possibly a second motive. Among the reports or rumours there is one that says Putin's presidential plane flew a similar route to that of the Malaysian airliner within 37 minutes of one another [NB I suggest this is unlikely, NK]. This report has led to speculation that Washington decided to rid itself of Putin and mistook the Malaysian airliner for Putin's jet. RT reports that the two airplanes are similar in appearance.'[179]

The area 'held by rebels' was very small and the weather was cloudy, so MH17 was not visible from the ground. Do you want to believe that rebels could hit a plane flying over six miles above the ground, *for no reason*? Having it crash into that small area way off the proper flight path must have involved skilful co-ordination between the war-gaming powers.

Strafed by Two Jets

"Eyewitnesses in the Donetsk region saw Ukrainian warplanes near the passenger jet. They say they heard sounds of powerful blasts and saw a Ukraine warplane shortly before the crash. (ITAR Tass)" That info came from a Spanish Kiev air traffic controller working in the Ukraine.[180]

An unexplained change of course of the Malaysian MH17 flight took it directly over the Eastern Ukraine warzone. A Spanish air controller confirmed that the MH17 flight was escorted by Ukrainian fighter jets minutes before it was downed. The presence of the Ukraine fighter jets reported by the Spanish air traffic controller was confirmed by eyewitness reports in the Donetsk region. He was soon taken off duty as a civil air-traffic controller along with other foreigners after the Malaysia Airlines passenger aircraft was shot down. The air traffic controller suggested in a private evaluation and based on military sources in Kiev, that the Ukrainian military was behind this shoot down. Radar records were immediately confiscated the event. Military air traffic controllers in internal communication acknowledged the military was involved, and some military chatter said they did not know where the order to shoot down the plane originated from.

Data released by the Russian military showed a Ukrainian SU-25 fighter jet gaining height towards the MH17 Boeing prior to the catastrophe. "[We] would like to get an explanation as to why the military jet was flying along a civil aviation corridor at almost the same time and at the same level as a passenger plane" asked Lieutenant-General Andrey Kartopolov, head of the Main Operations Directorate of the HQ of Russia's military forces, speaking at a media conference in Moscow on 21st July. He added, "It's equipped with air-to-air R-60 missiles that can hit a target at a distance up to 12km, up to 5km for sure." A US surveillance satellite was overhead at the time, and he urged the US to publish the space photos and data captured by it: "This may be a coincidence, but the US satellite flew over Ukraine at exactly the same time when the Malaysian airliner crashed."

"The starboard (right-wing) jet engine was badly damaged and caught fire, pointing to a hit by a smaller air-to-air missile launched from a fighter interceptor, flying at about the same altitude"; and the midsection had been "blown outward and not inward," indicating a bomb blast inside the cargo bay. These expert observations suggest that a NATO interceptor fired a heat-seeking missile at a jet engine, triggering a fire.[181]

Various sources have confirmed the SU25 Ukrainian Fighter jets on radar, trailing MH17 at the same altitude, some 4km behind it. Even OSCE officials (Organisation for Security and Co-operation in Europe) have (on July 31) confirmed evidence for a spray of bullets shot through the cockpit of the plane. They are agreeing with aerospace expert Peter Haisenko as follows:

> * The crashed Boeing photos showed clearly multiple bullet holes from machine gun bullets, which consistently showed a frontal angle and hardly could result from a ground-air missile.

> * This aircraft was not hit by a missile in the central portion. The destruction is limited to the cockpit area.

> * It becomes abundantly clear that an explosion took place inside the aircraft.

> * Very few photos can be found from the wreckage with Google. All are in low resolution, except one: The fragment of the cockpit below the window on the pilot's side. Both the high-resolution photo of the fragment of bullet riddled cockpit as well as the segment of grazed wing have in the meantime disappeared from Google Images. One can find virtually no more pictures of the wreckage, except the well-known smoking ruins.

- i.e., whoever is responsible for the event has the ability to remove images from Google.

THE SU25 is equipped with a 250-round magazine of anti-tank incendiary shells. These penetrated the cockpit from both sides. A SU25 doesn't normally go above 25,000 feet, however experts reckon it can stay at 33,000 feet for a limited period - why the Malaysian MH17 was not allowed to cruise at its normal height of 36,000 feet, but was given a limit of 33,000 feet.

An authoritative German report likewise concluded: 'Surface-to-air-missile attack ruled out, as calibre of cockpit bullet holes puts Ukraine pilots in the frame for MH17 murders':

> You can see the entry holes and some exit points. The edges of the bullet holes are bent inwards, these are much smaller and round in shape. The exit holes are less well formed and the edges are torn outwards. Furthermore, it is visible that the exit holes have torn the double aluminium skin and bent them outwards. There is only one conclusion

one can make, and that is that this aircraft was not hit by a missile. The damage to the aircraft is exclusively in the cockpit area.… The cockpit of MH 017 was hit from TWO sides, as there are entry and exit holes on the same side.…'

The BBC has deleted its own news report on this matter - a report with the too-shocking title, "Ukrainian Fighter Jet Shot Down MHI7 - Donetsk Eyewitnesses". The original BBC Video Report was published by BBC Russian Service on July 23, 2014. Earlier on July 17th, the BBC had reported on confiscation of the pilot's voice recordings with the pilot just before the shootdown: "Ukraine's SBU security service has confiscated recordings of conversations between Ukrainian air traffic control officers and the crew of the doomed airliner, a source in Kiev has told Interfax news agency."

Way Off Course

Planes since April have stayed clear of the East Ukraine battle-zone. MH17 was NOT supposed to over fly Eastern Ukraine - it should have flown over Western Ukraine. Jim Stone wondered: "How come it disappeared from trackers in west Ukraine and appears to have travelled about 1000 km into eastern Ukraine some 200 km off route without being challenged by Ukrainian authorities?"

> MH17 deviated from the civilian flight path, which should cross close to the exit mouth of the Azov Sea, away from the current battle zone between the Ukraine military and militant ethnic Russian irregulars. Instead its navigation steered the jetliner on a more northerly course in contested airspace, where Ukraine military aircraft conduct both air strikes and troop transport missions, putting the Malaysian Airlines jet into jeopardy.

This flight was 300 miles off its normal course, reported *The Telegraph*, much further north than it should have been. *The Telegraph* quoted Robert Mark, a commercial pilot who edits Aviation International News Safety magazine, as saying:

> I can only tell you as a commercial pilot myself that if we had been routed that way, with what's been going on in the Ukraine and the Russian border over the last few weeks and months, I would never have accepted that route.

Malaysia Airlines had filed a flight plan requesting to fly at 35,000 feet throughout Ukraine airspace but was instructed by Ukraine air traffic control to fly at 33,000 feet upon entry.

A video blaming Russia for the shootdown was made apparently by the Ukraine government on the 16th *the day before.* It has since been deleted, however memory remains on the Web. This is typical for SFT events: a hiccup in the time-sequence. Likewise, a supposed intercepted radio transcript of rebels discussing their shootdown of the plane was found by an audio analysis expert to be fake:

The tape's second fragment consists of three pieces, but was presented as a single audio recording. However, a spectral and time analysis has showed that the dialog was cut into pieces and then assembled... the audio file has preserved time marks which show that the dialog was assembled from various episodes.

- the view of award winning former Associated Press reporter Robert Parry as reported on Prison Planet.[182]

Amsterdam Airport

Some months prior to this event, a Malaysian tribunal had found Israel guilty of genocide. Malaysia had been an outspoken voice in the UN and the world media on Palestinian rights in Gaza. Clearly, a price has to be paid for this kind of thing. The plane was shot down at around 13:20 UTC, close to the time when Israel's assault on Gaza began that day, close enough to knock news reports of Israel's massive assault upon Gaza off the front pages. "Security at Schiphol Airport is operated by ICTS, an Israeli-owned airport security company based in The Netherlands founded by former officers of the Shin Beit intelligence agency. Its subsidiaries are also involved in key security functions there, including ProCheck, Ramasso and I-SEC" Source: Yoichi Shimatsu, who earlier discovered "many aspects of the Israeli security set-up at Schiphol International Airport and the role of the Mossad intelligence agency in secret operations there, one of Europe's business transport hubs." (Y.S. was former editor of *The Japan Times Weekly* in Tokyo.)

The flight of MH17 was registered with two different departure times. The official report has it taking off from Schiphol Airport at 12.15 Central-European local time (i.e., 10.15 UT), but other sources had cited fifteen minutes later at 21.31. A normal flight would have only one departure time: we here bear in mind that the official record has no MH-17 flight that day, i.e., it was cancelled and never departed.

For some days Malaysian airlines were denied access to the wreckage. It would be "inhuman" if *"we are not allowed"* to the site of the crash in Donetsk Region, eastern Ukraine, said Malaysian Transport Minister Liow Tiong Lai on 19th July, adding that Malaysian authorities *"are concerned"* over the security zone of the area as evidence "hasn't been secured." Anyone was allowed to visit the crash site. The Malaysian transport minister added "There is no confirmation on who has flight recorders." But then on the 21st July they received both of the black boxes, but were not able to hang onto them and they ended up in the possession of the UK Ministry of Defence at Sevenoaks (that is where the remains of the 30 bus from the London bombings also ended up) as if the Malaysian authorities could not be trusted to read out their own aeroplane black boxes.

A Fabricated Event

The BBC news correspondent on the crash site the following day reported bloated bodies and the stench of rotting flesh. Bodies *don't bloat and stink after a day.* Russian sources confirm this BBC report that the bodies found in the wake of this crash DID NOT BLEED and hardly burned: as if they were old, having died some time ago.

Figure: Stench coming from trainload of rotting bodies, picked up from crash site.

A Russian commander stated: "a significant number of the bodies weren't fresh," adding that he was told "they were drained of blood and reeked of decomposition."[183] A total of 283 passengers were reported as dead. These days, fabricated terror events need not always have real dead bodies.

Intercepted e-mails showed an intention to set up the event.[184] On March 9, 2014, from 'Ihor':

> Events are moving rapidly in Crimea. Our friends in Washington expect more decisive actions from your network. I think it's time to implement the plan we discussed lately. Your job is to cause some problems to the transport hubs in the south-east in order to frame-up the neighbor. It will create favorable conditions for Pentagon and the Company to act. Do not waste time, my friend.
>
> Respectfully,
> Jason P. Gresh
> Lieutenant Colonel, U.S. Army
> Assistant Army Attaché
> U.S. Embassy, Kyiv

The Pentagon and 'the Company' were planning something.

> Proceed with caution. Speak only Russian… There is a lot of scrap metal, with it you can do anything. Damaged aircraft you specify. It is essential that all was as real attack. Neighbors, special forces, but without corpses.

A fabricated scene is here being envisaged, where 'corpses' would have to be provided.

> 'Remember, you need everything to be as real attack of the Russian Special Forces' Igor Protsyk (commander of General Staff of Armed forces of Ukraine) to Basil

It will seem like a real attack by the 'Russian Special forces'.[185] The morphing of the war-game/terror drill into the real thing is the secret crux of state-fabricated terror.

Buk Missile System Government-Owned

The surface-to-air missiles in the vicinity and possibly used were state-owned and not held by rebels: A division of Buk missile systems of the Ukrainian Armed Forces was, according to Pravda, deployed to the Donetsk region on July 15, two days *before* the downing of the Malaysian airlines MH17 flight. Russian Defence sources confirm the presence of several missile batteries in the Donetsk operated by the Ukraine armed forces:

> "The Ukrainian military has several batteries of Buk surface-to-air missile systems with at least 27 launchers, capable of bringing down high-flying jets, in the Donetsk region where the Malaysian passenger plane crashed, Russian Defence Ministry said." (RT, July 17, 2014)

Of significance, the Prosecutor General of Ukraine, Vitaliy Yarema, confirmed that the Donetsk rebels did not have Buk or S-300 ground-to-air missiles which could have downed the plane. According to the *Kiev Post* report: "Ukrainian prosecutor-general says militants did not seize Ukrainian air Defence launchers" Members of illegal armed units have not seized air Defence launchers of the Ukrainian Armed Forces in Donetsk, Ukrainian Prosecutor General Vitaliy Yarema said. (Kiev Post) Mr Yarema also confirmed that according to military sources: "After the passenger airliner was downed, the military reported to the president that terrorists do not have our air Defence missile systems Buk and S-300," (quoted by Itar-Tass).

The Mirror-Illusion

Has Malaysia Airlines has lost two Boeing 777 planes or only one? Did one airline lose two identical 777 passenger planes in four months? Let us consider this sequence of events:

<u>November 2013</u> Kuala Lumpur commission finds Israel guilty of crimes against humanity and genocide.

<u>March 2014</u> Plane traveling from Kuala Lumpur vanishes over Indian Ocean, MH370, a Boeing 777-200, ID No. M7-MRO.

<u>July 2014</u> Plane travelling to Kuala Lumpur blows apart over Ukraine: MH17, Boeing 777-200, ID No. M9-MRD

Is it likely, that one and the same airline should happen to lose two machines of exactly the same type, over four months, without a single survivor? Both the MH17 and the MH370 appear to have lost radio contact and veered off course onto an unusual route, before meeting their fate. No previous Boeing 777 flight had ever experienced a catastrophic accident.

Did the first plane land secretly at Diego Garcia, and then reappear four months later at Schiphol airport in Holland? One finds a degree of consensus on this matter, amongst experts. This might have the implication - which some might find unduly conspiratorial - that fragments of the plane wreckage have been removed and placed in the Indian ocean, where they have been 'found,' as evidence of a crash which never happened.

The experienced naval and commercial pilot, Field McConnor, was interviewed on the Richie Allan show about this matter, and declared he was 'nearly 100% certain' that the two planes were one and the same (31.7.15 interview, at 4 minutes). The MH370 flight that took off from Kuala Lumpur had landed secretly at Diego Garcia, he explained. I spoke to a Dutch investigator, who likewise assured me on the basis of photos of the MH17 plane taking off from Schiphol airport that day, that it was indeed the very same MH370 that had vanished earlier that year over the Indian Ocean.

There was a slight modification in the design whereby the MH17 plane had an extra window compared with the earlier one, and in this respect the plane wreckage was found to match the window configuration of the MH370. 'MH' here signifies Malaysian Hospitality. A Malaysian Airlines Boeing 777, the same type that was used by MH-17, was seen stored in a hangar at Ben Gurion International Airport in Tel Aviv, no doubt a part of the story.

There is a need for an intercontinental symposium on this matter, to ascertain whether these two planes were indeed one and the same. Such a conference might help to avoid WW3, insofar as the shoot-down is being presently blamed on Putin, whereas rather the scheme is looking like a proposed Operation Northwoods event whereby a plane apparently (but not really) full of passengers is made to crash and look as if it had been shot down by a notional 'enemy.'[186]

Let's return to the alleged 'passengers' of the crash. A local news service asked about the Dutch bodies on the plane and the answer was that 'almost all' of the bodies were Asian: 'I personally have not seen a single European-looking body.' They were all bloodless, with smelly liquid oozing out of them, probably formaldehyde. A witness described a 'mortuary smell.' At night time the bodies shone with a greenish hue - this is a sign of decomposition. Decomposing bodies were reported on the 18th, less than 24 hours after the crash. The weather was warm, not hot, such that one would only expect the first sign of decomposition after some three days. Torn limbs and shattered skulls lay around - but no blood.

A lot of mobile phones and cameras were lying about. The phones would either not turned on or their display was broken. Not a single photo from 2014 could be found and the images seemed to come from the period August to October 2013. There was much luggage, but it was packed with winter clothes, none for the summer.[187]

In September after a couple of months there came the Dutch Accident Investigation Safety Board's 'Preliminary Report - Crash Involving Malaysia Airlines Boeing 777-200 flight MH17'. This just said that 'impacts from a large number of high-energy objects from outside the aircraft' had caused the explosion, and that the plane wreckage was 'distributed over a 10 km by 5 km area' indicating it had been blown apart in the sky.

Figure: New passports being scattered on the ground

I suggest that that Preliminary Report was an honest document, which one can hardly say for its final report which emerged in October 2015. As Gerhard Wisnewski pointed out, it lacked any information about the dead, for example, the cause of death, or how many bodies were recovered, i.e., there were no autopsy reports, not even for the pilots: normally a major point of interest for an air-crash. It claimed to have a readout of the cockpit voice recorder for the last half-hour of the flight, obtained by the British MOD at Farnborough who had the black boxes: this showed how the conversation was quite normal until 13:20:03 hours when it abruptly went silent, i.e., no panic or alarm could be detected.[188] Considering that the plane was way off course and air controllers had reportedly lost contact shortly before the explosion, that seems odd.

A dozen or so passports were seen as being scattered on the ground, by the MH-17 wreckage - a site which was not cordoned off or protected in any way. Some of the passports had holes punched in them, i.e., they were out of date. People were asking: 'Why is he scattering a bunch of passports from the Netherlands all over the ground?'[189] - why indeed? 'And why are they all intact if they were in this crash?' The pristine passports tell the story: 'there was not one recovered that looked the least bit used" (from Jim Stone). The video showed some character taking these passports out of the back of a car, before scattering them on the ground!

Reuters has shown a picture of a big explosion with a fireball, supposedly of the plane hitting the ground. We have no images of the plane coming down, nor of the BUK missile going up, but only a distant fireball on the horizon. One would hardly expect pristine passports on the ground after that. One is bound to add, that modern false-flag terror events are renowned for having passports and/or I.D. proving remarkably endurable through explosions and infernos!

An initial report had 108 AIDS-expert doctors killed, on their way to a Melbourne AIDS conference, which suddenly went down to only 6 the next day - suggesting that no actual list of passengers existed for that plane. (Emirates Airline was the official airline for that AIDs conference in Melbourne, offering steep discounts). 192 Dutch nationals are said to have been killed.

War Game Goes Live

Two NATO-Ukraine 'exercises' were running in the days leading up to July 17: 'Sea Breeze' and Rapid Trident' . They *ended on July 17th (according to* RT's Cross Talk, July 4th). Those war-games are what morphed into the terror-drill.

The Malaysian government took the view that the Ukrainian government in collusion with NATO shot down the Malaysian MH-17 aircraft over Ukraine, in its August 6th *New Straits Times,* Malaysia's flagship English-language newspaper. Given the tightly controlled character of the Malaysian media, it appears that this accusation has the imprimatur of the Malaysian state.

These details do matter, as the Western media have been trying to generate a WW3 situation out of what is just another false-flag terror event - and doing so over the 100-year anniversary of the WW1 Outbreak, August 1914. Comparing with the earlier Malaysian Airlines tragedy - the MH370 shot down March 8th over Indian Ocean, there is evidence that contact with Malaysia Airlines flight 17 was lost in advance of the wayward event. Next, and once more like flight 370, there is evidence that the pilot of Flight 17 actually diverted-purportedly on the basis of a vague sense of being "uncomfortable"-the craft into the dangerous warzone region where it was shot down.

This was the 100-year anniversary of the outbreak of WW1, as it brewed up in July 1914 - in exactly the same part of the world, the Balkans. Then later on, Russia's last ruling monarch of the Romanov family Tsar Nicholas II, together with his wife Tsarina Alexandra and their five children Olga, Tatiana, Maria, Anastasia, and Alexei were executed on 17 July 1918 - a subliminal message to Putin? The MH 17 crash also shares an anniversary with the demise of TWA 800, which some view as having been brought down by a missile on July 17, 1996 and subsequently covered up by the US government. The maiden flight of MH17 was on 17 July; also a funny synchrony with the mystery death of David Kelly, the UK gas-warfare expert, on 17th of July, 2003 just as the US-UK was starting the war with Iraq.

Russia has called for a non-political investigation of the crash - the one thing which cannot be allowed to occur after state-fabricated terror. Instead, the Netherlands, Australia, Malaysia, Britain, Belgium, Germany, the Philippines, Canada, New Zealand, Indonesia, the United States and Ukraine agreed to a joint 'prosecutor' team, said a 'Eurojust' statement.[190] Absurd 'Eurojust' statements appeared, concerning which we may ask, what is America doing in this team, as it neither had any casualties nor is it in Europe, and why is Russia excluded, as it had much relevant evidence and is moreover in Europe?

Several days after the event, (on July 24th) the Kiev parliament and its entire cabinet collapsed with Prime Minister Yatsenyuk ('Yats') resigning, maybe caused by the demoralization of realising it had been party to diabolical state-fabricated terror? Ostensibly this collapse was due to the parliament's refusal to go along with the IMF's 'shock therapy' - selling off national assets to repay debts. Yats explained: "Our government now does not have an answer to the question how to pay salaries," adding, "How to support the army and armed forces? How not to demoralize the spirits of those tens of thousands of people who sit not in this hall, but in trenches under bullets?"

Soon after the incident, British news outlets floated, on no evidence, the bogus story, that MH17 had been diverted to "avoid thunderstorms in southern Ukraine," and that went onto Wikipedia. A certain Dutchman Nico Voorbach, president of the European Cockpit Association, the man used to brew up this fiction, told *The Guardian*, "I heard that MH17 was diverting from some showers as there were thunderclouds." The story was refuted by *Malaysian Airlines* in a Malaysia News report: 'MAS operations director Captain Izham Ismail has also refuted claims that heavy weather led to MH17 changing its flight plan. There were no reports from the pilot to suggest that this was the case." So Western media have acknowledged that a change in the flight path did occur - later admitting that their "heavy weather" narrative was a fabrication.

Rage of the Empire

Some good news for Planet Earth happened on July 16th in Brazil with the formation of a BRICS bank. As Webster Tarpley commented, concerning the BRICS bank being established: "MH17 is US-UK answer to launch of BRIC bank at Fortaleza summit - the biggest challenge to IMF and World Bank since 1944." The shoot-down also happened to be on the anniversary date for the flight TWA flight 800 being blown out of the sky, viz., July 17th, 1996. A few months earlier Russia had been informally expelled from the G8 summit, however after the BRICS banking system was established a more intense demonization of Putin, even his 'Hitlerization' one may say, has followed. The establishment of a non-Rothschild controlled banking system is a major challenge to the Empire: the Obama administration could not convince a single South American leader to avoid the BRICS summit in Brazil. In some degree we may see the shoot-down as a response to this event.

Dutch Report   October 2105

The Western media unanimously accepted the Dutch Safety Board report on the MH-17 shoot-down, blaming Russia. We here quote Gordon Duff writing for *Veterans Today*:[191]

> Today, Dutch investigators came up with their long predetermined solution, that a BUK missile shot down MH17 no matter how impossible that might be. Any other answer would have brought down NATO.
>
> The Kiev-backed SU25 pilots following MH17 "from below" have never admitted to seeing anything though the plane, according to them, nearly fell on them.
>
> Then again, the American AEGIS radar imagery units, one in Constanta and two more on ships in the Black Sea, though they recorded everything, were withheld along with American satellite imagery. Only one answer for this, because they recorded planes shooting down MH17, as is consistent with the German report.
>
> Other than the simple issue of impossibility, there is rock-solid evidence that MH17 was trailed by two SU25 aircraft that Kiev claimed could not be responsible, because they were not capable of flight at that altitude.
>
> In the article below, based on live interviews on *Russia Today*, pilots debunked this, pilots who have flown the SU25 to nearly 50,000 feet.
>
> This is the crux of the story. The other "crux" of the story is not only the predetermined insanity the Dutch have come up with - long expected - but the behaviour of the media, including the very weak Russian media, *Russia Today*, *Sputnik News* among others, who quickly lose focus.

This is a story all about control of the media.

The respected US political advisor Paul Craig Roberts reached this sad conclusion, about the downed MH17 plane and the attempt to blame Russia:[192]

> The Western media have proved for all to see that the Western media comprises either a collection of ignorant and incompetent fools or a whorehouse that sells war for money.
>
> The Western media fell in step with Washington and blamed the downed Malaysian airliner on Russia. No evidence was provided. In its place the media used constant repetition. Washington withheld the evidence that proved that Kiev was responsible. The media's purpose was not to tell the truth, but to demonise Russia...
>
> The same group in Washington and the same Western "media" are telling the same kind of lies that were used to justify Washington's wars in Iraq (weapons of mass destruction), Afghanistan (Taliban = al

Qaeda), Syria (use of chemical weapons), Libya (an assortment of ridiculous charges), and the ongoing US military murders in Pakistan, Yemen, and Somalia.

The city upon the hill, the light unto the world, the home of the exceptional, indispensable people is the home of Satan's lies where truth is prohibited and war is the end game.

Many question-marks remain. Was it in fact the vanished flight 370 plane? Europe does need to have a debate on this matter! A real investigation would have looked at serial numbers on parts that identify the plane, and would not be limited to photos of an air crash. Consider the following possible scenario. The old Boeing-777 of MH flight 370 was remotely flown out via pre-programmed autopilot from Schiphol airport with a transponder identifying it as MH17, and then received two fighter jet escorts when far enough away from the originating airport not to arouse suspicion. These fighter escorts stayed close enough to conceal their radar signature and provided "pilot feedback" from the pilot-absent zombie flown flight 370, which at the appropriate time was shot down.

A prime-time vampire series called "The Strain" began on July 13th 2014, directed and written by Guillermo del Toro. Its first episode featured a Boeing jetliner arriving at Kennedy airport from Europe with everyone dead on board, drained of blood and already decomposing.[193] The Empire, or so one gathers, must tell us in advance what it is going to do.

They call it 'predictive programming.'

11
Paris: Charlie Hebdo
2015

She was practiced at the art of deception
Well I could tell by her blood-stained hands

The Rolling Stones, 'You can't always get what you want'

There has been a succession of state-fabricated terror events in Europe, starting with say the Bologna bombings in 1980.[194] I suggest that French intellectuals need to use these as a basis for evaluating what has happened in the 'Charlie Hebdo event' and to classify it correctly. Did anyone die in that event? Did terror strike France on that day, or was it just done by actors? Did the event have a purpose, and if so, what was it? Did Muslims play any role in the event, or not?

What Ostensibly Happened in Paris

On 11th January an estimated 3.7 million demonstrators took to the streets with 'Je Suis Charlie' placards - the largest ever show of French 'solidarity' since the liberation of Paris in August 1944. Those creating these events know how to pull on the heartstrings of a people! Let's hope that some small proportion of those who then came out to demonstrate now feel like complete idiots over how they were duped. How were a million placards so quickly printed, as the event itself only happened on Wednesday, 7th January?

'Je suis Charlie' events were going strong on French radio by about 12.30 Paris time on the 7th, *one hour* after the event which was at 11.30 Paris time. One hour after! That invites comparison with the 9/11 event, where the name of Osama Bin Laden was being broadcast over the airwaves a mere hour or so after the Towers had collapsed.

An ailing satire magazine quickly printed a few million copies - after its staff had supposedly been shot. Somehow it was well able to handle the huge excess demand. On January 13th the next week's edition came out, with a three million print run at three euros a time. Overdraft, what overdraft? The spectral staff must surely have savoured this supreme moment of success.

A fabricated photo flashed around the world's newswires, together with headlines like, "Global leaders join 'unprecedented' rally in largest demonstration in history of France" - *Independent* on 11th Jan. Whereas what had really happened was - - a photo-op on an empty, guarded street where a small, hired crowd was surrounded by security officers (as *The Independent* admitted to its readers a day later on 12th).[195]

The world leaders might want to be popular, but … they are not. Maybe if they made some effort to speak words of truth to us, that might change.

This whole story is ostensibly about a satire magazine. So let's hear a bit of satire, if that's the word, concerning France's huge demo, quoting my favourite Muslim, Kevin Barrett. ('Je suis brainwashed', *Veterans Today* on 12th - the day after the march)

> Million morons march for big lies. Call them sheeple. Lemmings. Zombies. New World Order mind control slaves. Whatever you call them, the drooling dimwits chanting "we are Charlie" are the all-time greatest argument for Rockefeller-style eugenic euthanasia.
>
> And don't get me started on those "world leaders" who led *le défilé des idiots*. These scumbag-psychopath "leaders" are the worst terrorists on earth. Take Netanyahu - please! Where are the black ski-mask guys with AK-47s when we need them? Somebody call in a drone strike!

This Charlie Hebdo thing (dramatic drum roll) is the most obvious freakin' false flag imaginable... throw-down ID in an abandoned getaway car, Police Commissioner conveniently suicided, intel-cutout patsies murdered, blatantly fake "terrorist kills cop" propaganda video...it doesn't get any better (or should I say worse) than this.

Netanyahu had been instructed not to come, which did not prevent him from turning up and hustling his way to the front of the photo-op. Once it was known he was coming, France's security minister sternly advised him that this "would have an adverse effect on ties between the two countries as long as Hollande was president of France and Netanyahu was prime minister of Israel" (Haaretz). The latter's war-of-civilization remarks were of just the kind the French authorities were keen to avoid, plus he urged French Jews to move to Israel, where they would be safe!

By way of contrast, here is what the French President, François Hollande, had told the people of France on national television, on 9th January. Looking shaken and fearful, he briefly stated:

Those who have committed these actions, these terrorists, these illuminati, have nothing to do with Islam. ('Ceux qui ont commis ces actes, ces terroristes, ces illuminés, ces fanatiques, n'ont rien à voir avec la religion Musulmane')

- leading to fervent web-debate over whether he had just alluded to 'the Illuminati' as the perpetrators, or whether this French word was being used in its more casual sense as just meaning, e.g., 'idiots.' But whatever the answer, he had made some attempt to avoid blaming Muslims.

Kevin Barrett successfully brought out his *Je Ne Suis pas Charlie Hebdo* with twenty-two contributors within months after the event: it was, as the US professor David Ray Griffin observed, "A breakthrough in the study of State Crimes Against Democracy (SCADS). Never before have truth-seekers countered with such a comprehensive response to a likely false-flag operation so soon after it happened" - a testimony, one could note, by a Christian theologian concerning a book edited by a Muslim.

On 12 January the French Parliament approved with almost unanimity (one abstention only) a budget for France's continuous and enlarged involvement in the new war on Iraq, a new war-engagement led by Washington and supported by the UK, Canada, Australia and France. Aircraft carriers and troops were mobilised, not losing one day. French lawmakers agreed to display 10,000 troops throughout the country to protect 'vulnerable places' - i.e., spying on citizens, for their protection. All this is looking very pre-planned.

There was, however, one Frenchman who spoke the words of truth: Jean-Marie le Pen, 86-year old leader of the French National Front party. The event, he said, was *the work of Western intelligence*: "The shooting at Charlie Hebdo resembles a secret service operation ... I don't think it was organised by the French authorities, but they permitted this crime to be committed." Pointing to the fact that one of the Kouachi brothers (allegedly, the terrorists) left his identity card in a crashed getaway car, he sagely compared this to the 'miraculous fact' that one of the passports of the 9/11 hijackers was found on the ground in New York after two planes collided with the twin towers of the World Trade Centre in 2001.

His daughter, Marine le Pen, dissociated herself from him on this matter. His house was *set on fire* on Monday 26th January. Although somewhat injured, he managed to escape. That fire was the Empire's way of telling him, that he was on the right track.

Punishment for 'Wrong' French Policy?

On December 2nd, 2014, the France Parliament had passed a resolution asking that France recognize a Palestinian state - even though Netanyahu had earlier warned them that such a move would be a 'grave mistake'. Its lower house voted to recognize Palestine with 339 MPs voting in favour and 151 against. Then - almost as bad - on 6th January, the French President, François Hollande, called on the West to end sanctions against Russia. France was openly stepping out of line from the Empire's policy.

One week before the event, Israel informed France that it was "deeply disappointed" with France's vote on a UN resolution that would have required Israeli forces to withdraw to their pre-1967 borders by 2017.

On the 5th of January, two days before the event, Hollande put forward on France Inter-Radio a shockingly pro-Putin viewpoint, calling for sanctions against Russia to be abolished:

> I think the sanctions must stop now. They must be lifted if there is progress. If there is no progress the sanctions will remain … Mr Putin does not want to annex eastern Ukraine. He has told me that…

and rejecting the idea that France should militarily occupy Libya. Did he need to be taught a lesson for daring to express these sensible, humane, and anti-war views?[196]

The US commentator Paul Craig Roberts said on January 10th that: "French President François Hollande this week said that the sanctions against Russia should end. This is too much foreign policy independence on France's part for Washington…. the attack on Charlie Hebdo was an inside job and people identified by NSA as hostile to the Western wars against Muslims are going to be framed for an inside job designed to pull France firmly back under Washington's thumb."[197]

With France taking such a measure decisively sympathetic to Islam, would it make any sense at all for Muslim zealots to choose that moment to murder a dozen French citizens? Such an act could only turn French public opinion against Muslims and in favour of Israel.

A comparable view was expressed in Russia: *Komsomolskaya Pravda*, one of Russia's leading tabloids, ran the headline: "Did the Americans stage the terror attack in Paris?" and posted a series of interviews on its website that presented various reasons why Washington might have organised the attack. In one interview, Alexander Zhilin, head of the pro-Kremlin Moscow Centre for the Study of Applied Problems, claimed the terror attack was US retribution against President François Hollande for a January 6 radio interview in which he urged the EU to lift sanctions against Russia. Washington had used the attacks as "a quick fix for consolidating" US and EU geopolitical interests in Ukraine, Mr Zhilin claimed.

One may here be reminded of the Breivik Oslo event, when the Norwegian government was advocating sanctions against Israel. In the summer of 2011, the Norwegian AUF (the Labour Party's youth movement) was poised to have Norway's government impose a complete unilateral economic embargo on Israel, but that anti-Israel embargo never materialized: the project was pre-empted when the entire leadership of the AUF was slaughtered, allegedly by lone Zionist Anders Breivik, in July;[198] or indeed the Fukushima event when Japan was likewise adopting undue criticisms of Israel;[199] or Malaysia, which had dared to hold a court which found Israel guilty of war crimes and genocide![200] Soon after, three of its passenger planes fell out of the sky.[201]

Pro-Zionist Charlie Hebdo Office Destroyed - *Again*

Our story begins upon a specific date, that of the first 'attack' upon the CH offices, on November 2nd, 2011:

2.11.2011

when the CH issue number was

1011

Both of the attacks happened on a Wednesday, which was when the magazine appeared. The CH office was then half a million euros in debt, while a couple of months later they were a comparable amount in the black, i.e., the attack rescued them from bankruptcy. 'Muhammad' had been listed as the Editor in Chief, and pretty much the whole issue (2.11.2011, issue number 1011) was an attack on Islam. Making this issue as offensive as possible meant they could attack their own offices, then blame it on Islamic fundamentalists. A single Molotov cocktail (a petrol bomb) had allegedly been thrown through the window, but no one was arrested and no one claimed responsibility. The CH staff quickly blamed Islamic fundamentalists, however given the state of their finances, the word on the street was that it was an "insurance job". Some sort of explosion may have taken place in that office, but as most of the paper and wood had not been burnt it could not have been a Molotov cocktail. We are here following the insightful analysis of Sheila Barr.[202]

The CH office has moved through four addresses: It used to reside at what we'll call *Address 1,* namely 44 Rue Turbigo 75003 (see image below), until the 17th of October 2011. Just before the first alleged Islamic attack it apparently moved to *Address 2,* 56-62 Boulevard Davout 75020. But NB there are no photos of the CH staff at that address. Following that alleged attack this subversive magazine moved to their *Address 3,* namely Rue Serpollent, which happens to be where the Head of Police in Paris resides.

Figure: CH staff outside 44, Rue Turbigo

As regards to the event in January, 2015, an analysis of Facebook activity concluded that, "It would seem that the day before the shooting, January 6, the staff at CH spent the whole day on Paris business directory sites, changing their address status from Rue Serpollent to Rue Nicholas Appert.' The address of the Charlie Hebdo office, on the day of the 'shootings', was given as 10 Rue Nicolas Appert, *Address 4.* But NB an analysis of the photos from that day reached the conclusion: "Apparently, there have never been any pictures of the Charlie Hebdo staff at 10 Rue Nicolas Appert," and instead, they all seemed to come from 44 Rue Turbigo (*Address 1*) - as if they were back at their original home.

This is all rather puzzling. Let's quote wise words from Sandra Barr: "I have not been able to find one picture of any CH staff member at number 10 Rue Nicolas Appert." From careful study of nearby buildings she concluded: 'Nearly all the pictures that were shown in the press of the CH staff were taken in this Rue Turbigo building.'

She concluded: "It is my honest opinion, that Charlie Hebdo was never located at either Boulevard Devout, or 10 Rue Nicolas Appert (Addresses 2 & 4), I think both of these addresses were used to stage false flag events that would incite hatred towards Muslims, and give governments an excuse to impose draconian laws on the people." Thereby we may in some degree apprehend what the CH office was doing moving in with the Parisian Head of Police.

For both alleged attacks, the company moved into the alleged premises just prior to the attacks. The company name is Charlie Hebdo Hara Kiri, and Hari Kiri means to end one's life - could this subtly allude to its twice-used self-destruction procedure?

The bankrupt CH magazine was purchased by Edouard Baron de Rothschild (a major shareholder in the French daily *Libération*), one month before the event, in December 2014.[203] Prior to the 2015 attack CH was two hundred thousand Euros in debt. To remedy this, they decided to repeat what they had done successfully in the past - except that, this time some 'deaths' would be needed - apparently.[204]

Alleged Deaths

After the attack, at 11 am on 7.1. 2015, we saw no blood or dead bodies, or any pictures of the dead being loaded onto ambulances, and then later on, no post-mortems or coroner's inquests.

The CH Editor Stephane Charbonnier is or was fervently pro-Jewish: his magazine produces obscene anti-Christian and anti-Muslim cartoons, but for anyone who doubted 'The Holocaust', he said "I'm for cutting off their balls. No need to waste time discussing".(quoted in *Libération*, a daily newspaper owned by Édouard de Rothschild, in its tribute to Charbonnier on 7/1, the day of the event) His partner, the crisis actor Jeannette Bougrab, is a Mizrahi Jew and member of the French Council of State. In the view of Gilad Atzmon, CH "was a neocon, philo-Semitic magazine that supported Zionist wars, and was dedicated to minorities and Muslims in particular, while at the same time silencing criticism of Jewish power and the American war machine. Charlie Hebdo went about acting as the Israeli cultural attaché in Paris." (Atzmon, 12.1.15) We may compare this verdict with that expressed by Sandra Barr:

> It would seem that publishing cartoons of the Prophet Mohammed was a nice little earner for CH. Their stupid magazine was juvenile, vulgar, and offensive to anyone anywhere that had any religious beliefs. (except Jews) I do not follow any religion, and I found their depictions of Jesus, the Virgin Mary, and the Prophet Mohammed extremely offensive. Their magazine was first created just after the first gulf war, and if they were given a brief by intelligence services, it was to spread fear of Muslims, and create divides between religions. They were frequently accused of serving the Zionist agenda, and going ever so lightly on Israel and Jews.

One cartoonist in Charlie Hebdo had been sacked for a comparatively innocuous remark, accused of 'antisemitism'.

There were two Jews on the CH payroll, which matters, because of the huge meaning that was overlaid onto the event, as security cars patrolled every French synagogue, and Netanyahu called for Jews to emigrate to Israel. One of these employees, Elsa Cayat, had her cousin Sophie interviewed by *The Independent,* (12th January) where she disclosed that in 2014 she had travelled to Peru with various CH "contributors." Would a small magazine greatly in debt really want to send at least four of its staff to Peru, to take drugs in the jungle? George Wolinski a cartoonist at CH was also Jewish, while Bernard Maris who allegedly died in the attack, was a Mason initiated at the Grand Orient de France lodge in Paris, and also had a connection with the Central Bank of Peru. Another victim of 7/1, Michael Renaud, was also a member of France's Grand Orient Lodge.

The offices of Charlie Hebdo normally had a couple of security guards outside its offices, who were not there prior to the shooting. The CH journalist staff were gathered for their weekly editorial meeting, and as a CH reporter told the French newspaper *Le Monde,* the attackers would have had to have been informed that the meeting was taking place, because otherwise there would not have been many people on the premises. Corrine Rey**,** a CH cartoonist who goes by the pen name Coco, had apparently encountered the masked shooters at the buildings entrance with her daughter. She provided the digital code to enter the Hebdo offices. Rey said that, "the men 'spoke French perfectly' and 'claimed they were Al Qaeda terrorists." Thus, at the building's entrance - timing their arrival exactly for the weekly editorial meeting - the two armed men requested the digital entry code, speaking with perfect French accents, and were given it, allegedly shouting 'Allah Akbar!' they entered.

Another (unnamed) witness of their arrival at the CH office recalled one of them having blue eyes - he allegedly forced her to recite the Koran. Yemeni citizens do not have blue eyes.

Had CH staff vanished to Peru? The columnist 'Lasha Darkmoon' published on 11th January an alleged statement from Ellie Katsnelson, aka Madame Rothschild, an aristocrat of Rothschild parentage who had fallen out with her "family," living in France:

> Muslims had nothing - I repeat, nothing - whatever to do with the carnage that took place in Paris last week… Ahmed Merabet, the first French policeman purportedly shot dead, is actually not a Muslim at all: his real name is Avigdor, and his brother's name is Maloch, recently changed to Melek - all of them crypto-Jews in the service of Israeli intelligence, i.e., Mossad agents. Avigdor is in Buenos Aires right now, and will remain there for six years, a standard operating procedure with those deep in Israeli psyops. After this he will resurface with a new

identity. The amount such players get paid is 666,000 euros or dollars.'[205]

If indeed Ahmed Merabet died from that shot -with an AK-47 fired, pointing at his face - do we have a body? Will there be an autopsy? Why are there no search results whatsoever for Ahmed Merabet before January, 2015?

Escape

The two main suspects were named Cherif and Said Kouachi. Despite both being under watch by French security forces, they managed to execute the attack on CH office with military precision, unobstructed in one of the world's most heavily policed cities. Military forces were searching for both men. How could they, under security watch, successfully execute a commando-like attack in broad daylight, then leave the crime scene with apparent ease? They were seen dispatching a police vehicle with multiple shots in its windshield, killing two policemen, wounding another, then driving off unhurried in their car, according to reports.

Wearing bulletproof vests, they had clearly been well-trained for their mission. One of the attackers Said Kouachi left his ID in the getaway car - which also conveniently contained jihadist flags and Molotov cocktails. What kind of criminals would be well-disguised and yet take their ID, then leave it in a car? They then escaped completely, while shooting at police all over Paris. They seemed calm, well trained and handled the automatic firearms with experience.

Sporadically shouting "Allah Akbar" throughout the duration of their onslaught, the two attackers were caught on video making a spectacle of themselves as they paraded down the Paris street guns blazing. It is hardly usual for terrorists to make it publicly known who they are and what they stand for before concluding their dirty work, 'an anomaly the mainstream media refuses to emphasize for obvious reasons.'[206]

Though the perpetrators escaped and defied capture, that did not prevent the French police from identifying them within hours. Heading north, they abandoned their car for another and quickly left Paris. Manhunt operations continue, but both men remain free with Paris put on maximum terror alert with civil liberties suspended, widespread searches, cars stopped, homes entered, etc.

One suspect named, the 18-year old Hamyd Mourad, alleged car driver, quickly handed himself to the police at around 11 pm, after he saw his name mentioned on the news, which saved his life. He had a sound alibi, of being present in a classroom that morning.

Driving up north through Paris, the getaway car, to quote Kevin Barrett, 'headed straight to the area where the largest Jewish community in France lives, and they decide to change "stolen" vehicles in front of a shop run by Zionist extremists collaborating with the Israeli Ministry of Defence.' Around noon in the Rue de Meaux, the change of cars had happened in front of a patisserie shop used by the Israeli army.[207] The masked Charlie Hebdo killers drove their car to that Jewish Kosher restaurant 'Patisory' that was popular with Israelis/Mossad in Paris - then laughably 'by accident' are said to have left the ID of Kouachi in that car.

When we first saw that car, it was a black Citroen C3 with bright, shiny chrome wing-mirrors. This car was then 'dumped,' enabling the 'ID left in the getaway car' story to work - just as in the 9/11 event, where Korans, wills, etc., were supposedly left in hired cars outside the airport. This stage of the story *confirms the Islamic identity* of the alleged terrorists. But, as many pointed out, the left-behind black C3 Citroen containing the ID was a different model which had *black* wing mirrors. The whole event is looking rather staged.

One of the attackers "was trained" at an Al-Qaeda camp in Yemen in 2011 according to a top US official - how should a US official suddenly know about this case? Reportedly they were both veterans of Obama's war on Syria, brought back for what looks like a classic false-flag attack. Then as Paul Craig Roberts commented, 'The Charlie Hebdo and Boston bombing have in common that the police decided to kill the alleged perpetrators rather than capture them.'

One Real Death

A police chief investigating the event suddenly 'committed suicide' on the night of Wednesday/Thursday (the mock-terror event was on Wednesday 7th). Helric Fredou was in his office, just completing his report:[208] he had dispatched the team of police officials under his jurisdiction, and had them return for a debriefing, and was urgently working through the night to prepare his police report. There was a news blackout on his death, except only that an autopsy 'confirmed his suicide' i.e., that he had shot himself in the head with his own gun for no reason. His mother refused to believe the story and was informed that she would not get to see the autopsy report. Under French law if a death is declared a suicide, the next of kin supposed to be allowed to attend the autopsy - but, that didn't happen here.

Staged Video of Phoney Shootout

At 8.30 am on the morning of January 7th, the police cordoned off the street, adjacent to the CH office to prepare it for the coming drama. A citizen asking the police about this was told, that it was for the purpose of making a movie - which was true enough.

On that morning, a posse of photographers were gathered up on a rooftop, waiting for the exciting events to begin. What a surprise that Amchai Stein, the deputy editor of Israeli IBA Channel 1, happened to be there, and as soon as the action started. Just after 11.30 he was posting photos of the shooting. *All video initially posted was shot from rooftops.* This was for a scene that lasted less than a minute! The films had several people shooting from different places. These were normal roof tops with no reason for anyone to be up there. The rooftop crowd wore bullet-proof flak jackets.[209] The crisis actors getting out of the car were captured in full

- leading not a few to wonder, why would anyone have a camera ready and rolling to capture a scene when they were not supposed to even know it was going to happen?

Figure: Note trainer shoe dropped outside car door, a kind of indication that actors were involved. They soon picked it up before leaping back into the car. Also, note the mark put onto the road indicating where the car should stop.

At the 9/11 event for comparison, we recall how one of five Mossad agents explained on Israeli national TV, 'Our purpose was to document the event' - as to why they had set up their camera on the other side of the Hudson River, opposite the world trade centre, *on the morning* which altered our world forever, as the planes went into the Towers. Those Israelis were arrested on that day of 2001, as the Towers were still smouldering, because of their very suspicious behaviour, but then released after a flurry of diplomatic activity and returned to Israel. The Israeli TV presence at the Charlie Hebdo event surely has to remind us of this. Mossad enjoys a certain reputation of foreknowledge concerning suchlike events, for example, the London 7/7 event: Netanyahu was not only in London on that very morning, but he claimed to have been warned of the event just before it happened.[210]

A well-photographed scene shows no blood on the pavement around the policemen when shot. Video sequences show the AK-47 rifle being shot with no recoil, no blood on pavement - actors are here involved. E-mail forums discussed how YouTube videos of this scene rapidly vanished in the wake of the event. I have personally never seen videos vanish so fast as these Charlie Hebdo ones did!

The officer falls down for the first part of the show, and *to prove how bad the terrorists are*, is "killed" while wounded and laying down. As a staged drama, it makes them look more 'wicked' to stop the car and kill a defenceless policeman. In the video, we see far too much white smoke coming out of guns - blanks produce all that white smoke, loaded rounds do not. No blood was anywhere on the pavement - shades of the Lee Rigby fake death in UK! Although the instant of shooting is whited out, we still see the blood-free aftermath. We hear too much echo in the sound of blanks being fired. Also at that close range the head would have been blown open. There was no ricochet effect when the gun is fired.

Figure: no blood on pavement as actor is shot with AK-47 rifle.

By the next day, 'blood' had been put onto the pavement! Soon after the psy-op street-theatre of a policeman being 'shot,' the pavement area was cordoned off, and some 'blood' put there - as a journalist inadvertently explained on Sky News,[211] "You can see the blood on the ground, which has been put there..." We could indeed, and also that it had not been there the day before.

The 'bad guys' should have been running away and trying to escape - why would they want to pull up, get out of the car, and finish off the hurt policemen? The *purpose* of this 'terror' video sequence was that it made the 'terrorists' visible: no film was available of what had happened around the CH office, nor were any bodies or blood available to view, so there was an immediate danger of public scepticism. We therefore could be shown the bad guys killing a defenceless policeman in the aftermath of that attack, already lying down on the pavement. It served to *confirm the narrative.*

Dynamite in Jewish Grocery Store

On the same day a few hours later, a car exploded and went up in flames right outside a synagogue in the Paris suburb of Sarcelles. News reports said this was unrelated, but I suggest otherwise, that it was, in a general way, part of the story. And what was the story? Netanyahu's speech made in a Paris synagogue appealing to Jews to come to Israel, where they would be safe, could here be a central *motif.*

Two days later on Friday, the scene shifts to a Kosher grocery in the Port de Vincennes district of Paris. Film of this event shows a lot of armed police gathering outside the supermarket, which is closed.[212] Amedy Coulibaly is reported to be holding hostages in there. A metal grille then rises to open it and the police all start firing into the shop, and start to enter it. There seems to be no return fire and it is unclear who the police are firing at. Then a man tries to leap out, with his hands tied together - and falls on the ground. There is no weapon in his hands and yet the police continue shooting: as if they did not want him still alive for questioning, which would doubtless have been inconvenient. As Paul Craig Roberts commented, "The connection between Muslim murderous ire against French cartoonists and Coulibaly's alleged attack on a Kosher deli is asserted, but not explained."

The suspect entered the Kosher grocery in the Port de Vincennes district of Paris and took up to 14 hostages, at least four of whom are alleged to have been killed by the gunman. Police claim they found 15 sticks of dynamite inside the store after they stormed the shop. A video of the police outside that store makes it clear that they are firing blanks.[213]

The chief suspect Amedy Coulibaly was apparently killed along with several of his hostages, but his accomplice Hayat Boumeddiene evaded capture - despite being surrounded by literally hundreds of police and security personnel with the whole district locked down and the site of the siege was under intense scrutiny. The police, TV cameras, police helicopters, etc., were all watching, yet somehow Coulibaly's partner and accomplice at the scene of the siege managed to escape undetected. Was she allowed to escape and maybe even assisted, because she was Amedy Coulibaly's handler? She had lived with Amedy Coulibaly for several years. She reappears, of course, in Syria ...

The four allegedly killed by Coulibaly were Jewish, and their bodies were flown over to Jerusalem for burial, leaving a whiff of suspicion that there had been no real deaths, no real corpses. In London, on the days following the CH event, Shomrim 'Jewish police' (Shomrim means 'Pride' in Hebrew) cars, painted yellow and blue to resemble police cars, were prowling around, no doubt hunting for anti-semitism.

This event 'bears all the hallmarks' of state-fabricated terror with major Israeli input. Use of actors, a poorly-done staged shootout, pre-prepared photographers, no possible motive for Islamic attack just as France adopts pro-Palestine position, detailed knowledge of security and timing of journal staff meeting, a perfect escape, etc. Also leaving ID in a car with other 'Islamic' gear - 'clues' - would journalists fall *again* for that one? The road was cordoned off beforehand, kept traffic-free, just like the Lee Rigby event.

12
Bataclan: Paris Again Hit by (Fictional) Terror 2015

The outrage occurred on Friday, 13th November 2015, just two weeks after Halloween (31st October), when a Russian civilian plane had been blown out of the sky. The date - 11/13/15, in US terms - was a remarkable sequence of odd numbers.

A year earlier in November 2014, *The Economist* published their 'The World in 2015' issue with a front cover widely surmised to contain 'Illuminati' symbolism. Let us inspect its bottom right-hand corner.

Here is a close-up of the relevant image. We see:

- A missile and two arrows, indicating AN ATTACK.

- A painting in The Louvre indicating PARIS.

- The magazine was pre-viewing the year 2015 so '11' would tend to indicate THE MONTH OF NOVEMBER.

- Alice (portrayed as in 'Through the Looking Glass') alludes, I suggest, to a *mirror-delusion* whereby a true enemy creates a virtual enemy that is an image of itself, i.e., the reference to 'Alice' is a coded confession that THE STATE ITSELF IS THE TERRORIST.

- The two arrows have numbers on them (11.3 and 11.5) which are on the same level, suggesting they should be put together. Rearranged we are shown THE VERY DATE OF THE ATTACK 11/13/15.

Nothing else happened in 2015 relating to these numbers. **Thus, the prevision of the Paris Event Is Unequivocal.**

The manufacturers of the 'War on Terror' laugh in the face of humanity as they lead us through lie after lie and war after war towards their desired end.

We gather that there is a mysterious law, whereby the perpetrators of the fabricated-terror events have to tell us in advance, i.e., they have to give the warning! Let us now run through the evidence, indicating who did it.

Following the Charlie Hebdo attacks in January, the French regime implemented a despotic anti-terror bill that gave authorities virtually unlimited surveillance powers. France essentially declared martial law, dispatching tens of thousands of troops into the streets. The authorities could wiretap phone communications and snoop on Internet traffic of ordinary citizens.[214] Despite this power to spy on just about anybody, they once again failed to stop 'a highly sophisticated, multi-faceted attack that would have required so much logistical expertise and know-how that it is palpably unfeasible such a plot could succeed without the help of insiders within the French state (and possibly other states).'[215]

Pre-cognition of Event

The Event as *predicted* by *Paris Match* on October 2nd was to be a French Style 9/11, "un 11 septembre à la française." Not only was it coming, but it was *difficult to avoid:* "impossible a déjouer"! Judge Trévédic explained in that issue of *Paris Match.* "The attacks in France will be on a scale comparable to 9/11." Will be?

It is fair to ask … 'How can a person, a senior figure, be so confident that a unique event in French history is about to occur?'

Intelligence? If they had the Intelligence, they should have been able to prevent the attacks rather than have the shooters reportedly shooting up the city at their leisure, unmolested, for hours on end.

Drills on the Day

  '…that very night. A chilling stroke of fate.' - Patrick Pelloux[216]

  '…a simulation of essentially what happened that night.' - Pierre Carli

It had been thoroughly prepared. As is usual for state-fabricated terror events, drills were planned to simulate the event on the very same day: as with 9/11, as with the London bombing, as with the Oslo/Breivik event, as with the Boston Marathon bombing, etc. - we expect this as the normal signature of state-fabricated terror.[217]

Patrick Pelloux turns up as France's version of Peter Power: he had been involved in the earlier Charlie Hebdo events, just as Power was for British terror events, and who then becomes a chronicler at Charlie Hebdo. Conveniently, his book on the subject *just happened* to come out a couple of days before the next event, on Friday 13th. He explained on *France Info Radio* that Paris police were prepared because, "as luck would have it", they'd **planned an exercise to train for multi-site attacks on that very morning,** November, Friday13th, 2015: '*Précisément le même scénario.*'

Les avertissements se multiplient autour d'un «11-Septembre à la française»

Robin Panfili   **France**   02.10.2015 - 10 h 45   mis à jour le 02.10.2015 à 12 h 45

Utilisée dès 2001, l'expression est devenue récurrente dans la bouche des spécialistes du terrorisme ou des médias depuis le 7 janvier.

Figure: *Paris Match* on October 2nd

Estimates of the 'actual' number of dead kept changing, hovering between 125 and 130, yet are we not astonished that Thomas Loeb, who was responsible for leading the drill's medical services, explained how it had been planned for '*Quelques heures avant la tragédie*' - a few hours before, and that **it planned for 129 dead** -[218]

> The eight SAMU Ile-de-France met on Friday [13 November] for an exercise pertaining to the simulation of a terrorist attack in Paris.[219] We gathered in the Coordinating meeting room of the Defence area Ile-de-France, that morning, to work on the hypothesis [scenario] of an armed group involved in attacks in several locations Paris. This is what we call a tabletop exercise to consider the coordination of our actions… a very

clear working hypothesis for months, the idea of multiple simultaneous attacks.

One of the drills was at the actual hotel where the German football team were staying.[220] The very next day, the UK's *Metro* newspaper reported that the attacks left 129 people dead - the same number!

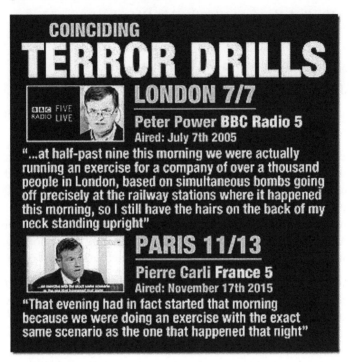

COINCIDING
TERROR DRILLS

LONDON 7/7

BBC FIVE RADIO LIVE

Peter Power BBC Radio 5
Aired: July 7th 2005

"...at half-past nine this morning we were actually running an exercise for a company of over a thousand people in London, based on simultaneous bombs going off precisely at the railway stations where it happened this morning, so I still have the hairs on the back of my neck standing upright"

PARIS 11/13

Pierre Carli France 5
Aired: November 17th 2015

"That evening had in fact started that morning because we were doing an exercise with the exact same scenario as the one that happened that night"

Wiki Up Too Soon

The *Wikipedia* account was posted up *while the event was in full swing*! The police did not storm the Bataclan music hall until after midnight, and yet within two hours from the onset of the attacks, at 23.06 a full and detailed account appeared. It was complete with footnotes, and specified "Syria" as being mentioned by a witness at the Bataclan. It had "5 or 6 terrorists", and "3 suicide bombers." That initial version specified that in a televised statement at approximately 23:58 (local time), French President François Hollande declared a state of emergency and closing of borders for the whole of France. That was *too early* - rather like the BBC reporting the collapse of Tower 7 before it had happened, on 9/11. Was that a confusion over time zones? Most are viewing this as, so to speak, 'precognition.' The too-soon Wikipedia account with its unduly-detailed narrative then hardly changed as events unfolded and we infer that its purpose was (again, as is the usual practice in False-Flag attacks) to *define and stabilise* the narrative.

Timeline, Evening of 13th November, Paris time

9.17 Explosions heard in the vicinity of the Stade de France.

9.20 Shooting outside Casa Nostra, pizzeria.

9.45 Bataclan shooting, as 'anthem to the devil' being played

9.50 Suicide bomber blows up near Stadium

10.10 A 'hostage situation' in Bataclan.

11.06 Wiki site goes up

00.44 Police storm the Bataclan

Jewish Precognition and Israeli Bataclan Owners

The *Jewish Telegraphic Agency* confirmed the details of the Bataclan owner's pro-Israel credentials in an article headlined "Before terror, Paris':

> Before Friday's bloodbath at the Le Bataclan concert venue in Paris, this centrally located hall from the 19th century had received numerous threats over pro-Israel events hosted there. From at least 2006-2009, Le Bataclan was the venue for the annual fundraising gala of Migdal, the French Jewish non-profit group that supports the Israeli Border Police. Last month, the theater served as the meeting place for a gathering of some 500 Zionist Christians who came there in support of Israel.

The Zionist ownership of the targeted venue in Paris has kindled much suspicion about the Bataclan's proprietor, Joel Laloux, and what he may have known about the attack in advance. Quoting from *The Times of Israel*, the Jewish owners of the theatre, who had had it for forty years, decided to sell shortly before this event - and did so *on September 11th*.[221] They emigrated to Israel after selling it. The co-owner Joel 'told Channel … he took a call from the theater at the time of the attack and I could hear the gunfire.' He added that a member of the Eagles of Death Metal was "hit by a bullet and killed." "There is blood everywhere," he said. "It will take three days just to clean that up." That claim of the band member being hit was incorrect, but it shows a desire to appear knowledgeable on the part of the old owners. After selling the property, did they just happen to be on the phone to the new owners, and hear the gunfire? Would the new owners really have wished to phone Israel at such a moment?

The 'Jewish community' in Paris apparently knew of the event on Friday morning. 'Just Friday, security officials in France's Jewish community were informed…' wrote *The Times of Israel* the very next day November 14th. But, that paper seems to have had doubts, had they not gone too far? So online that text was soon altered to 'for months, security officials….' Those who design these events remain hidden, but is seems they cannot resist adding their signature, as it were.

Bataclan

If there was a major terror-drill going on that day, then what happened at the celebrated concert given by the pro-Zionist, devil-worshipping band 'Eagles of Death Metal' (EODM) at the Bataclan theatre in Paris that night? Did a terror-attack happen there, with ninety members of the public shot dead - or not? According to the police report,[222] the band started at 8.45 pm, with 'terrorists' arriving at around 9.40 pm, then the police came at 10.00 pm. A stand-off took place for a couple of hours until after midnight, at 12.20 pm, when the police freed some hostages.

The police described how they fired at the belt of one hostage and he blew up, implying that he was wearing a 'suicide belt.' Most accounts have the various Kalashnikov-brandishing killers wearing suicide belts, however there is a credibility problem here: in the real world, no one has ever seen such a thing. One appreciates that the story cannot have the police bringing live 'terrorists' out of the Bataclan, who would then be able to talk. Lead singer of EODM Jesse Hughes gave a dramatic account of the event whereby "I saw fear fall like a blanket on the whole crowd and they fell like wheat in the wind - the way you would before a god." Did the audience suddenly lie down on the floor? There were no chairs in the main arena. Would you really do that in the event of such an attack, rather than, say, run for the exits? He added: 'The first thing I needed to do was find my girl. Fear took a backseat and "where's my girl?" took over.' According to one eyewitness report, it had been very dark during the concert, but then somebody put the lights on when the killers arrived. Jesse Hughes added:

> The terrorists would go up to bodies and stick them with the gun. If they budged, they'd shoot them again. One girl got up and said she was scared. The guy said, "Don't be scared, you'll be dead in two minutes," and then he shot her, BOOM.[223]

Are these just delicious death-fantasies? Remember the audience was supposedly joining in the chorus of the EODM song 'Kiss the Devil' - after all it was Friday 13th - when the shooting started. Let's go through the unfolding sequence.

Within an hour of the attacks becoming news, Fox News ran a story alleging that a "suspect" arrested at the Bataclan theatre told the police, "I am from ISIS." Fox hyped the story multiple times on their live news coverage and it was picked up by other mainstream media outlets and soon spread across the Internet. Fox News anchor Shepard Smith said on air:

"There is one man who has been arrested in Paris tonight. Arrested by French authorities who told French authorities, 'I am from ISIS.' I now have further information: that suspect has just told French police within the last hour or so, 'I am Syrian, I was here with two others, we were recruited by ISIS and this is ... an ISIS mission.' [The man] was quoted from inside the [Bataclan] theatre saying, 'This is for Syria. Allahu Akbar.' "

The story cannot be true (as Brandon Martinez pointed out) because none of the alleged shooters/bombers at Bataclan or any of the other sites were taken into custody. In the aftermath of state-fabricated terror, the patsies used cannot *ever* be allowed to speak to the media, or to any public figure - they are killed or jailed, or if deemed to be valuable may change their identity after apparently dying.

This Fox News report at once established the "ISIS" connection in the public mind, which may remind us of the US news proclaiming Osama bin Laden as the culprit, an hour or two after the Towers crumbled on 9/11. It thereby tells us about the perpetrator of the event.

At the Bataclan, a radio presenter witness, Pierre Janaszak described how the gunmen took 20 hostages and heard one of them tell their captives that 'it was Hollande's fault for intervening in Syria.' An alleged link to Syria was maybe the first 'fact' to emerge.

According to *Daily Mail* one of the suicide bombers that blew himself up (in the Bataclan) was identified after his finger was found (15 November). Is this not a mere insult to their readers' intelligence? Can the story get any sillier?

Immediate responses, before the official story has stabilised, are valuable. We quote three: "I also knew last night watching Kelly's File on FOX that the "parade" of "survivors" on camera with Space Blankets looked very fishy - at least four of these people coming out of the Concert Hall were smiling? laughing? Would you be smiling after witnessing a blood bath massacre as we've been told? People fall back into the same trap and believe the media. Some of it is real. Some of it involved crisis actors….all of it involved the Elite who have been planning this for a long time." (Barbara Joshua).

One must here agree that the groups of 'survivors' seen wearing their gold 'space blankets' did look very casual and unharmed. Here is another thoughtful comment made the next morning:

> In the very early hours there were no bloody scenes reported, no eye witnesses telling us what happened, lack of activity from emergency responses (I expect to see a mass rush of emergency calls, but nothing.) ISIS constantly being blamed, captions in the headlines saying immigrants were shouting for Syria when attacks happened and how emergency measure and tighter control will be needed to deal with this threat. All this is the call sign of a false flag event and is very similar to the London bombings. Within minutes it's all being confiscated and kept under national security.

Soon, 'survivors' were seen emerging from the concert theatre back door: 'No one is in shock to any degree. People are moving slowly. Others are milling around. No one is in obvious pain. There are no raw gunshot wounds from an AK-47 to be found… No one is suffering from burnt, shredded flesh and/or amputations…These people are crisis actors. The wounded are *fake* wounded. There are no wounds visible anywhere. The corpses are also fake.' Notice the body on the pavement that people have to step over as they emerge from that back door: when they're gone, he/it, still lying down, switches on his mobile phone! These French crisis actors just don't look stressed-out enough!

The next morning, newspapers carried a happy image of the Bataclan's audience. The concert hall takes up to about fifteen hundred people. We were assured by The *Mail* that this was taken 'moments' before the bullets started flying.

Figure: Groovy satanists?

In the middle foreground region but nowhere else a lot of characters are making the 'devil's horn' sign. The image looks as if every character is separate, has been overlaid on a separate Photoshop layer, comparisons here being made with the old *Sgt Pepper* album cover. Thus, there is no real sense of depth in the image. Everyone looks in a different direction, each in his own private world. Some are sharply in focus, others not. The crowd goes too far back under the main balcony, and is too brightly lit there. Readers may wish to check out the colour image of this 'happy satanists' picture, to help decide. In contrast, an alleged video of the band as the shooting began shows everything as being very dark.

Journalists were not allowed to enter this theatre after whatever had happened. After all, they might have seen the theatre not riddled with bullets and no blood anywhere, and that would never do.

Over the next few days various other images were released of this alleged EODM audience, and a remarkable fact emerged: all of the characters depicted in the various pictures were *different*. One German investigator I spoke to said he had found one image, *just one person,* that might have duplicated between two of the images. In the above, viewed in colour, one notes how the ginger-bearded fellow to the centre-left holding up a glass of beer duplicates further back and to the right. Every expert I have spoken to has taken the view that these are composite, layered images. What are we to infer from that?

A further problem concerns the ninety-odd persons who are said to have died in the concert, where none of the facial images we're given, not one of them, show up in the various audience pictures that have been released.

Figure: Dummies or real deaths?

If tickets were sold for the event, would that not prove that it was a real concert, with genuine members of the public attending? The trouble is, there are just three of these shown on the Web, each being very different from the others. That again fails to inspire us with confidence. The concert was indeed publicly advertised, in a music magazine.[224] *Was the Bataclan then riddled with bullet-holes*? That's the kind of physical-material evidence we'd all really like, but never get. "Helen described how the killers chillingly dispatched disabled fans ..." (*The Mail*, 16th November) - why am I not believing these stories?

Not until Sunday morning, two days later, did the mystery photo of the Bataclan floor appear, with the 'bodies' scattered around. The French press were strangely silent as to where it had come from: "NO media from the mainstream press has tried to learn more about the origin of the photo."[225] *The Telegraph* said it had come from an unnamed Dutch blogger. As these are about the only dead-looking bodies we were shown in the entire Friday 13th drama, its source is not without interest.

We see no blood on the clothing, no beer cans or broken glass, no bullet casings, no police or emergency workers - and the faces are nearly all turned away from us. The white shirts in foreground show no wounds. No bodies are wounded, yet some of them lie over the 'blood'-swept corridors. The low image resolution contrasts with the previous picture.

There turned out to be one Frenchman with some moral fibre, who was prepared to enquire as to the origin of this image. One month after the event, Monsieur Hicham Hamza posted the following onto his 'Panamza' site. The Dutch blogger in question, Bart Nijman, was being quizzed over the source of the photo, and finally admitted that a reporter called Bosch van Rosenthal (aka@eelcobvr) had been the source of his post. Bosch van Rosenthal had posted this image at 10.35 that Sunday morning. His source, he declared, was "Israel News Feed" led by "@IsraelHatzolah". That is the twitter tag of United Hatzalah, a paramedical group affiliated to the Israeli army, chaired by Mark Gerson, the former executive director of PNAC, the US Project for a New American Century.

Naturally, M. Hamza was arrested by the French police for this shocking behaviour, charged with "violating judicial secrecy, publishing images in grave violation of human dignity, and premeditated willful violence." He had "violated the secrecy of the investigation," i.e., blown the cover of the perps. Kevin Barrett ran a *Veterans Today* article on the subject, entitled, "Bataclan Carnage: The shocking photo was disseminated from Jerusalem." M. Hamza was, Kevin Barrett affirmed, "the only investigative journalist in France with the courage to question the official stories of the Charlie Hebdo and 11/13 attacks." (VT, 1.3.16) That *Veterans Today* article came out mere weeks before the 'United Hatzalah' struck again, or rather turned up in the Brussels airport, on the morning that that blew up - see next chapter.

This strangely-fabricated image is the only one the world has been shown of the apparently dead bodies that night. It is a *very* low-resolution screen-capture image, deliberately so. No emergency medics attend the bodies, nor are any police there, as they would have been, were it real. Five unidentified people stand in the background on the upper balcony. If four or five killers had been shooting for ten to fifteen minutes, should there not be a larger number of dead? Ninety or eighty-nine were reported at the Bataclan. Some claim that freshly-killed dead bodies were dragged in to lie there, which accounts for the blood being 'swept' on the floor: but closer inspection reveals that they are mannequins or dummies, with 'blood' splashed about - and swept strangely around the floor, swept into a huge heart-shape, upon the unsightly bare concrete (or, maybe a tarpaulin that covers the carpet): none of the normal carpets and chairs for concerts are present - as if the owners did not want them spoiled by this macabre theatre.

We quote Olé Dammegard on the dummies:[226]

> If you zoom in, you see the body of a woman, she's lying straight
> … look at her legs. You cannot do what she's doing with her legs.

Not with a human body. What she is, and what these bodies are, I would strongly suggest, are what are called capper bodies, stunt bodies, used for film stunts, not real bodies. … Here, on most of these bodies, there are no holes at all, no blood.[227]

Blood-chilling 1st moments of Bataclan attack, police shoot-out with terrorists emerge (VIDEO)

French special forces evacuate people, including an injured man holding his head, as people gather near the Bataclan concert hall following fatal shootings in Paris, France, November 13, 2015. © Christian Hartmann / Reuters

Figure: Unharmed layabouts outside the Bataclan, 'including an injured person holding his head'

Those are more or less the only 'dead bodies' seen anywhere over the Friday 13th Paris event. There are one or two images of blankets covering 'corpses,' maybe left over from the drill earlier that day. Suspects are either allegedly dead or escaped, as with Charlie Hebdo event. No cellphone pictures of the alleged drama is up on YouTube: *not one.*

Of all the people in that concert hall, did not one of them take a photo or record the screams? No video shows the killing spree.

From the Bataclan comes the testimony of the British soft-porn actress Ginnie Watson, which changed on different narrations: she was with one friend, then she was with her two friends. In her Fox News interview the Sunday after she looked as if she could hardly keep a straight face. Such fake testimonies indicate a set-up job.

White Male Killers

On the Rue de la Fontaine au Roi in the 11th arrondissement a gunman was reported as opening fire on patrons inside the Casa Nostra café.

Figure: Actress Ginnie Watson 'remembering' the trauma[228]

From a *Guardian* report:

He was standing in a shooting position," Colclough said. "He had his right leg forward and he was standing with his left leg back. He was holding up to his left shoulder a long automatic machine gun. It was fully intentional, professional bursts of three or four shots. Everything he was wearing was tight, no zippers or collars. Everything was toned black. A man in military uniform: black jumper, black trousers, black shoes or boots and a machine gun.

Despite the heightened security around Paris in the wake of Charlie Hebdo, despite the prediction a month before that something like this could happen, a man dressed all in black could walk along a street carrying a machine-gun, set it up, and start spraying restaurant-customers …. and then get away. He allegedly killed five or six diners - but, do we see any trace of dead bodies?

Here's a different witness in the *Mirror*:

At about 9.30pm a new-looking black Mercedes pulled up outside with dark tinted windows at the back and the passenger and driver windows down. I could clearly see the passenger's face as he was not wearing a hat or mask. As soon as the car stopped he quietly opened the door and got out in front of the restaurant. That is when I saw he was holding a machine gun that was resting on his hip. I could not take in what I was witnessing.

People outside spotted the shooter approaching with his gun and tried to run inside but he shot them down in the doorway. Then people inside moved forward to see what was happening and he sprayed more bullets into them. I was trying to catch them on my camera phone, but the gunman saw the light on my mobile and I ducked down behind the wall as they fired at my hotel. The gunman calmly reloaded his weapon several times. He then shot up at the windows in the street to make sure nobody was filming anything or taking photographs. It lasted over six minutes.

He fired lots of bullets. He was **white, clean shaven, and had dark hair neatly trimmed.** He was dressed all in black except for a red scarf. The shooter was aged about 35 and had an extremely muscular build, which you could tell from the size of his arms. He looked like a weightlifter. He was not wearing gloves and his face was expressionless as he walked towards the bar.

The driver had opened his door shortly before the shooting began and stood up with his arm and a machine gun rested on the roof of the car. He stood there with his foot up in the door acting as a lookout. I would describe him as tall, with dark hair and also quite muscular. They looked like soldiers or mercenaries and carried the whole thing out like a military operation. It was clear that they were both very heavily armed and the gunman was carrying several magazines on him. They both then coolly sat back in the car and sped off in the direction of the Bataclan Theatre.

These sound like SAS killers, hired mercenaries, trained commandoes. Of course, they are not caught, as they vanish into the night. That account rather negates any concept of assassins coming over from Syria. But, was it a real event? No corpses appear around this café after the event, nor does a single photo record this amazing sight. No one records their car registration number.

One survivor told *Sky News* that he had been in the Bataclan concert hall and saw the attackers who murdered hostages. He added that one of the gunmen had white skin and blond hair. Another *white male killer* - as reported the next day in the *Metro* newspaper. Another café nearby had its CCTV working - *the only* CCTV working in the whole event - showing what has been interpreted as some actors pretending to be wounded. The room is nearly empty, a window is broken and some smoke enters the café.[229] Actors huddle under fragile tables, outside: as Dr Eowyn asked, would you really hide under these tables if a killer were on the loose?

Football Stadium: Passports

The attack included a football stadium at which the President was attending: foreknowledge of his location would have required significant planning and preparation. The three suicide bombers (or two on other reports) at the stadium were the unluckiest in history, as they blew themselves up with only one victim.

The *Guardian* laughably reported, 'A suicide bomber approached the gate with a match ticket when he was frisked by a security guard who turned him away'. This was at 9.15 French time, i.e., he was attempting entry some two hours after the game had begun. The guard said the attacker was discovered wearing an explosives vest when he was searched at the entrance to the stadium![230] We are indeed in some fairy tale from Hell, whereby a 'suicide bomber' allows himself to be frisked - and then what happens? We hear nothing of course from the two hundred CCTV cameras in use around the stadium.

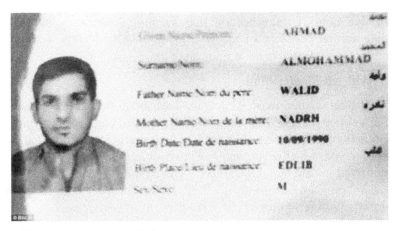

Two 'suicide bombers' who allegedly detonated outside of the Stade de France were identified by their passports conveniently "found" by police at the scene, having survived the explosions in pristine condition. A headline in the *Independent* read: "Syrian and Egyptian passports found near bodies of suicide bombers at Stade de France." Just about every state-fabricated terror event features a passport in pristine condition, so this new report stimulated widespread scorn and derision. French authorities conceded that the Syrian passport they had "found" in Paris was fake and bore the name of a Syrian Army soldier, Ahmad al-Mohammad, who died months ago. It remains wholly unclear who was the real bomber, if there even was one.

Is that the best that French Intel can manage? The image would hardly get anyone through passport control.

Inside the stadium, Hollande and his German counterpart were sitting together. Bangs were heard, presumably coming over the PA system, but *nothing was seen* and the game continued to its end. Hollande was moved to the most conspicuous part of the stadium, inside a big glass case - just what one would do with a President in case of a deadly terror attack. At the end of the match the exits were closed and the spectators are seen milling around on the pitch. No witness outside sees the 'bombers' or any remains of them - it's the usual story.

Cyber-Attack Beforehand

Paul Craig Roberts received 'a report from European security' that there had been a massive cyber-attack on French systems 48 hours prior to and during the Paris attacks.[231] This took down the French mobile data network and 'blinded police surveillance'. It was 'a sophisticated attack that targeted a weakness in infrastructure hardware' this being beyond the capability of most organisations. An attack of this nature could suggest state involvement.

For comparison, it has been observed per the Sandy Hook hoax: 'the entire CT State emergency communications system was 'hijacked' and 'unplugged' on December 14th., 2012, per an elaborate frequency change plan implemented merely five hours in advance on that morning, effectively supplanting and replacing normal police and EMS with FEMA/DHS 'shadow' command centre personnel.'[232] That sounds quite relevant.

Alleged Mastermind

'Europe's most wanted man' Abdelhamid Abaaoud was allegedly among those killed in a police raid on Wednesday 19th. A mangled corpse was identified as that Belgian national. They also shot dead 'a female suicide bomber,' if that makes any sense to you, who died crying 'I'm not his boyfriend.' As an innocent girl she was murdered in cold blood by police.[233] Her death was real, maybe the only one. The general policy here appears as, 'Let's kill all these terrorists. It's not as if we want information from them.

A witness, Amel Alla, claimed she is "99.9 per cent sure" she saw Abaaoud with eight to ten other men "smoking joints and drinking beers" on the street *after* the attacks. Another witness, Jean-Jacques, claims Abaaoud "was sitting in the street with a bottle of whisky and he offered some to me." That doesn't sound quite like a man who had just organised the deadliest attack in France since the Second World War.

SET UP PATSIES?

WWW.LIGHTONCONSPIRACIES.COM

> Figure (from Olé Dammegard) of two patsies: above, Abdelhamid Abaaoud and below, Ibrahim Abdesalam. Note man on stretcher with hand lying comfortably behind his head: can't they get *anything* right?

Ibrahim Abdesalam, who allegedly blew himself up outside a Paris café - without killing anyone[234] - reportedly "smoked cannabis every day while he stayed at home listening to Arabic hip hop and claiming unemployment benefits," according to his former wife, Naima. The ex-wife told the *Daily Mail* that Abdeslam smoked pot ("three or four joints a day") and "never went to mosque or prayed." She also claimed her ex-husband was not the least bit interested in politics or current affairs and "never watched the news, because they did not have a TV." She further suggested that he "had no gripe with the West." This is rather reminding us of the Mohammed Atta character, billed as the 9/11 mastermind; also the 'no interest in politics' reminds us of the four patsies framed for the 7/7 event in London.

Instant National Response: War Declared

Right away, the authorities knew and were proclaiming who had done it. Let's listen to professor Chossudovsky, on *Global Research:*

Within minutes following the attacks, which were launched simultaneously, and prior to the release of a preliminary report by the police, France's media went into overdrive. News commentators and intelligence analysts on France's network TV stated with authority that the attacks emanated from Syria and Iraq...The attacks were described without evidence as an act of revenge and retribution against France for having bombed ISIS strongholds in Syria and Iraq as part of Obama's counter-terrorism air campaign.

Are we really meant to believe that starving, travel weary, ill and weak people with no money, somehow managed to pull off a military-precise attack in five different locations without anyone in the French forces knowing anything?

Shortly before midnight on that same day November 13, France's president announced drastic police state measures against an alleged terrorist network operating nationwide. He surely did not take that decision spontaneously that evening - prior to the holding of any cabinet meeting. His speech averred that jihadists were behind the attacks, but gave no evidence from police sources to support his claim. We note his words:

This is a terrible ordeal which once again assails us. We know where it comes from, who these criminals are, who these terrorists are.

hat is almost identical to the phrase Tony Blair used on the afternoon of 7/7! **We accept the absolute truth of his words - he did indeed know who these criminals are, and where 'it' comes from!**

Hollande declared a "state of emergency," effectively putting the nation under martial law - that is to say ,military rule with enforced curfews, totalitarian opinion-monitoring, and widespread mass surveillance of the citizenry. French media immediately started comparing the November 13 attacks in Paris to 9/11, intimating that France was at war and that the alleged Islamic State attack was from abroad, i.e., the Middle East. Without debate in France's National Assembly, a State of Emergency was declared throughout France - lockdown under military law.

Geopolitical Perspective

France's largest warship, the nuclear-powered aircraft carrier, the Charles de Gaulle, was anchored off the coast of Syria, and it was somewhat in need of a script, of a role. Some Western military intervention was needed 'in order to save a proxy war that has been all but lost by the West.'[235]

It was clearly state-sponsored terror, but by whom? "The scale of the attack is that of a military operation. It would have required a large group of well-trained militants, well-armed and funded, with experience in planning and executing coordinated military operations, moving large amounts of weapons clandestinely, experts in the use of weapons and explosives, as well as possessing intelligence capabilities used to somehow circumvent France's increasingly colossal surveillance capabilities.

> Like the terrorists and their supply lines pouring out of NATO-territory into Syria itself, clearly with immense state sponsorship behind them, those involved in the most recent attacks in Paris are also clearly the recipients of state-sponsored funding and training. (Tony Cartalucci, Global Research)…

adding:

> Just as the Islamic terrorist mercenaries always "accidentally on purpose" leave their calling cards behind, so are the dirty CIA-Mossad fingerprints left indelibly written all over virtually every state sponsored terror event on this planet.

That's true enough.

On the 15th, French planes struck the Syrian town of Raqqa. It was announced that thirty air strikes had destroyed an ISIL training camp and munitions dump in Raqqa. However, a media activist in Raqqa told *Al Jazeera* on the Tuesday after,

that these air strikes had just targeted abandoned ISIL bases in the suburbs of the city where there were no civilians or ISIL fighters. "It has been two insane nights. Abandoned ISIL posts were targeted at the entrance of the city, along with ISIL checkpoints and several other points. Electricity and water have been cut off as supply lines were hit too."

Figure: the desolate Syrian city of Homs

As usual, the French and American strikes claim to be attacking ISIL/ISIS, while actually hitting Syrian towns and villages, knocking out their water and electrical supplies, etc. The desolate and abandoned Syrian cities appear as being the strategic goal of the bombing cam–paign: depopulation, as the refugees teem across to Europe.

A new Theatre of the Absurd is needed, so we can experience collectively the demented stories we are being given: the suicide bombers who were not allowed into the football stadium, because they had not got a ticket, so they instead blew themselves up outside; the terrible attacks outside lovely cafes, leaving no corpses lying around; the people teeming out of the back exit of the Bataclan, to the sound of bang-bang-bang, stepping over a body lying on the pavement by the exit - who later gets up to consult his mobile phone: while a pregnant woman hangs out of a window, by one arm. We are being invited to *suspend our disbelief* if you'll excuse the expression. The crisis actors get to wear smart gold thermal-shock foil and all look unstressed, unwounded: in vain we search for anyone with a real gunshot wound or with real blood coming out.[236]

View of Ken O'Keefe

The thing that is most important with regard to the latest manipulation in Paris is not whether it is a hoax or not. It is however a very interesting issue, that I will not deny. But the most important matter is that this is a manipulation, staged or not, and those responsible are as always, very easy to identify because essentially they all work for the same masters, whether they know it or not. Getting caught up in technical issues that are truly inferior to the bigger issue of what is at play is a mistake in my view. I am in no way saying we should not look at every angle, hoax, not a hoax, Mossad/CIA responsibility, Russia in on it or not, etc., indeed we should, but let us not be distracted by issues that are more of a footnote than a primary issue of the event. It is an active attempt to manipulate us into yet more war and always it is based on lies, this is the most important matter and we need to guide people to the primary relevance of this fact and not let details marginalize this critical-for-humanity understanding.

Aside from that, it is in my opinion a classic false flag, hoax or not. It is yet another "evil Muslims did it" manipulation. Even if those who carried it out are "ISIS" dipshits who were just successfully shepherded to carry out their silly little delusional "jihad", while probably having no idea at all who they actually work for, it is still a classic state-orchestrated false flag. This is not blow-back, which means unfortunate and unwanted; this is most definitely wanted and encouraged, if not overtly carried out by our so-called "intelligence" services". The big white gunman being a pretty good sign of this. The bottom line is, no matter what the details, it is just another sad and transparent act that is consistent with the agenda of setting the Middle East alight and fostering a third world war by fanning the flames of a clash of civilizations. That theme/agenda is primary. How it ties into Greater Israel is also, in my opinion, hugely relevant and critical for people to learn (18 Nov.)

If Hercule Poirot were investigating this case, he'd probably start off by enquiring

- How the police managed to take two hours before storming the concert theatre.

- How could a killing spree go on that long in central Paris.

- Who and where are the two burly white men dressed in black that turned up in a new-looking black Mercedes with tinted windows, with a machine gun on the roof of the car, etc. - and calmly started shooting at the diners.

- How did a new-looking passport survive after a suicide bomber blew himself up with a huge bang in a football stadium

- How a terror-drill came to be conducted that same day in Paris.

- He might interview the two Jewish-Zionist owners of the Bataclan theater, who had owned it for forty years, then sold it on … September 11th, two months before the event.

- He might then visit the Paris mortuary to enquire about their records of corpses from that night: where he would surely receive an 'access denied' notification.

Of course, we are just being nostalgic here: police no longer need to search for clues in that old-fashioned manner. Why, they can read in the newspaper who did it… like the rest of us.

13
Mock Terror in Brussels
2016

Europe is indeed under attack - but not, I suggest, by Islamic terrorists.

Shortly before the event in Brussels, the largest-ever terror-drill took place in England. On the day of the spring Equinox, March 20th, the Metropolitan Police were working together with special forces troops from the SAS regiment, preparing their response for up to 10 simultaneous terror attacks on the streets of the British capital!

<u>Figure</u>: Emergency services members wearing decontamination suits attend a simulated terrorist attack in the centre of London, getting ready for a 'multiple-target attack.'

Normally, the spring equinox is a time of new hope, optimism, and growth as we recover from the rigors of winter. But the date this year was being imprinted with Fear. The event was billed as a follow-on from the Paris attacks:[237]

> It is understood that the security services are concerned that Islamist terrorists returning from Syria with military training could attempt to execute multiple attacks across London, similar to those seen in Paris in November 2015. In doing so, the attackers would force authorities to spread resources across the city. The Sunday Times reports that army

regiments from outside London are now readying themselves to be deployed to assist the SAS and Metropolitan Police in the event of a Paris-style multiple target attack. A minister said that preparations are now in place for such an eventuality, explaining: "We used to plan for three simultaneous attacks, but Paris has shown that you need to be ready for more than that. We are ready if someone tries with seven, eight, nine, ten."

A fortnight earlier, 'Europe's largest terror drill' had been rehearsed in England:

Hundreds of 'dead' bodies were today strewn across the horrifying scene of carnage, the victims of this major disaster. These are the traumatic sights that scores of emergency services were faced with as they took part in the first day of Europe's largest-ever disaster response training exercise.

Figure: a mock 'Waterloo Station' recreated near Dart–ford in Kent, Feb 29th to March 3rd. Seven train carriages were wrecked as a tower was imagined as crashing onto it.

Hundreds of trained emergency workers from four countries took part.

Seven tube trains were buried under thousands of tons of rubble, as a huge tower block collapsed onto Waterloo station! Frightening screams were heard from trapped passengers… but don't worry, it was only a drill. The images emerging from this new, 21st Century *theatre of catastrophe* were assuredly far more gory, realistic, and frightening than anything to emerge two weeks later from Brussels. This four-day event transpired in a 'disused power station' at Littlehampton near Dartford in Kent: 'Over the next four days, 2,000 blood-covered volunteers will act as victims, with fake sliced limbs and open wounds recreating the blood and gore of such a large scale incident.' *Europe's largest ever disaster drill* was EU-funded to the tune of almost a million pounds. What effect does it have upon our culture for such a huge and realistic terror-drill to be conducted in a secretive manner? Will it not provide video footage for fake terror events in the future?

Such disaster-planning has a tendency to acquire undue realism.

Ceiling Collapse at Brussels Airport

At 8 am in Brussels Airport two bombs were reported as going off only seconds apart, and then at 9.11 am a third bomb was reported as exploding on the Metro. One may compare that time of *eleven minutes past nine* with the first of the 7/7 London bombs that went off, in 2005, at exactly 11 minutes before 9, at Aldgate station. That timing gives us the signature of the perpetrators:

> The Brussels metro authority, STIB, said a single blast occurred at 9.11am in the second carriage of a train that was stopped at Maelbeek.

This date of 22/3 we may compare with that of the Madrid bombing of 2004, viz., 11/3. The numbers 11 and 7 do especially turn up in 21st Century SFT events. The Madrid bomb happened 911 days after 9/11. Adding up the numbers of the date 22/3/16 gives 7+7 or 77. This date has been widely compared to the Skull-and-Bones lodge number 322: in American usage the date is 3/22. These events normally happen early morning for maximum media coverage, and also when people are most emotionally vulnerable.

Figure: Logo of Skull and Bones society at Yale

We have the usual situation of *NO CCTV RELEASED*. One very blurred image was released of three people in the departure lounge casually wheeling trolleys, with no time-and-date stamp as a CCTV should have. We are advised that two of these *might* be wearing just one glove. What more proof could one need? These two are meant to be carrying the huge bombs in their trolleys and to have detonators in their alleged-single gloves. One of them was supposedly about to blow up the Metro station, some distance away - in which case what is he doing here? If the detonator was in the glove, then why would they want to commit suicide - why not just walk away from the trolley before pressing the button? At no level does this story make sense. The media harps on about 'suicide bombers', but no evidence for such exists.

That image was first released at 10.27 a.m. by *Dernière Heure,* part of Belgium's media giant Groupe Multimédia. Twitter-feed comments confirm the early timing. The Airport was closed down at eight o'clock, so this photo came out rather too soon. It is taken from above, not from floor-level, so is presumably an old CCTV image with the timestamp clipped off.

Figure: two alleged terrorists with trolleys, taken at an unknown date, at Brussels departure lounge.

CNN ran a clip of a chaotic scene of a smoke-filled subway tube with people running about, released at 9.07 am, just an hour after the first explosions. It soon turned out that this had not come from Brussels on that day, but from years earlier in Russia! It came from an April 11, 2011 bombing of the Minsk Metro in Belarus. Another fake video was released on that day to the news channels, taken from an i-phone (of the alleged tube bomb blast) likewise coming from Russia, from Domodedovo Airport in 2011.

An Eyewitness Report

In a conference at Amsterdam ('Open Minds'), I and Olé Dammegard spoke to a witness who we reckoned was credible.[238] He had listened to an online discussion between the two of us on the subject, and reckoned it was not quite right! So he came to correct us. He plus girlfriend had entered with their baggage via the entrance opposite Check in Till Number 5, and had then turned right and walked towards the far end. As shown in the first image (used here with kind permission), a bomb with a very loud blast and bright flash went off, in that waiting room at the end, when he was not far from it: they were then around the Counters 9-10. His ears felt damaged by the noise, however he was not thrown backwards by it, so it may not have been a 'real' bomb. The couple started running back with their baggage, towards the gateway whereby they had entered, during

which they were aware of a second blast behind them seconds later, maybe from the same place as the first one (second image). They are sure that no bomb went off around the Checkout Counters 1-6.

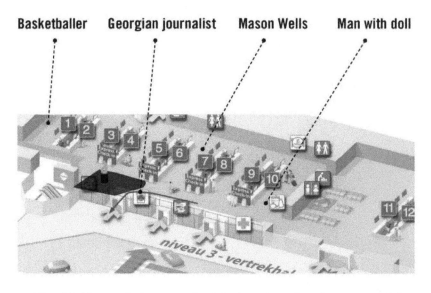

The third image helps us to find the location of various parts of the story. Thus we see how far away the crisis-actor basketball player was from any explosion. The position where the photo-journalist Ms Kardeva claimed

Figure: Ceiling tile collapse at Brussels departure lounge, showing undamaged walls and sculpture.

to be is also shown, as is that of the 19-year old Mormon Mason Wells who also coincidentally survived the Boston and Paris attacks ('feet away from the explosion…there was fire around my face and by my feet … I was covered in blood' … But he felt 'the presence of God').

The second blast[239] was reported as being between Counters 2 to 5. There is a huge difference here, with our eyewitness testimony. The images of broken windows we have been shown, are by that entrance. Olé has taken the view that the images we have been shown, which all come from around the Checkout Counters 1-6, were prepared some days before. Many tiles are seen as having fallen from the ceiling, while the walls and the display panel for the plane arrivals are unscratched. The large sculpture in the centre of the hall (see figure) was also undamaged.

The Departure Lounge was closed down a few days before on the 17th for general renovations, in preparation for opening up a new wing, called 'the Connector.' This would have given time to prepare for the event, or indeed to film it if, as is possible, much of the photography was done beforehand.[240]

A smoke bomb may have gone off quite early on, as rooms were seen full of smoke, which caused passengers to flee from the departure lounge. Pictures of abandoned luggage are seen amidst the smoke.

Crisis Actors Arrive on the Scene

As with the Paris events, various of them made up with fake-blood wander around looking casual and unshocked. One of them carries a doll. Under these circumstances the one thing the authorities cannot do is 'release the CCTV,' because that would greatly fail to endorse any 'suicide-bomber' story. Over the night of March 16/17, a major re-organising of the Brussels Airport had taken place, with a new 'secure zone' introduced, which would have been convenient for introducing any explosives.

Following the attack, the airport was closed, so there was no way the media could have got hold of the surveillance videos in the immediate wake of the attacks. The airport surveillance video could not have been available to the media less than one hour after the terror event. Instead, what *Dernière Heure* did was to take one Moscow International airport video, remove the audio in Russian, change the date, and broadcast it on the Internet and network TV at 9:07 am. Clearly, they would have had to have done all that beforehand.

The Independent reported the video the next day as being fake - which is in itself quite remarkable - but averred that it was the fault of social media that had somehow got to use an old one by mistake! In fact, however, as *Global Research* pointed out:

> *The Independent's* report is based on a fallacy. It was the mainstream media that published the Moscow and Minsk video footages. It was

thanks to incisive social media blog reports that the use of fake videos by the mainstream media was revealed.[241]

The Independent's report was thus a damage-limitation exercise. CNN interviewed a fake-sounding journalist "Chris Cuomo" reporting the Metro event who had not seen the blast, but felt some wind coming though the tube, etc.

At noon, a Kalashnikov rifle was 'found' in the airport, beside the body of a 'dead terrorist,' then later a 'suicide vest' was reported. How did a Kalashnikov get inside the airport, and who is supposed to have wanted to discard a 'suicide vest' in an airport? Who would bother, if a bomb in a trolley was good enough? Then a laptop was found in a litter bin, with some sort of message from the alleged suicide bomber about how insecure and frightened he was. How could they have found that message in the computer, or infer to whom it belonged?

We are hardly surprised to hear that security at the airport was run by ICTS Europe, operating in Belgium through its wholly-owned subsidiary ICTS Belgium. ICTS International is owned by the two Israeli Jews, Ezra Harel and Menachem Atzmon, and has been implicated in various false-flag terror events mainly 9/11, 7/7 and the 2009 Schiphol Airport 'Underpants' bomber.

All three bombs are said to have been 'nail' bombs, which means that a lot of people should have wounds from flying nails, which was clearly not the case. Over three hundred people are said to have been wounded by this event, with 32 dead, but can we see just one single person, either wounded or dead, with nail-bomb type injuries? One could draw an analogy here with the Madrid bombing of 2004, where nail bombs were alleged but none of the wounded had any nail-bomb type injuries. It seems that the mental condition of modern journalists is such that the scriptwriters can add in 'nail bombs' to their story without needing to provide any backup evidence.

I suggest that we have not seen one single person who was either wounded or dead, in this entire Brussels theatre of terror.

Huge amounts of bomb-chemicals - the usual suspects, hydrogen peroxide, acetone, etc. - were allegedly found at a swiftly-located address in a northern suburb of Brussels - plus, of course, a black ISIL flag, just what you would leave behind in a rented room if you were intending to commit suicide. The quantities reported include 15 kilos of the unstable acetone peroxide, one hundred and fifty litres of acetone and nearly 30 litres of hydrogen peroxide.

But, that will generate the same problem as those constructing the London Bombings storyline experienced - how strong was the peroxide supposed to be, and where could they possibly have obtained it? Did they buy bottles of hair bleach at the chemist? In today's terror-obsessed society, no one can buy strong hydrogen peroxide anywhere, without a special license. It is here being implied that TATP had been made - and Wiki assures us that this was the explosive used - which would have needed a coolant to keep it stable and a detonator to make it explode. There has to have been apparatus for using quite strong sulphuric acid, and cooling vessels during the preparation: can we see this please? Traces of the ingredients, for example, acetone, should have been readily detectable at the airport, which no one has suggested.

Hydrogen peroxide which can be used to make explosives is something around 70% proof. It's a viscous and quite heavy liquid (formula H_2O_2), made using low-pressure fractional-distillation apparatus. Our fictional 'terrorist' not only has to be able to make it, but also know what strength it is. If it's the wrong strength, it won't go bang. This part of the story is just barking mad.

Had this been a real investigation, the police would have a signed statement by a professional analytical chemist, to say he had been given a sample from such-and-such address in a northern suburb of Brussels, and had confirmed it to be TATP.

Two Crisis Actors Compared

Here are images from the Bataclan in Paris on 11/13/15 and Brussels, both "victims" looking remarkably casual and unhurt, both with lots of fake blood. As to how the girl's fingers are all red, has she not dipped them into a red pigment-jar on bottom-left of the image?[242]

The NATO-linked photojournalist, Ketevan Kardava, played a key role here, taking most of the photographs the world was shown from inside the airport that morning. She also reported from the Paris Friday 13th event the year before, and at the Oslo event some years earlier, so she's a real *crisis photographer*. She claimed to have been standing a mere five feet away from the huge, 2nd bomb in the airport, which allegedly went off in-between the Check-In Counters 4 and 5. Five feet from this epicentre, she kept taking the photos: "Everyone was covered in blood. They lost their legs. All of them … The people I photographed were not able to run and I wasn't able to help them. It was very, very difficult for me to leave them. I was the only person on my feet." Oddly enough she didn't photograph one dead person, nor did she receive a scratch from those awful nail-bombs.

One could compare this with Martin Buxant tweeting how a witness had told him: 'We saw bodies go up in the air and then falling down heavily.' The *Daily Mail* reported - "I heard a man shout some Arabic words, then an explosion.. then a second explosion, a massive explosion, much bigger…. It was a horror. I saw at least seven people dead. There was blood. People had lost legs. You could see their bodies but no legs,' he said." So the dead were all around, bodies thrown up into the air, everyone losing their legs - but, Ms Kardava just carried on photographing? None of her photos posted up on Facebook show people with missing limbs, or missing anything else. We get no hint of her having seen or being able to photograph a 'suicide bomber' standing right next to her. She is said to have taken the iconic pictures we have all seen, e.g., the two women on the

bench.

The shocked lady to the right in that picture is Nidhi Chaphekar, who works as inflight manager of the Indian Jet Airways. She was "due to leave Brussels for Mumbai, where she is based, when the attacks hit". (ibtimes.co.uk 23 March) The yellow jacket ripped open is her in-flight uniform. But, there were no Jet Airways flights[243] from Brussels to Mumbai that day (as observed by Reddit), the nearest was on the 26th. The story is baloney.

A tall and well-known basketball player was lying down by the Checkout Counter No. 1, near to the wall - a long way from the blast wherever you reckon it was. It was fairly obvious that some fake blood had been put beside his leg. Stories appeared as to how he had been sent flying through the air, doubtless because of this distance he was located, from any blast.

Wiki Up Too Soon

The Wiki site was up within a couple of hours. As with the Paris Bataclan event, had it gone up too soon? The Wayback Machine had over a dozen screen captures for that day the 22nd, the first of which went up at 9.45 am. That first page had 17 references, it knew who was to blame: "shouts in Arabic were heard before the explosions occurred" and it knew the time of the metro blast to within a minute, at 09.11 CET. It ended with a comment about Israeli flights: 'Israel issued a temporary ban on all flights from Europe. The ban is in place from 10:30 am until midnight Israel time.'

Patsies Take the Blame

The day after the event, two suspects were being fingered by newspapers: the brothers Khalid and Ibrahim El Bakraoui, but as 'suicide bombers' they could fortunately not be questioned. The single, blurry photo of the two of them casually pushing trolleys in the airport showed no hint of guns or suicide. One of these, Ibrahim, had we learnt just thrown his laptop into a trash can …with a suicide message about how he was unsafe and lonely, a variant of the theme whereby such patsies leave wills and Korans in a hired or left-behind car. The reason for them wanting to commit suicide, rather than just detonate the bombs remotely, remains obscure, as usual.

A few days earlier, on 16th, "these two were reportedly detained according to the media when one of the brothers showed up at a hospital with a broken leg. The other brother was found hiding in a house police were searching. The two brothers were known to have links to violent crime in the Brussels area." As usual, the patsies are *known to the authorities*.

Israel Science Minister Links Attacks to 'Foolish Rebukes of Israel'

After France, Belgium appeared as being the next country likely to make a move toward recognizing the state of Palestine. Back in December 2014, the

Belgian government had "agreed to recognize Palestinian statehood unilaterally," and that was soon due to happen.

Israel's "Science, Technology and Space Minister Ofir Akunis" drew a *connection on the very day of the event* between the deadly attacks in Brussels and Europe's frequent condemnations of Israeli policies, which he suggested diverted attention away from cracking down on Islamist terrorist cells growing in its midst.[244] In a post on his Facebook page, Akunis, who belongs to the Likud party, sent condolences to Belgium and wished the wounded a speedy recovery, and then adds: "many in Europe have preferred to deal foolishly with condemning Israel, labeling (settlement) products and boycotts."

Also, Israeli security claimed to have known in advance of the event, to have had 'advanced and precise intelligence warnings': "The security services knew, with a high degree of certainty, that attacks were planned in the very near future for the airport and, apparently, for the subway as well" (*Haaretz*, 23 March). as with 9/11, just like 7/7, Israeli intelligence in the only one claiming foreknowledge of the date. We can surely believe this claim.

The Belgian authorities asked the media to halt all reporting on the investigation into the bombings, "so as not to harm the inquiry".

Predicted Four Days Before

This new terror event was predicted by Turkey's President Erdogan on March 18th. Speaking at a ceremony to commemorate the 101st anniversary of the Battle of Gallipoli in the coastal town of Canakkale, he said: "there is no reason why the bomb that exploded in Ankara cannot explode in Brussels, or in any other European city." Erdogan's statement followed the deadly terrorist act of March 13, when a car bomb had exploded at a bus stop near Ankara's central Kizilay Square, leaving many dead and injured. The Turkish head of state blamed Kurdish radicals for the attack and berated European leaders for their refusal to recognize certain Kurdish organisations as terrorist groups. "The snakes you are sleeping with can bite you at any time," he warned.

ISIS had done it - or so it was averred by the hitherto-unknown 'Amaq Agency'. The self-proclaimed news agency 'amaqagency.wordpress.com' allegedly representing the ISIS reported on the day that Islamic State fighters had 'carried out a series of bombing with explosive belts and other devices...' in Brussels. Reuters quoted this mysterious, unknown agency as an authoritative source. I noticed that nothing on this WordPress site was more than two or three days old, and wondered why anyone would want to take such a message seriously?[245] Thus *The Guardian* reported that 'The Isis-affiliated news agency AMAQ said its fighters carried out...'[246] Thus a spanking-new anonymous WordPress site is alluded to as an 'Isis-Affiliated News agency.' Not surprisingly, it vanished soon after.

We may compare that with a *Daily Mirror* revelation of December 2015:

Hackers have claimed that a number of Islamic State supporters' social media accounts are being run from Internet addresses linked to the UK government's Department of Work and Pensions. A group of four young computer experts who call themselves VandaSec have unearthed evidence indicating that at least three ISIS-supporting accounts can be traced back to the DWP. Every computer and mobile phone logs onto the Internet using an IP address, which is a type of identification number. The hacking collective showed *Mirror Online* details of the IP addresses used by a trio of separate digital jihadis to access Twitter accounts, which have been used to spread extremist propaganda. At first glance, the IP addresses seem to be based in Saudi Arabia, but upon further inspection using specialist tools they appeared to link back to the DWP. The British government sold a large number of IP addresses to two Saudi Arabian firms.

That sale was completed in October 2015. It is thus clear that ISIS accounts and IP addresses were being supplied by HMG's Department of Work and Pensions. Does that maybe include the above 'Amaq Agency'? As with the Paris attacks, suicide bombers are alleged by the authorities, but no scrap of evidence is ever presented. These fictional "terrorists" have no demands, nor do they benefit from the attacks, they leave obvious trails of evidence, and attack people who are no threat to Islam.

United Hatzalah and Purim

That day March 22nd saw a full-moon lunar eclipse around midnight, signifying the Jewish holy day of Purim over 23rd-24th. "What makes this particular festival of Purim so disturbing are the overt cannibalistic overtones dominating the festivities. Besides the religiously-mandated drunkenness, Jews gather at homes and eat prepared foods made to resemble the body parts (ears, eyes, feet, internal organs - you name it, they make it) of Haman, the Persian ruler described in the book of Esther who conspired against them. Compare and contrast this with what Judaism's two main competitors - Christianity and Islam who have no equivalent where they devour the symbolic body parts and organs of their enemies nor revel in the despoilment, gloating over the suffering of others. In fact, no other religion of any civilized people on the planet engages in something like this. The closest we could possibly come to finding something like this would be some of the voodoo practices found in the Caribbean or West Africa."[247]

At the Brussels Airport, 'dismembered bodies everywhere' were reported.[248] One alleged 'eyewitness' Giulia Paravicini told how'… a police officer after he heard the explosion, he lost one leg' - uh, huh. But wait - 'another person I interviewed whose hands were covered in blood' - why would such a person want to be interviewed? And, '…he saw a man whose chest was completely open' - but hang on, we have not seen *ONE SINGLE PERSON* with a wound in all of this charade - just various actors with fake blood. Then 'Another man, with no head, whose body was still moving and shaking ...' - Give me a break![249] She interviewed a Ms Yassine Amrani, who claimed to have been present at the time of the explosions: "Everywhere there were bodies with no heads. There was a woman screaming while she was holding her baby and she screamed 'Where is my baby?' I told her she was holding her child, but she said she had one other that she couldn't find." Yassine said his friend went up on the third floor where, he said, the bomb exploded and screamed to him not to come up because there were dead people everywhere. "There was blood flooding on the floors I tried to help out, this is why I am covered up in blood," Yassine said.

These are unhinged necro-hallucinations.

The Purim story (in the Book of Esther) concerns the tactics of deception, as well as mass murder - as Kevin Barrett has explained.[250] For comparison, the Iraq war began on 19th March 2003, the day after the full moon on March 18th, so it was on the day of Purim.

The group 'United Hatzalah' turned up in the previous chapter, as having provided the image of dolls lying on the Bataclan floor. March 21st saw the huge AIPAC meeting in Washington, where Trump made his speech. United Hatzalah were flying back from that on their way to Israel, and had stopped off at the Brussels airport on their way. They were standing within earshot of the blast,[251] as we gather from this report in an Israeli newspaper:[252]

> Yaakov Yeret, an Israeli paramedic who volunteers with the United Hatzalah emergency services organisation, was praying at the airport's synagogue when the blast went off. "[After] we felt the explosion, we left the area to see what happened and joined the crowd that was being guided outside by the police," he recalled. "They assembled us on the other side of the airport, and now we're waiting for instructions."

There is no synagogue anywhere near Brussels airport. The twitter report on the day was by United Hatzalah EMT Yakov Y. at Brussels Airport, saying "At the time I was praying at the synagogue... we felt the explosion." It must have been an exciting Purim day.

There had been a major terror-drill the day before in Antwerp, Belgium's second largest city, with a thousand or so participants, and it ended at 10 pm. Then the events in Brussels began at 8 am the next morning. Nothing much is available on that drill in English.

Days after the event, it was announced that the entire departure hall would have to be rebuilt "until the last stone." The reason? "We want to prevent that at the time of the reopening there will be anything left to remind people of the attacks" - they did not want people wandering around trying to reconstruct the story. It has remained closed, while a large new arm of the airport has opened to take the traffic instead. This ongoing construction would have helped them to evacuate the terminal, except for the crisis actors.

Nice, Munich, & Mossad
2016

Evidence continues to surface that the terror attacks in Nice and Munich were government orchestrated false-flag operations by European Union governments in league with Mossad and the CIA, while the authorities waste no time clamping down on civil liberties in the wake of the events.
- Investmentwatch (24 July 2016)

The US film, 'Bastille Day', about an 'anti-terror mission in France' was released in France on the day before Bastille day - 14th of July, France's big national holiday. It was quickly withdrawn, as being unduly reminiscent of what transpired on that day. Thus, the Empire announces beforehand what is to happen - or, so we're told. One is here reminded of the UK horror film 'The Descent' which was due to open within days of the London bombing in 2005, but had to be withdrawn as being too similar to what actually happened: people trapped underground and dying. The advert for that film famously managed to get onto the side of the 30 bus which blew up in Tavistock Square that day. Or again, the film 'V for Vendetta' was filmed on the London Underground in the months leading up to 7/7, and featured a tube train being primed to explode: its launch had to be postponed to the next year, as being unduly reminiscent of what happened on 7/7.

What a Coincidence

A couple of state-fabricated terror events from July, 2016 six days apart are best viewed conjointly, being firmly linked by a Mr Richard Gutjahr, who was pre-positioned to film both of them, in Nice and Munich. His wife is the senior Mossad agent, Einat Wilf, a former foreign policy advisor to the Israeli government. As an ex-TV reporter for CNN[253] he holds various distinguished positions, e.g., he was honoured by the United Nations with a 'World Summit Award' in 2103. For *both* of these events, Gutjahr was interviewed on-site by the BBC! At the Nice event he said, 'It looked bizarre, it looked like it was … in the movies' and likewise the Munich event he described as 'something out of a bad movie, with the shopping centre completely surrounded by police, a helicopter overhead and police carrying semi-automatic rifles.'

Yes, it was just like a movie. And he was in it, all ready to start filming before the event happened. He thereby revealed to the world, the hidden logic of these events. Readers may recall the Charlie Hebdo event in Paris a year earlier, where the deputy editor of Israeli IBA Channel, a Mr Amchai Stein, happened to be up on a roof and all ready to start filming, just *before* the brief event - a mock street shootout, lasting only a minute or so - began.

Going back to the Paris-Bataclan story of 2015, on the night of Friday 13th of November (see Chapter 12), Mr Gutjahr phoned up a journalist in Paris at 11.15 pm, instructing her to go out at once and get the story, and even telling her *where to go*, which was presumably to the Bataclan. He then swiftly did a midnight interview with her on his German radio channel.[254] That was quick work indeed! We don't know where Mr Gutjahr was in that story, and it may even have been him who took the blood-heart photo of the Bataclan theatre floor.

Figure: a husband and wife team

Returning to events in Nice, Gutjahr was on the balcony of the Westminster Hotel, adjacent to the street where the Bastille day celebrations were being held. He filmed the very beginning of the staged-theatre event as the lorry came into view moving very slowly, and then started to speed up. Its journey finished outside the Hotel Hyatt, the big Regency Casino, so that (as Olé Dammegard pointed out) its total journey was some two hundred yards - not a mile as reported. While the lorry was driving slowly, his film shows a motorbike driver alongside it - and that featured heavily in news reports, with a claim that he was there killed.

The story of what happened in Nice on Bastille Day first appeared (as an English language report) on the website of New York Jew Pamela Geller. She is an arch-Zionist and strong proponent of the War of Civilization meme.[255] As the event happened around 10.30 pm at night, and her post was dated July 14th, i.e., the same day, she therefore had only a few hours to create the page. The video on her site was taken by someone wandering along the road - which we are to presume was the Promenade D'Anglais on the coast of Nice - and photographing a multitude of dolls, *inflatable rubber dolls*, lying along it, with fake blood here and there.

There seem to have been two distinct video cameras that photographed the scene and a couple of the dolls are here shown, with a view from each camera.

The limbs lie at impossible angles and the skin hardly resembles human flesh.

One of these images shows a mannequin in blue trousers, presumed to be female as it has a bra on, and with no head: it's been decapitated, but no blood comes out. It lies adjacent to what many have surmised to be a dead pig or goat. The other mannequin has a severed arm: maybe someone thought it might look as if a lorry had run over it, but it doesn't.[256]

Figures: two dummies on the road in Nice

People hang around these bodies, but we see no ambulances, no medics, nor emergency workers - of course not, it's just a drill. And why are these dolls all in the road, not on the pavement?

Ms Geller's site does seem an odd place for this story-forming video to manifest. She only had a few hours to get everything ready, so it has to have been prepared beforehand.[257] We may compare her video with the image of the Bataclan concert-theatre floor, released couple of days after the Friday 13th event in Paris: it showed dummy corpses lying around and was supposed to show persons who had been killed that night. As we saw in Chapter 12, no newspaper dared to ask where that video had come from, and eventually its source was traced to United Hatzalah, an Israeli source. Like that photo, the video was blurred and grainy as if not wanting to reveal undue detail.

French citizens awoke the next day with the news that 77 people had been killed by a berserk driver of a large white lorry, a number which soon changed to 84. Multiples of seven were here turning up, for an event on the day of 14/7.

An Imaginary Debate

Are we never allowed to hear an intelligent studio discussion on any of the countless TV channels available? RT will *nearly* go there, but not quite. Let us here imagine such. One guest starts off by saying: 'Have you noticed how we didn't see a drop of blood on the gleaming white paintwork of that lorry at the end of the alleged rampage, even though it supposedly rammed into at least two hundred and eighty people?'

Another adds: 'I examined all videos of that lorry, and they all showed it on that same road, the Promenade d'Anglais. It's still on that road when it ends up surrounded by police, after it's been stopped. So how was it supposed to have come off the road and careered into crowds of civilians?'[258]

'Stopping a lorry like that would have been simple for the police, they'd just shoot at the tyres - if they had wanted to stop it, of course.'

Another interjects: 'The next day the papers showed us an alleged 1.1 miles of beach road the lorry had driven along, saying that it had started at 10.25 and ended at 10.50pm. That is two miles an hour, on average, and how could it have mown down civilians at that speed? We do see a film of it driving along at maybe twenty miles an hour - thanks to Richard Gutjahr from his balcony - but, there's no sign of it hitting anyone. How could it, at that slow speed?'

'We recall Mr Gutjahr's testimony: "I stood on the balcony, right on the Promenade d'Anglais, and saw how people celebrated there, and how suddenly a truck drove through the crowd." He was about the only person who then gave such testimony, wasn't he? I suppose he was guiding the narrative. He also mentioned that "the streets were locked so there was no traffic whatsoever," which was true enough. His video was taken he claimed at "a little after 11 pm" which is questionable, other sources put the event a bit earlier.'

'Such a huge twenty-ton lorry is not easily manoeuvrable - it's path cannot twist and turn in order to hit people. Even if we grant that the lorry had managed to crash through the row of palm trees to get onto the pavement, it would hardly have been difficult for citizens to escape, either by leaping onto the beach which was next to them, or into side-streets. Instead, we saw crowds running *along the road* which hardly makes sense if a lorry is approaching. We'd expect a few old people to have been hit - but all those dummies lying there didn't look very old, did they?

'Then we saw a close-up of a couple in the crowd laughing as if they were hugely enjoying the experience:[259] I'm moving towards the idea of a travelling terror-troupe which stages these events.'

'If this fellow had been prosecuted for gun crime a few months earlier, as the police assured us, if he was a 'career criminal' as they said, how could he possibly have hired such a huge lorry? And even supposing he had done that, why don't we see a single i-phone image of the amazing scene, as it ploughed into civilians?'

'The police had to shoot dead the driver - or claim to have done so - after all they can't take the risk he'd speak to us, can they? Of course, they conveniently find his ID in the lorry next to him - the 'terrorists' stooges in these events always carry ID on them on their last trip to Paradise!

'And then it turns out he's still alive and was in Tunisia, not in France at all. The next day he posted up a video, protesting at the ID theft. A local online newspaper affirmed: 'Mohamed Lahouaiej Bouhlel serait vivant et témoigne de Tunisie, de Sousse plus exactement, affirmant ne pas être le coupable du massacre!'[260] Such ID theft seems to be a normal feature of these phantom-terror events - do you remember the French female 'terrorist' shot dead by police over the Bataclan affair, on Friday 13th last year? After being apparently shot dead by police, she turned out to be in Morocco, still very much alive, protesting that she had nothing to do with it - but having trouble going out of her front door, because everyone was asking her if she was a terrorist! (Search for Hasna Buolacehn, Morocco). How can they possibly get away with this and why can we not read a single newspaper account discussing how the alleged lorry driver is still alive?

'And Mr Bouhlel was no religious fundamentalist, he was just leading a normal life integrated into mainstream society[261] - like so many of these patsies. We are reminded of the four who were accused (posthumously) of having perpetrated the London bombings in 2005.'

Another responds: 'It wasn't only the alleged lorry driver who had his identity stolen - after the *Mail* published a list of dead with pictures, many of these objected that they were still alive.[262] It appeared that most of the people who went missing were either alive or had fake names and identities attributed to them. Most of the alleged casualties/victims did not have any verified user accounts on social media, and instead pictures were found to have been ripped off other accounts and plastered on websites with fabricated names. Who could have done such a thing? Why aren't they punished for it? It seems that some of the 'grieving relatives' are doing some very bad acting.

'There was a beautiful black girl named by the *Mail* as Lea as being dead, and it turned out her real name was Adamara Ajuzie. She was furious about this attempt to steal her identity and *The Mail* had to apologize - but that isn't really enough, is it? We the public need to be told why this identity theft happened in the first place.'

Another commented, 'All those dummies in the Pam Gellar videos, we see no sign of them having been run over or crushed in any way. I suppose inflatable dummies don't really stay crushed. And the blood is the wrong colour, it only stays that bright-red hue for a few minutes.'

Another observed that: 'We always expect CCTV to vanish, whenever state-terror happens. But this time, the police in Paris instructed the Nice authorities to destroy all of the CCTV and they refused to do so! That has never happened before. It seems that they have 30,000 hours of CCTV material, 24 hours either side of the event, not yet deleted. 'This is the first time we have been asked to destroy evidence' a Nice official commented, adding that such destruction of evidence could carry a risk of prosecution. He added, 'We do not know if giving a destruction order while we are in full backup is not going to curtail the whole system.' When *Le Figaro* contacted the Paris prosecutors office, they were told that they especially want 'the cameras in direct contact with the event' to have their film deleted. The police in Paris are pretending that the film might show too-shocking material that could be harmful if disseminated - whereas more likely it will *not* show anything much happening, or maybe only crowds being told to run by the police, dummies being laid into position, police cars moving about, etc.'

Another added: 'In the months prior to this event the unpopular French government had been struggling to contain huge citizen uprisings and mass protests. The state of emergency was just about to be lifted - whereas this event enabled its maintenance and extension for another six months. Also, a month earlier, France's Foreign Minister had organised an international meeting to relaunch the deadlocked Israeli-Palestinian peace process - so maybe he needed to be taught a lesson.'

Another commented: 'There were large-scale drills just prior to this event, which always seem to foreshadow major state-terror operations. In April, attendants at the Cannes Film Festival were unnerved by an intrusive anti-terror drill, spoilt the mood of the festival. Then in June a massive mock-terror drill was rehearsed in Lyon with couple of thousand people involved, ahead of a big football match. Such large-scale rehearsals do tend to invoke the event that is being drilled.'

Another remarked: ''Nice systems,' the company running CCTV in Nice, has its headquarters in Tel Aviv. It specialises in surveillance, security, phone recording, etc., i.e., how to snoop on everyone. A lot of these events seem to involve Israeli intelligence technology, for example, the companies running surveillance on the Underground at the time of the London bombings. There could be a decided risk in employing Israeli security firms.'

But such a discussion can never happen, can it? Normal, critical intelligence can never be allowed after these events on any media station. What is the censorship that stops such thought? Let us hope that alternative channels and radical playwrights will envisage such scenes. This could be aided by having the traumatised dolls supplied by LifeTech or some such company, lying around, with fake blood on the floor, etc. It is, after all, we who are the real victims of the attack, we who receive the devastating emotional impact, as the 'fear porn' hits us via the mainstream news.

Bogus 'Heroes' Emerge

When the lorry is first seen, outside the Westminster Hotel by Mr Gutjahr, there are various indignant-looking persons around it, maybe objecting to its presence there at such a moment of festival. The big firework display had just ended and it's 10.20 pm, when we see someone on a motorbike drive past it on its left-hand side, between it and the curb. He stops, puts down the bike and runs along beside the lorry, although we can't see much because of the trees and shadows. Various claims were made in news reports that he had been knocked down, however an astute analysis by 'Serebra Sana' suggested that he ran the couple of hundred yards beside the van to its destination, after which he found himself being beaten up by the police, next to the van, then dragged away.[263]

Several days later, some 'heroes' started to appear in media reports. A young man 'known locally' as Gwenelle Leriche (i.e., it was an invented name) leapt onto the lorry and managed to punch the terrorist through the cab window to try and stop the van - or, so the *Mail* averred. He chased the terrorist-driver down the street on foot! No trace of this individual appeared in any French media reports, it was only a British-American story. Then, a M. Alexander Migues had been pedalling along on his bicycle when he saw the lorry 'bearing down' on him, so he managed to throw down his bike and jump onto the cab. He then found that a gun was being pointed at him, so he backed off. That was a French story.[264] Both feature an 'ISIS terrorist' or 'ISIS killer truck' that is encountered.

Finally, the 49-year old 'Frank' appears in a French studio, claiming to have been the man on the motorbike. When he first arrived, he was with his family, and they all saw the van which 'must have been doing 80 or 90 km per hour.' Also, 'I saw people flying around, people being mown down.' He started to chase the truck, 'with my wife behind me' and managed to get onto its front cab. Then, 'Using all my might, I hit him. I hit his head.' He noticed that the terrorist was holding a gun in his hand and he was shot! Fortunately the gun didn't work, so he kept on hitting the terrorist. His last line (believe it or not) was 'I slide under the wheels of the truck.'[265] 'Frank' has here told a *very* tall story.[266] (N.B., 'Frank' is a kind of generic name for French people) None of these 'hero' stories happened, they are negated by the photographic evidence.

These heroic efforts to stop the truck may remind us of the 'heroes' of the 9/11 event on flight 93 - the flight where all the telephone calls came from - and the 'let's roll' story of the doomed passengers trying to storm the 'terrorists' who had taken control. They may well have had the same scriptwriters!

Some have doubted whether there was a driver of the lorry, as no one ever sees him: could it have been remotely piloted?

The driver is said to have stopped his lorry, got out, and started to shoot into the crowd. Nobody sees this, or records it, but it's important by way of proving how wicked he is. He somehow survived the various 'heroes' biffing him in the head as well as the hail of bullets going through his windshield, from police (a dozen or so stick-on bullet holes were plastered onto the lorry's windscreen. These were not very convincing, as no cracks appeared in the glass). The patsy must never be available for questioning, so that story of him shooting into the crowd justifies *their* story of shooting him dead. We don't see him dead, nor any blood around the stationary lorry - just bad actors hanging around.

The police have to give us some story about this patsy - it would not do for them to shoot him dead and then say that they knew nothing about him. He was, they averred, a 'career criminal' and to back this up some guns were found in the lorry. The problem then becomes that no person with such a record could have possibly hired a lorry, especially not in such an area and over the big public holiday, with France still being in a state of emergency and *de facto* military law.

The CCTV normally vanishes in these events, but not this time. Sandra Bertin in charge of surveillance for Nice refused to knuckle under when instructed by the Interior ministry to destroy it all. She was instructed to doctor her report, of what the cameras saw, and had the nerve to reply, 'I told him I would only write what I had seen.' She claimed that she was then 'harassed' for an hour, and asked to send in a 'modifiable version' of her report! They objected to her report averring that 'no municipal or national police were visible' during the event. This is a common feature of state-fabricated terror events: had the real police been ordered to vacate the area to allow the street theatre to be performed? France's Interior Minister Bernard Cazeneuve has filed a defamation lawsuit against her, and there is a general feeling that this is undue pressure on an honest policewoman doing her job.

In the week after this event, French fighter planes flew thirty sorties over Syria, killing over a hundred civilians - many of them women and children. Fried by bombs or crushed under masonry,[267] these are the real deaths, not the theatrical ones in Nice.

What Really Happened

A live report by 'I-Tele,' a French all-news station, gave coverage at 11.40 pm that night, live from the Promenade d'Anglais at Nice. That is the earliest coverage we have of the event. It started by showing crowds running along a couple of roads. Then it interviewed the owner of a restaurant, which was a mere fifty metres from the Westminster Hotel where the van stopped, so that the van did not reach the restaurant. The fireworks had been going off right in front of that restaurant. As to what the owner saw: 'We saw a big crowd rushing, followed by gunshots.' As the fireworks ended the lorry arrived, and the police stopped it. Were their gunshots going off with people all around? 'Non, non!' - definitely not, *the police stopped him right before he got to where all the people were watching the fireworks, 50 metres away.*' ('Et il a été stoppe à 50 metres avant d'arriver juste en face de vraiment là où il y avait la foule…')[268] The restaurant owner saw the van with the police around, but *makes no mention* of the truck running over people.

That live interview was one hour after the event, when: 'Apparently there are still people in the truck, and the police are trying to stop them.'

The Horror, the Horror!

On the next day, President Hollande spoke of how:

'L'horreur… L'horreur de nouveau vient de s'abattre sur la France.'

And, to reinforce that sense of horror, a whole lot of low-credibility details of the last year's Bataclan event were released *on that very day*: although no one had reported this at the time, the three terrorists, who stormed the Bataclan theatre on the night of Friday 13th, had actually tortured and disembowelled several victims. Why, they had even chopped off testicles and placed them in the victims' mouths! The French Parliament had heard hours of such testimony from the police. The terrorists had even filmed themselves doing this, for Islamic State propaganda! And these stories had all been kept a secret … until the Nice event.

But then it turned out the testimony was mere hearsay and no witness who had seen such a thing or the bodies or even a sharp knife could be found. A mere two days later papers were having to print retractions: no, sorry, it didn't happen. The whole story was just, *fear porn*.

The Link with Hamburg

It was Germany's turn to be hit next. Most other middle-European nations had been targeted, had had to digest the untruthful narrative. And how simple it was.

The date, six days later, of 22/7, was the 70th anniversary of the blowing up of the King David Hotel in Jerusalem in 1946. That decisive event in the formation of modern Israel was a kind of payback or gratitude towards the British government for having formulated the Balfour Declaration, whereby Jews could go back to their 'homeland:' the hotel Britons were staying in was detonated. Then in 2011 the Oslo-Breivik event happened on 22/7. The multiples of 7 and 11 are important here. In 2014 a cryptic new message had appeared on the Georgia Guidestones: 'GAME ON 711.'

As before, Mr Richard Gutjahr who lives in Hamburg, was on the scene, being the main person interviewed by the media concerning this event. He provided major Western media outlets with extensive reports about the Munich attack, posting images and videos on his Twitter account - some of which he soon deleted.

He was probably (though no one seems to be sure) positioned with camera at the ready in front of a McDonalds entrance. Action! The 'terrorist' emerges wearing black, he seems to be coming out from the large Olympia shopping mall, then a crowd of young people appear, stage left. We hear the distinctive sound of blanks being fired, and the crowd of half a dozen or so rushes quickly away. No one drops to the ground, nor does any blood spurt, and we see no wounded. Can you see nine dead people from that video?[269] Conveniently, the terrorist then shot himself.

The next day, as the story started to explode on websites around the world, Gutjahr speedily removed his photos of the shooting from his Twitter feed, and they vanished simultaneously from a *Russia Today* article.

Cynthia McKinney, the former US senator tweeted, "Same Israeli photographer captures Nice and Munich tragedies" adding "How likely is that? Remember the Dancing Israelis?" She posted a video with the caption: "Same Israeli photo-propagandist pre-positioned in Nice AND NOW MUNICH." That tweet went all around the place: its message was just so simple!

Yes, indeed, we are reminded of the five Israeli-Mossad agents who were positioned on the morning of 9/11 on the other side of the Hudson river, all ready to start a-filming as the planes smashed into the Towers - or indeed whatever did smash into the towers, without wishing to pre-judge the matter. "We were there to document the event," they memorably stated on Israeli TV - Mr Gutjahr's sentiments exactly.

In Munich, Gutjahr's daughter was tweeting of the attack[270] live from the Olympia shopping mall. They tried to delete these, but it was too late, they'd been copied. Ditto for his wife having been trained by Israeli intelligence: 'Since the Munich shooting, Einat Wilf's Wikipedia page has been edited to scrub all reference to her links with Israeli intelligence.'[271]

Initial reports had several shooters in the Munich event which soon reduced to one. The number of dead fluctuated quite a bit which some found suspicious: initial tweets had six, then nine or ten, and it finalised at nine. The shoot-out in front of the McDonalds entrance on that day has to have been staged, it was even less convincing than the Charlie Hebdo street shootout - and it lacked fatal injuries, or any injuries come to that.

A professional police officer Scott Alexander scrutinised the sequence of events in Munich,[272] and the first thing he noticed was that dozens of police officers in full combat gear appeared on the scene *too soon*. They seemed to keep running about aimlessly, as if their aim was to be photographed, whereas no real team of tactical SWAT officers would behave in such a manner. Initially, he noticed, three men were reported to be firing weapons, and we were given 'eyewitness reports' from people who had allegedly observed them. But soon only one teenage shooter was said to be the cause of trouble, the others had just faded out of the story. That begged the question, why lockdown an entire city and deploy so much manpower for just one teenager?

He was alleged to have killed people both inside and outside McDonalds, in which case should there not have been yellow police 'crime scene' tape to secure the area and prevent public access? And why were only grainy, low-resolution photos of the alleged terrorists available?

A 'shooting victim's father' was seen walking through the streets of Munich carrying a bouquet of flowers and his son's photograph. He would go up to random people, show them the photo, and say: "This was my son." He showed no sign of distress nor shed a tear. That has to be an actor.

The police searched the dead suspect's room and, of course, found a 'manifesto' - a standard feature of these stories. One reporter spoke to various occupants of the apartment complex, but could not find anyone who remembered seeing the alleged terrorist. 'It was though he did not really exist' concluded the reporter, a Mr Alexander. The young 'terrorist' had supposedly shot himself dead.

As with other recent events, victims are seen left in the street and merely covered over with blankets, as people stand around unconcerned. Concerning the grieving relatives:

> In almost every instance following a false flag, staged, or contrived event you will always find mourners who have brought flowers, candles, teddy bears, etc. In addition, you also have all the hugging and crying with no one actually shedding a tear. It's fake! An interesting example in Munich is that at every memorial I came across I found the exact same kind of flowers and the same candles inside bright red containers.

- the sage judgement of Scott Alexander, the experienced police officer.

We remind ourselves that the state risks everything by indulging in such hellish theatricals, that deceive their own people, even with fabricated deaths - never again can it expect to recover that trust which ought to be a natural bond between citizens and the state.

We have reviewed one more time the way illusion is generated, admiring the creative artistry of Those Who Create Delusion. And, one more time, we are startled by the gullibility of the goyim.

Phantom Terror over Westminster Bridge 2017

> Earth has not anything to show more fair:
> Dull would he be of soul who could pass by
> A sight so touching in its majesty
>
> *on Westminster Bridge,* by William Wordsworth, 1802

For a country like the UK, with a huge military budget and no real enemy, care has to be taken for the 'Phantom Menace' to be sustained and promoted.

An audacious 'terror' event happened over Westminster Bridge in London, on 22nd of March, a year to the day after the Brussels airport terror event of 22nd March, 2016 – likewise as we have seen, a state-fabricated terror event. One may doubt whether any real deaths were there involved.

It is becoming known as the Westminster 322 event, this being the Skull-and-Bones number: the date American-style being 3/22 (compare this with 9/11). Did it use rubber dummies and crisis actors, or were there real deaths, real people in hospital with broken bones? It would be hard to have both. Various people have told me they saw some sort of terrible thing happen. I here argue that, as a state-fabricated terror event, it served a globalist agenda; and that the story we've been told did not and could not have happened. As always in these events, an illusion of some sort was set up. It is possible that the only definite death here was the patsy, the alleged perpetrator - killed by the Deep State up in Birmingham.

As usual, the story makes no sense. A crazed killer is supposed to have driven a hired car, mounted up onto the pavement of Westminster Bridge in order to hit and mow down a load of people, then crashed his car into the railings of the House of Parliament, at the end of the bridge - then leap out with two knives (but no gun) and run along a very crowded street, in order to enter the House of Commons – then full of MPs debating – through a heavily-guarded gate which happened to be wide open. After entering he stabbed a policeman to death! We can surely perceive this as a nightmare-hallucination and not a feasible sequence of events in the real world.

Two days earlier, as on the previous year, there had been a major terror-drill. It was said to be 'terrifyingly realistic' with boats speeding by on the Thames right underneath Westminster Bridge, teams of black-clad agents shooting each other with guns and blank cartridges and people taken hostage in a cruise-boat. As usual, the terror-drill *precedes* and *foreshadows* the actual event. These events were timed around the Spring Equinox. We saw how in 2016 there was a huge anti-terror drill in London on 20th March with black-clad security police roaming around, just two days before the Brussels event.

The spring Equinox should be a joyful time of celebrating the fertility of Spring arriving, and we should reject the implanting of fictional terror-drills on this time. Whoever is making these things happen was even able to get inside the gates of Britain's House of Commons to create the realistic-looking (but impossible) drama.

We saw a car with its front crumpled-up *as if* it had slammed violently into the House of Commons railings at the end of Waterloo bridge – the railings being hardly scratched, an event which has to remind us of the Lee Rigby event (22.5.13), where a car on the pavement had its front crumpled-up, *as if* it had slammed into a road-sign post next to it – which was however unscratched, so that the whole scene resembled a theatre-prop (Chapter 9). Outside the House of Commons the heavy load of traffic and large crowds meant that no car could ever have driven across the flow of traffic to make such an impact. Nor did anyone see any blood on the front of that car, which may also remind us of the Nice event the previous year (14.7.16), when a huge lorry had allegedly ploughed into a seaside crowd, but was found to have no speck of blood on it (Chapter 14). After such a crash, do you want to believe that the driver had really then leapt out – unseen by anyone, there are no witnesses – brandishing two knives, and desiring to kill a London bobby?

As usual in these events, the CCTV was all switched off – this being around the seat of Government, in Westminster, one of the richest districts of the UK, at a supposed time of risk and danger! It had been switched off months earlier, we were told, because of its 'cost'. This absence of CCTV is a defining feature of modern, state-fabricated terror in the UK. We have been shown only one blurred video of the bridge taken from a great distance, showing a moving, ghostly grey speck, supposedly the car driving along the pavement.

The various pictures of the Westminster Bridge after the event all show a pavement clean and free from blood plus a large, yellow road-sign in the middle of the bridge, on that very pavement that the car had supposedly sped along. *All* the videos and picture show it – there can be no doubt it was there. Walking along a week later (I was in a video deconstructing the story[273]) we walked past it, a big sign saying the road would be closed the following weekend. No car *could possibly have driven* along the pavement past that sign.[274] Westminster Bridge has no lamp-posts, bollards or fences by the kerb to impede a car which wished to do such a thing so that, *were it not for the yellow sign,* a drive along the pavement would have been feasible. Street-lamps are on the outer edge of the bridge, along the balustrade.

Let's hear from an eyewitness, 'Stephen', interviewed by *The Sun* reporter (scroll down to bottom of the Sun page, 'Eyewitness who was on Westminster Bridge') who I suggest sounds genuine enough, though in a shocked condition. He was on the bridge, when:

Suddenly a bus stopped right in front of me and everybody started screaming. I saw a trainer in the road [i.e. a shoe] and I thought, somebody must have been hit by a car, then I saw a body on the other side of the road... Then I looked over the side of the bridge there was another body lying in the water.

He was asked, as to whether he had seen any indication of what had caused those people to be injured – had he seen a car come though? He replied,

No, I didn't see anything...

He *did not see any car.* As regards the shoe he alluded to, shoes play a bizarre part in these stories, and they are seen removed from people who are supposedly victims. Often only one shoe is removed, and placed nearby.

A young student interviewed told of *a drill* ongoing on that week:

I was on my way to film a University project and we just got to Westminster Abbey where a load of armed police officers jumped out of cars. I would say maybe 50 of them or so. I basically thought it was a training exercise, which they've been doing all week.[275]

A security agent is seen glowering at him as he says that.

Russia Today has its office in Westminster, and were on the scene right away. Their man Rattansi was looking at the car crumpled up by the railings, and wondering if it could be the same car as had allegedly driven along the Westminster Bridge pavement? He had heard about only two deaths: a policeman killed inside the House of Commons premises, plus a civilian, under a bus on the bridge. This latter image (which we come to shortly) thus played a pivotal role by way of directing the narrative.

The postcard kiosk

A tourist kiosk is at the far side of the bridge, away from the House of Commons, and close to St Thomas' hospital and the Marriott hotel.The pavement of the bridge can just be seen on the far-right of this image (with the yellow sign in the background). People are strolling on it in a normal kind of way. The balustrade we see here is parallel to the river. The body of Melissa Cochran is supposedly lying there, with postcards lying about as if the kiosk had been hit. Her husband Kurt is supposedly lying down dead further to the left and down some steps.

Ms Cochran later appears in hospital with her right leg immobilised as if its bone had splintered – however, in the pictures where we see her lying on the pavement, we do not notice any damage to that leg.

No car could have hit them there, because the space is inset away from the road – it would have had to slam into the balustrade. It was around here that the car supposedly drove up onto the pavement, the last traffic light on the pavement being just prior to this kiosk. The car could not have been driving very fast, because of the uphill slope and the heavy traffic. It could not possibly have impacted two people so that they fly through the air, some distance. Nor could it have struck the tourist kiosk, because that is inset away from the bridge pavement.

The picture we've been shown of Mr Cochran lying down has a bendy-looking left leg suggesting a dummy. The knee bends outwards, an anatomical absurdity. No face or even head is visible, and compare this with images of the shot PC in the House of Commons, who has no face or even head visible. Mr Cochran's Facebook page was converted into a fundraising appeal in less than 24 hours, which also appears with other 'victims' of this tragedy. They were a US couple travelling in the UK, so who other than Kurt's partner could have known his password? Macabre death-type clues had been posted on his Facebook page a week before this event. His appeal fund raised at least $70,000.

The couple had come to London to celebrate their 25th wedding anniversary, a poignant tale which remind us of the fate of the charming Andrea Christea (31 years, see image) who was expecting her fiancée to propose to her, that very day, 22nd of March! She was Romanian, and the two of them agreed that they had to be on Westminster Bridge, for their moment to remember. A picture shows her on the bridge, with the shimmering lights of London, romantically reflected upon the Thames behind her, in the evening-time (photoshopped?). Instead, she was alas bumped off the bridge by a car into the Thames and died a week later – or, so they say. The Masters of Deception know how to pull upon our heartstrings!

That picture must have been taken sometime before, when the sky was blue – not grey and cloudy, as it was on the day. It featured in newspapers *the very next day*, 23rd of March, so where did they get it from, and should they not have told us on what evening it was taken?

There is one video-sequence of traffic crossing that bridge as the 'car' drove along, we see (from a great distance, and very blurred) something fall off the bridge, a couple of seconds *after* the car has gone by: it falls down, and a large splash appears, much too large in fact. Slowing the video down to one image at a time shows the splash developing too soon, *before* the figure has impacted the river surface. Falling off that bridge tends to be lethal and one may greatly doubt whether anyone then did.

I'm A-Frade it's just a hoax

The bus number 53 had been driving towards the House of Commons, and film of the traffic crossing the bridge shows it moving quite slowly. It then stopped, and did a lot of crisis actors then disembark from it? We see it empty and driverless, but with the posterior of a 'body,' some sort of mannequin under its back wheel. Why is it in black tights and with no shoes on? Various bodies we see on the pavement had their shoes removed and this seems to have been part of the narrative.[276]

A 'policeman' or some yellow-clad security guard walks past the stationary, empty bus taking little notice of the 'dead' human posterior protruding. It has to be a dummy, because it's uncrushed, as if it has just re-inflated after the bus drove over it! (But NB, people disagree on this matter). There is a problem with using dummies in that they don't stay crushed. After being driven over by a double-decker bus, any human or animal would be squashed, with its blood all over the road and on the bus's wheels. Here we see no speck of blood. We see a hand that looks unnatural.

London Transport should be obliged to make a statement explaining why the back wheel of one of their buses was jammed against a lifeless dummy – or whatever they claim it was. They should also tell us what happened to the passengers and driver, and why none of them have come forward. The only woman allegedly killed in this 'terror' event was Ms A. Frade ('are you afraid?') and will London Transport comment upon whether she died under one of their wheels? Did she impact the front of the bus and do her relatives accept that this is her?

London Transport should either admit that one of their drivers killed a civilian on Westminster Bridge, *or* that one of their buses was used in a hoax terror-event to fool the public. Clearly, they prefer to remain silent, but by doing so they betray the trust which Londoners have placed in them.

A later picture shows the bridge without any blood on the pavement or sign of persons having been run over by a speeding car, and the 'body' under the bus has merely been covered over with a sheet. Why is it being left under the bus? Police and security agents are around, but no hospital staff. The huge St Thomas' hospital is just around the corner.

Images of that No. 53 bus show another couple up ahead lying in the gutter.[277] A dummy lies on its back with limbs wrongly-positioned: one hand vertically in the air and its posterior not touching the ground. A crisis actor on top of it pretends to be giving treatment. Nearby on the pavement we see a pair of shoes (see image). Olé Dammegard interprets this aspect of state-sponsored terror as 'product placement':[1] Adidas and Nike shoes were especially on view in this Westminster event. For comparison, he describes how, when we are shown the 'ISIL' terrorists in the Middle-East they normally appear with a row of gleaming-new Toyota trucks.

Another dummy lies on the pavement, at the House of Commons end of the Bridge, with one shoe off and one shoe on and a pool of blood by the left shoe. A close-up does not show the blood as coming from the leg. His feet are splayed outwards at an anatomically impossible angle. One would need rubber joints to lay both feet flat against the pavement, in opposite directions, while the legs are also lying flat on the ground. (Try it – one simply can't keep one's knees and ankles both flat to the floor at the same time.)

Figure: Adidas shoes, with crisis actor in the gutter, Westminster Bridge

For comparison, here is a dummy at the Nice event. Was it maybe the same dummy? One is here reminded of Ole Dammegard's thesis of a 'travelling terror troupe' which goes around doing these things – 'a sort of Rocky Horror show on steroids.'[279]

Figures: Dummy in road from the Nice (14.7.16) event, compared to a figure on Westminster pavement

The question of what the shoe symbolism so prevalent in these events is here supposed to 'mean' remains obscure, but for a fine comment on the matter, see Olé Dammegard's interview 'The soulless shoes of death.'

The London Eye, the world's highest Ferris wheel when it was built in 1999, is a three-minute walk from Westminster Bridge. Tourists high up on this wheel would have enjoyed the best possible view of whatever had happened. Were they asked? Slow traffic was chugging over the bridge at say ten miles an hour, and did they see a car mount the pavement and then start to drive much faster, causing mayhem? They were in the very best position to tell us. But instead, the wheel was frozen for nearly *three hours,* entrapping all of the passengers, after which they were allowed off one by one with police frisking them, and presumably removing any film. No one heard their testimony.

Identity of the perpetrator

If the car had been hired a few days before, as we were told, then surely hire documents would be inside it, or at least the car-hire company name would be inscribed upon it. The identity of the perpetrator could at once have been ascertained: police would simply have checked the number plate to trace the car-hire company, and thereby ascertained its driver.

Did the police find the ID of the perpetrator, either on his person or in the car? They announced right away an identity of the 'killer', and he *did look just like* the only picture we were shown: Trevor Brooks or Abu Izzadeen, aka the 'Hate preacher' from Hackney. But then his brother announced that he was still in jail – so someone else had to be found pronto. Fast action was then required, because the public had already been shown a 'dead' body on a stretcher plus a hired car crumpled up, so the police could hardly claim, not to know who it was.

<u>Figure</u>: Trevor Brooks (Abu Izzadeen) lying on the stretcher?

An hour before midnight on the 22nd, the police broke down the door of Khalid Massood's home in Birmingham. How did they obtain this address so quickly? The next day, we were told the killer was Khaleed Masood or Adrian Russell Ajao, a father-of-three English teacher from Birmingham, 52 years old – and *known to MI5*. African-looking, he did not credibly resemble the man on the stretcher: no one would derive him as 'Asian looking' which was the statement the police had earlier put out concerning the 'killer.'

The police had at first wanted to use Abu Izzadeen *keeping him still alive* but that had gone badly wrong. The patsy now had to be dead. I suggest they went up to Birmingham and killed Khaleed Masood, this being the only real death in this story. The Deep State is the killer, because it needs a dead body for its narrative.

Normally in a murder investigation the identity of a suspect is not released, to avoid biasing any future jury. But in 'terror' cases such as this one, the suspect gets damned and demonised by the media right away. When reading the terrible things he is alleged to have done, one should recall that no-one will ever defend him or rebut such charges, nor will he ever have a functioning defence lawyer at a trial. I suggest that no scrap of evidence puts him in London on the day of the event, that the police security agents killed him around midnight on the 22/23rd, and that he was living alone so that there was no-one who could testify to seeing him on that day. His name could only be released after they had entered his flat. He had to be dead before he could be named.

The story is that Mr Masood hired the car in Birmingham, drove it down to Brighton beforehand, then drove up to London to do the deed. It makes no sense and *doesn't have to,* because it will never be challenged: no-one will ever have to demonstrate it, in a court of law.

The BBC interviewed someone who knew him well, who described him as:

> the antithesis of a violent radical: he was a middle-aged man, focussed on his family and his career.[280]

His former wife testified that she could *not recognise him* in the picture:

> The wife − 14 years his junior − did not recognise her ex-husband despite watching footage of him on an emergency trolley outside Parliament, where he had just been gunned down by armed police after killing four people.

Neighbours were incredulous:

> One neighbour said she was "very surprised" that Masood could commit such an act of violence. His former neighbour Iwona Romek, said she could not believe her eyes when she realised the man who had lived near her was the same person responsible for the attack. She said: "I am very surprised, I cannot believe it. Because when I saw him, I couldn't even see that he could do something like this. Now I'm scared that someone like that was living close to me."

If we turn to the only image of the 'killer', inside the grounds of the House of Commons, it shows a man on a stretcher still alive at 2.50- 3.00 pm.[281] He was supposedly shot three times around 2.45, then for ten minutes or so they were looking after him before the ambulance came. Yet, we see no drop of blood underneath him and two knives on the cobblestones near him (circles have been put around them in the picture) again have no drop of blood on them. Why would he have wanted two knives? His shoes and one sock have been removed, like some strange Masonic symbol.

Most people believe that the stabbed policeman Keith Palmer really died. But how could that be, with no blood on either of the deadly daggers lying about? It was just a show. Why in his final moments did we see Foreign Office MP Tobias Ellwood 'heroically' attempting to resuscitate him by pumping his chest, while qualified medical personnel just stand around, watching? They would *never do that* if it were for real, as such massage is the worst thing for someone stabbed in the chest. If he really died, why are there no images that can identify the stabbed police officer, why is his face obscured? Why did he not wear a protective vest? As a Londoner, I'm aware that no member of the public could ever run in through that House of Commons gate, which is always heavily protected, and *especially* not brandishing a knife – guns would have been drawn immediately! Ellwood was swiftly promoted to the elite Privy Council (an inner clique of government) after this 'heroic' act. What was he doing out there when all the other MPs were locked up in the Westminster building, unable to get out? The charity appeal for that dead policeman's memory swiftly rose to over a million pounds. We here question the story.

Figure: the supposed terrorist still alive, waiting to be taken into an ambulance.

An early tweet at 2.48 pm had "Reuters BREAKING: Two people shot outside UK parliament, building in lock down – parliamentary official." Early reports featured two killers, which soon changed to the inevitable 'lone nut' narrative.

Figure: knife on the cobblestones, with no blood on it.

Videos available in the immediate aftermath show clusters of crisis actors on the bridge, standing over and generally obfuscating the injured person on the ground, usually with no blood visible, and with faces conspicuously turned away from the camera. Half a dozen or so wounded persons are seen being looked after, far less than the forty wounded and more killed we were told about. The crisis actors are later seen proceeding into the Marriot Hotel, which is adjacent to the St Thomas' Hospital, on the other side of the bridge from the House of Commons.

Elite photographers

The VIP Radoslaw Sikorski, former Harvard fellow and Polish foreign minister, member of the Council on Foreign Relations, and of the Bullington club at Oxford University – where he mingled with the likes of David Cameron and Boris Johnson - had attended the Bilderberg conference in 2016. He was there 'by chance' taking the main video, which captured the 'raw video aftermath' of the event.

<u>Figure</u>: Masonic helicopter lands on grass of Parliament Square, ten minutes after the event.

Also, the professional Reuters photographer Toby Melville, photographer of the elite - the Royal family, the Obamas etc. - 'just happened' to be standing by the river at the south side of Westminster bridge when: "I heard a thud, turned round and there was a man lying about 10 yards away from me" (supposed to be the US tourist Kurt Cochran). This he recalled was around 2.30 pm, while the main event was at 2.40 pm. This event with the two Cochrans may have been before this, and so would have been the beginning of whatever happened.

The list of casualties was strangely international: twelve British, four South Koreans, three French youngsters, two Romanians, two Greeks, and one each

Polish, Irish, Chinese, American and Italian. They added up to 23, whereas newspapers had announced at least forty injured. On the bridge, after the event, we saw about half a dozen. This vague, fluctuating number of killed or wounded is a characteristic of these staged events.

A red Masonic helicopter – which no one had ever seen before – made a dramatic descent onto the grass in front of the House of Commons, at 2.50pm, the time shown by Big Ben. The Freemasonic logo was prominently inscribed upon it, plus it had 'Advanced Trauma Team' painted on its side! Nobody was seen emerging from it and after a while it took off again, so that its purpose was less than clear. Turning up mere minutes after the event, it had to be pre-arranged. Its free-and-easy action contrasted notably with all the trapped, panicking MPs locked up inside the House of Commons. Did some 'Advanced Trauma Team' design this whole, thrilling event? Three hundred years ago, in 1717, the world's first public Freemasonic Lodge was opened, in London, making this a tercentenary event.

Four years after the Boston Marathon state-fabricated-terror hoax, the wise American Paul Craig Roberts wrote: "I am convinced that the only victims of the Boston Marathon bombing were the framed Tsarnaev brothers."[282] Those two innocent patsies had to die, taking the 'blame' with them. I suggest that is what happened here: the innocent Khaleed Masood is now dead, that being the sole real death in this story.

The next day, Theresa May made a speech in the House of Commons, about how the UK must stand firm in the face of Islamic terror. This was surely the aim of the exercise: the 'Phantom Menace' has been reinforced, emboldening the PM and improving her ratings, and she then announced a snap general election. We the public have been told what to fear, and the war(s) will continue.

Ole Dammegard had predicted this event (*Daily Star*, 24 March: '"Big Ben is next": London Terror Attack predicted') on an American radio show, one month beforehand. His words were: 'It's February 21st. Should there be a hit against Big Ben, then let it be known that this was pointed out beforehand.' He does have a reputation for predicting these events.

Reflections on the Inquest

At the Old Bailey in September of 2108, a month-long Inquest was set to reconstruct what had happened on Westminster Bridge a year ago. It featured the same lawyer Hugo Keith, who had earlier conducted the 7/7 Inquest, representing the Metropolitan police.

The story had centred on the notion of a car driving up onto the pavement of Westminster Bridge, such that its shocking trajectory went *all along* the bridge. This mysteriously changed at the Inquest and instead we were told how the car surged up onto the pavement, drove twenty yards, then *returned to the road* in order *not* to knock over the yellow sign. It then climbed back onto the pavement again and continued, slamming into pedestrians and tossing them into the road and into the river.

Can the story really change in this manner?

No British journalists reported such a mutation: the amnesiac and obedient British journalists print what they are told to.

Could that change have resulted from objections to the narrative as given, e.g. by me in the 'Kent Freedom movement' video done on Westminster Bridge a week after, where we pointed out the manifest impossibility? If we are to imagine a deranged 'terrorist' surging along at thirty miles per hour on the pavement and slamming into pedestrians left and right, then why would he bother about a light and flimsy street sign, that would easily have been knocked out of the way or flattened? The answer here has to be, because it was still there after the event. I believe that no journalists even mentioned that street sign when reporting the event, or at least did not suggest that it posed any impediment to the narrative.

A made-up story can always be changed and I suggest that has happened here: somewhat as, for example, the inquest on the Lee Rigby event switched the whole manner in which a car allegedly impacted into him, in response to online criticism.

Initially the car mounted up onto the kerb, we were told, just as it impacted Kurt and Melissa Cochran at the southern end of the bridge, travelling at over thirty miles an hour. They were standing just by a tourist kiosk, and the last traffic light is just before that: so turning left out of the traffic, going uphill and mounting up onto a 3-4 inch pavement I could not see how it could do more than ten miles per hour (Londoners may wish to visit this spot and decide for themselves). It could have impacted the couple, but not hurled them anywhere. Kurt was supposedly hurled right over the bridge and landed far below, at the bottom of some steps.

It may be a small point, but while doing the video on the bridge a week later, I had gained the impression that Aysha Frade had been photographed under the bus well before the yellow sign, i.e. due south of it: images of the stationary bus with her under the wheel appear as being south of the yellow sign, i.e. near the St Thomas' hospital, do they not? But the Inquest (Day 14) has this impact happen only after the car has passed by that yellow sign.

The dying moments of PC Keith Palmer formed a dramatic highlight of the whole story. At 2:50 pm he was dying (supposedly) of stab wounds, as a red helicopter landed on the grass of Parliament Square. We saw pictures of the 'hero' MP Tobias Ellwood pumping the chest of the dying policeman, while various police and medical personnel stood around watching him. He attempted mouth to-mouth resuscitation, as he later recollected, but to no avail. Eventually a doctor said there was no hope, and Ellwood recalled, "I remember looking at him and saying, 'you're going to have to tell me to stop, sir, because otherwise I'm going to keep doing this.'" No wonder he was promoted to Ministry of Defence Under-Secretary a few months later.

At the Inquest, the story had suffered a strange mutation. The red helicopter is 'London's Air Ambulance' and upon landing two medical personnel leapt out of it, crossed over the road into the House of Commons, swiftly set up a blood-transfusion for PC Palmer, opened up his thorax by cutting though some rib-bones, and 'one of the doctors then grabbed the heart directly and started squeezing it.'[1] Here we are in some unlikely B-movie script, more like an Aztec ritual than modern medicine. And what about the blood? It would have been everywhere, but no drop was seen in the original pictures, nor did any media source get to hear of this astounding finale to the PC's life, as his heart was seized a-hold of.

"He had lost a huge amount of blood .. the sheer loss of blood.." (from day 6 of the Inquest) while the body was lying on the cobblestones at the front of the House of Commons. We all saw (to remind the reader) the two allegedly-used knives lying on those bloodless cobblestones, with no drop of blood on them. The narrative is here seriously defective.

An intravenous infusion cannot be given once the heart has stopped beating. But the main point here is that no trace of the new narrative existed in the earlier and original version. Given that the helicopter landed at 2:50 about eight minutes after the event, we could be forgiven for assuming that its passengers hardly had time to grab their jackets, let alone bring a pint of warm blood with them suitable to go into PC Palmer. Would they have had time to be briefed as regards what had happened, and indeed would anyone have then known what had happened? The original narrative had no suggestion of an ambulance next to PC Fletcher, or that he was taken into one.

PC Palmer was wearing a protective shirt made of chain-mail, the Inquest was told, and we were shown images of the attempted stabbing which could not penetrate it: we were told how the assassin had to stab under the arm and in the neck, in order to avoid the protective vest. He did all this while holding two knives. It is not easy to picture the various heavily-armed police officers standing around while this was happening.

Coming back to reality, let us recall the sedate and overweight fifty-two year old English teacher who was Khalid Massood, recalled by his neighbours as happily pottering around his garden. According to a BBC interview, he was an 'Excellent teacher, who got on very well with his non-Muslim colleagues, a very friendly, stable kind of guy. He was not interested in the politicised version of Islam. He had no contact with any of the extremist groups. He was a Muslim who was committed to his faith, committed to his family, and was focussed on his career. ..In fact I'd go so far as to say that he was the antithesis of a violent radical. He was a middle-aged mature man…' Given the media stories about his wicked,

---

[1] September 17, Day 6, section 16: Search for Westminstrer terror Inquest transcripts

criminal past which have been proliferating during the Inquest, we should recall this.

The Inquest heard of the obligatory 'clues' left in the hired car: a map of England, with notes scribbled on it such as 'Hatred motivation,' 'Mum,' and 'Exciting opportunity.' These seem like contrived comments, made for public consumption, and remind one of the Korans and wills left in the hired cars of the 'terrorists' at the airport, for the 9/11 event; and again, why did no-one earlier report this?

A year and a half after the event, we have some different storytellers, who wish to give their own spin and colour to the narrative.

Conclusion

In acts of false-flag terrorism the perpetrators behind the deception come out with information very quickly to create a false narrative, which is then spread by the mainstream media. In the case of the terror attacks of 9/11 this early planting of the false narrative was done by the former Israeli prime minister and chief-of-staff Ehud Barak, who appeared on world-wide BBC World television blaming Osama bin Laden and calling for "an operational, concrete war against terror" - before the Twin Towers had even fallen.

By appearing on BBC World right after the planes had hit the towers, Barak was making use of the primacy effect and presenting the desired narrative first, before any evidence could even be examined to determine what had really happened on 9/11. In this case, Barak evidently had prior knowledge of the attacks and was prepared to be in the London studio of the BBC World to give the world the Israeli narrative of the crime - and the Israeli cure for the problem: the global War on Terror, something the Israeli military had been pushing since at least 1979. Barak's early analysis became the official version of 9/11, of course.

Christopher Bollyn, *Orlando False Flag* (2016)

It is indeed a remarkable fact - here presented by that tenacious investigator, Mr Bollyn - that a worldwide War on Terror was called for, via BBC television, on the morning of 9/11, in the year 2001, *before the Towers had even fallen*. The BBC had Ehud Barak in its studio in London just minutes after the first plane hit the building - he was obviously there before it happened. He was doing a PR job, in order to cement the narrative in the public mind. His account even included the upcoming wars against Iraq and Afghanistan! That could well remind us of the message put out merely hours after the 7/7 event in London in 2005, in the online *Jerusalem Post*, by Ephraim Halevi, former head of Mossad (see Chapter 5), calling for a 'war of civilization' to be waged in response, against the Muslim world - before any perpetrators had been identified. The shock value of the event leaves us traumatised, and thereby we are made receptive to the false narrative that is then given to us.

The BBC was on scene to report the 9/11 event, and famously its correspondent Jane Stanley reported the collapse of Building 7 in the afternoon, at 4.21 pm EST, while that building was still visibly standing right behind her! She was reporting the event 26 minutes *before* it happened. Her on-the-spot report faded away a mere five minutes or so before Building 7 actually fell. The BBC managed to lose this video for years, but eventually it turned up on Prison Planet, and a clamour arose for the BBC to explain how come its reporter had announced this event before it had happened. All they would say in response was, 'We don't do conspiracy theories.'

We may indeed wonder, how come the BBC was calling for a worldwide War on Terror before the Towers had even fallen, and then reported the collapse of Building 7 before it had happened?

A study of 9/11 truth remains the best possible introduction for evaluating the unfolding sequence of state-fabricated terror events: now appearing as *the primary art-form* of the 21st Century. They will remain so, until *Homo Sap* sees through the shabby trick. Political Science students need to demand that their courses feature a module on this topic.[283] So quickly are these events directing our modern world towards a place where no one wants to be.

The world divides between those who believe that, on the morning of September 11th 2001, the Towers in New York fell because of 19 Arab hijackers, and those who understand that it was, in one way or another, 'an inside job.' I'd surmise there would be quite an IQ difference between these two populations. As much as 30-40% of the populace may hold the latter belief (much higher in Islamic countries) and yet no political party or even politician can exist which expresses this view. Why should that be?

Sociologically speaking, ninety percent of the population will believe the official lie, as it comes through their TV screens, and around ten percent don't, while three percent *will fight actively* to expose the lies. You, gentle reader, are part of that three percent. It only takes those three percent to carry conviction for the ten percent to accept their view. Once that ten percent comes to strongly believe something, it's only a matter of time for a majority of the populace to come around to accepting it - but, it does take time.

A pathological form of politics has developed in this 21st Century, whereby the ladder of political promotion involves perjuring one's immortal soul to terrible, war-ratifying Untruth. Let's hear a woman's view:

> People that consciously believe in and accept lies as truth are making a statement to life, to the real objective universe, that they do not desire to exist in such a universe where truth is valued over lies. While very often we do not get what we desire in life, we can be sure that, in the end, we will get back that which we give to life. For those people that align themselves with illusion, with that which is not real, they will become just that - "a dream in the past." Those who pay strict attention to objective reality right and left become the reality of the 'future.'

> The fact is that the conditions of the present day are ideally suited to the acquisition of real knowledge. But why, you may ask, do we consider discovering the closest approximation of the truth of our past to be a worthy occupation?

It's quite simple: in a universe where the observer is as important as the observed, the closer they are in alignment, the more order is possible from the side of the universe which - being unimpeded by the barriers of lies - allows creation to manifest unlimited possibilities. When there is great disparity between the observer and the observed, it naturally creates disorder, chaos, and destruction, due to this conflict. This is why all the efforts of the New Age to have "harmonic convergence" that focus on "peace and brotherhood" - while the true foundation of our civilization is based on lies and greed - has only served to add to the chaos and disorder. It is also the reason why those who turn their backs on the horrors of the world, hoping that if they only "focus on the positive", they will be spared, will be one day confronted with a very rude awakening.[284]

If we don't bother to make any such endeavour, if journalists just grab a beer and then get on with the next job, then what happens?

Britain is now living in a post-truth political environment. Public statements are no longer fact-based, but operational. Realities and political narratives are constructed to serve a purpose, dismantled, and the show moves on... Public discourse becomes meaningless. It ceases to be about seeking a common solution to the problems that affect us all, and instead, becomes an exercise in manipulation, intrigue, and brutal power.[285]

Here is Paul Craig Roberts on the meaning, with which we are all familiar, assigned to the phrase, 'Conspiracy Theory':

A 'conspiracy theory' no longer means an event explained by a conspiracy. Instead, it now means any explanation, or even a fact, that is out of step with the government's explanation ... as truth becomes uncomfortable for government and its Ministry of Propaganda, truth is redefined as conspiracy theory, by which is meant an absurd and laughable explanation that we should ignore. In America today, and increasingly throughout the Western world, actual facts and true explanations have been relegated to the realm of kookiness. Only people who believe lies are socially approved and accepted as patriotic citizens.[286]

A political-social rift has developed, between those who derive their views from the Web, which is not controlled by the corporate media, and majority, mainly employed, family people, who obtain their views from the TV and newspapers. The latter are alas hardly worth reading and their rapidly-declining sales are an expression of this.

We've seen how the government and media-approved view on the topics here surveyed is well expressed in Simon Aaronovitch' book, *Voodoo History, How conspiracy theory has shaped modern history,* which adopts an attitude of dismissal towards everything here discussed, i.e., it is a polar opposite view. It opens with the 'conspiracy' notion that no one went to the Moon, the Apollo moon-landings were hoaxed.[287] then proceeds to bracket all other quests for a deeper meaning in history into the same category.

Mr Aaronovitch appears as reticent over public debate. He will dismiss for example as an absurd 'conspiracy theory' the idea that biochemist Dr Kelly was murdered, and will appear on the BBC saying this, but will he debate this matter in public? There has been to date only one public debate about 'conspiracy theory' in the UK, and that was in London's Conway Hall alluded to in the Foreword, when Goldsmith college psychology department was holding forth about alleged psychological characteristics of conspiracy theorists,[288] and Mr Aaronovitch backed out. Here is my colleague Kevin Boyle's account:

> In its original formation this 'conference' was set up as a very one-sided affair indeed, with all contributors firmly in the establishment camp. David Aaronovitch, he of *Voodoo Histories* (and foremost media tub-thumper for bombing Iraq) was to give a presentation in the afternoon. Many were looking forward to confronting this fellow, but discovered that he had 'pulled out' a few days earlier.
>
> Here is a media favourite, a columnist for the *Times*, whose every conscious utterance is broadly promoted by our mainstream media.
>
> Yet, when the opportunity arises for him to present his ideas before people who are ready, willing and able to challenge them (albeit in the very constricted form of short questions) he chickens out. That's how I saw the situation anyway, whatever excuses he came up with.
>
> The point is that this serial liar is always free to make his preposterous and dishonest statements unchallenged. For instance, in a recent article he wrote the following sentence:
>
> "…..the conspiracy theories over Israel's mistaken bombing of the USS Liberty in 1967……"
>
> Given the massive amount of evidence presented by those sailors on the USS Liberty who survived this attack and the astonishing political aftermath of the outrage, this statement can only be perceived as an obscene and deliberate lie."[289]

The USS Liberty was flying an American flag, it was an American ship, it put out American distress signals when attacked, it was in international waters, yet Israeli jets kept shelling it for a couple of hours - from which it was only rescued by a Russian ship appearing in the neighbourhood as a witness. That has to be intentional. Had it been sunk, it would have been blamed upon Egypt - with unthinkable, cataclysmic consequences. This is surely an issue where any British 'peace movement' should encourage open public debate. There is no doubt that the Israeli attack was deliberate and that it involved high-level complicity.

We should believe in Socratic dialogue. Socrates debated in the *agora,* market-place, with the sophists, and these were intelligent, well-educated persons, sophisticated one could say, who were fairly sckeptical, tending to believe that one view was as valid as its opposite and that there was no 'real' truth to be found. These are today's media pundits who scoff at 'conspiracy theorists.' Mr Aaronovitch' book reminds me of Jean-Paul Sartre's view that 'Things are entirely what they appear to be, and behind them ... there is nothing.' (*La Nausee*)

The 'lie' as described in every chapter of this book, in different forms, works so well because of the *silence of the Muslims.* Every time they are falsely demonised, falsely accused, do we hear their protest? We do not, at least not the UK - rather they display a doormat-like passivity, waiting for Allah to sort it out. They mainly appear as quiet, good citizens, who cannot manage a weekly newspaper between the five million of them, and thus make a perfect 'enemy:' *others write their script.* I have seen huge meetings of British Muslims about 'extremism' whereby they accept the British government's story of the 7/7 and 9/11 events, and agree to try and weed out 'extremism,' etc. However, when smaller 'truth' type meeting are held, they are assuredly not present.

Can Fake Terror Be So Cheap?

Around 2015, US Marines were putting up notices, saying they were not prepared to go and fight in Syria with Al-Qaeda. This meant that Al-Qaeda was finished, and so the Islamic menace had to be re-branded. A new fiendish enemy was developed called ISIS. These were formerly the initials of the Israeli Secret Intelligence Service, when Ephraim Halevi was its head. It may still be that! Its leader, the cleric Abu Bakr Al Baghdadi (actual name Simon Elliot or Elliot Shimon, yes, he's Jewish), seems to have taken military training for a year with the Mossad. (Source: *Veterans Today*, 4.8.14). A majority of the British people apparently favoured re-bombing Iraq, as well as Syria, because of what was suddenly being called 'Islamic State' - using acronyms ISIL or ISIS. These fulfil the comic-book concept of Pure Evil, so that everyone can hate them.[290] Politicians cater to the British need for a hate-and-fear enemy.

Syria needed to be bombed - after all, it has its own independent banking system, has no foreign debts whereby it can be manipulated, nor does it permit Monsanto seeds, etc. The pretext given in 2013 of its President Assad using gas upon his own people rather fell apart, as it was discovered that America had supplied the sarin gas and the rebels had used it.

<u>Figure:</u> Images from 2010 staged jihadist videos of 'Isis'

Crudely fake 'beheading' videos were issued, with a rubber knife and no real blood - but could these suffice to wind up people enough to start a new war? I'm not allowed to give you a link to this beheading video, even though it is the 'reason' for re-bombing Iraq, because - get this - the British police have warned, that merely watching it may be an act of terrorism.[291]

'Disclosures' about this newly-created enemy have been emanating mainly from a site called SITE which is allegedly 'monitoring the Jihadist threat,' by ardent Zionist Rita Katz. Her site was formerly involved in setting up the fake bin Laden videos, and is now producing low-cost beheading videos. I have intelligent, discerning friends who actually believe these. Can people still be taken in so easily - for *another war*?

There was a problem with a lack of shadow, absent behind the actor Steven Sotloff (a known Zionist mole). Was anyone bothered? Not a British journalist, to be sure. A shadow was cast by the fellow in black seen staging the murder, who was a Mr Abdel-Majed Abdel Bary, a former rapper from a wealthy family who left London to fight in Syria, who may well fit the profile of an informant for British security services.

Should there not be a punishment for this treasonous and unpatriotic mendacity? We should demand that, in the words of H.G. Wells:

> A time will come when a politician who has wilfully made war and promoted international dissension will be as sure of the dock and much surer of the noose than a private homicide. It is not reasonable that those who gamble with men's lives should not stake their own.

It's time for the secret *Gladio* structures that have generated so much terror to be dissolved. Maybe Europeans needs to engrave upon the walls of their halls of government the great and noble words of JFK:[292]

> The very word "secrecy" is repugnant in a free and open society; and we are as a people inherently and historically opposed to secret

societies, to secret oaths, and to secret proceedings. We decided long ago that the dangers of excessive and unwarranted concealment of pertinent facts far outweighed the dangers which are cited to justify it. Even today, there is little value in opposing the threat of a closed society by imitating its

arbitrary restrictions. Even today, there is little value in ensuring the survival of our nation if our traditions do not survive with it. And there is very grave danger that an announced need for increased security will be seized upon by those anxious to expand its meaning to the very limits of official censorship and concealment. That I do not intend to permit to the extent that it is in my control. And no official of my Administration, whether his rank is high or low, civilian or military, should interpret my words here tonight as an excuse to censor the news, to stifle dissent, to cover up our mistakes, or to withhold from the press and the public the facts they deserve to know.

Twenty-five centuries ago, philosophy began with Plato's image of the Cave, in which people were chained so they could view only flickering shadows on the wall, and could not turn around to see who was projecting them. Never has that metaphor been more savagely relevant than in this 21st Century. As the British philosopher John Michell wrote, in his last posthumous book:

This is the paradox of earthly existence, where authorities proclaim great lies to be true, and truth resides, as ever, amongst the few who dare to cultivate it.[293]

We become human by the act of discerning between what is true and what is illusory. Never has that been more difficult, or more necessary, than today. A virtuous person is one who endeavours to do this. A wise person is one who can. No carrot or reward is needed for this, only some degree of education into historical truth.

Recent publications by the Author

'Osama Bin Laden 1957-2001' in *And I suppose we didn't go to the Moon either* ed. Jim Fetzer & Mike Palecek (2015), pp. 237-250.

'Paris Again Hit by Fictional Terror' in *Another French False Flag?'* ed. Kevin Barrett (2016), pp. 55-68.

'Sandy Hook: Analogies with the London Bombing' 209-218, in *Nobody Died at Sandy Hook* ed. Fetzer & Palecek (2015), pp. 209-218.

'A European Context to Charlie Hebdo' in *And Nobody died in Boston, Either* ed. Fetzer & Palecek (2016), pp. 376-400.

More than forty articles up on *thetruthseeker.co.uk,* for background on how the present opus was composed.

Selected videos featuring the Author

August 2010: 'Windows on the World 7/7 Revisited' Part 1 with David Shayler, five thousand views.

July 2012: '7/7 Kollerstrom and Farrell Are Dead',[294] fifty-six thousand views.

May 2013: 'London 7/7 bombings, what really happened?' (NK on Rich planet TV) seventeen thousand views.

June 2013: 'Kent Freedom Movement investigate the Woolwich false flag psy ops', twenty-five thousand views.

August 2013: Interview by Richplanet TV on Drummer Lee Rigby - search for 'The show that allegedly caused its removal' - sixty-four thousand views.

January 2014: '7/7 London Bombings The lies Exposed!!' by 'We are Change', five hundred views.

January 2014: '7/7 Inside Job', with Muad'Dib, on TV: 'The More Show' (discusses train times that morning) six thousand views.

December 2014: '7/7, 9/11, Madrid, Bali and many more, all from the same False Flag Template,' Richie Allen Show, five thousand views.

December 2015: Paris Bataclan 'More Fake Terror Hits Paris?' with David Shayler, three thousand views.

March 2016: 'Brussels Hoax Exposed' with Ole Dammegard The Real Deal with Jim Fetzer, ten thousand views.

March 2016: Windows on the World, 'Brussels Attacks: Fake Reality', three thousand views

June 2106: Morris108, 'Jo Cox a psyop', twenty thousand views.

August 2016: Windows on the World, 'False Flag Terror in Europe', NK & Kevin Barrett.

Appendices

Magic Numbers

Strange numbers keep turning up in these events. The first July 7th bomb in London was at Aldgate station, and this went off at 8.49 am, i.e., 11 minutes to 9; the Madrid bombs went off on 3/11, 911 days after 9/11. Is there some clue here? Here are some that we have dealt with:

- Two allegedly-crashed planes on the 9/11 event were American Airlines 11 and 77.

- The date of the Bali bomb 12th October 10/12/2002 came from adding one to 9/11/2001 (US notation).

- The Madrid bombing on 11/3 was 911 days after 9/11, and had 191 deaths.

- The No. 30 bus that blew up on 7/7/05 in London had the serial number 17758.

- The first train to explode that morning (Aldgate) was at precisely 11 minutes to 9.

- The Mumbai terror attack was on July 11th or 11/7/06, when the news reported that *seven* trains had then been bombed over an *eleven*-minute period.

- The Breivik-Utøya massacre on 22/7/11 allegedly had 77 deaths.

- Paris (alleged) attack on 2/11/11, was the day of Charlie Hebdo issue 1011.

- The MH-17 crash of 2014 involved a Malaysian 777 Boeing aeroplane, flight 17, being blown apart on 17/7.

- President of the IMF Christine Lagarde declared 'Now I'm going to test your numerology skills by asking you to think about the magic seven … Most of you will know that seven is quite a number,' on 15 January 2014. She talked about how special would be the year ahead, and the Charlie Hebdo event was within a year of her making that speech.

- Writing appeared on the Georgia Guidestones around September 2014, "GAME ON 711."

- A song entitled '7/11' by American singer Beyoncé was released in November, 2014.

- Paris (alleged) attack 7/1/15, on day of the Charlie Hebdo issue 1177, with 17 people (allegedly) killed. Hebdo signifies 'Hebdomedaire' which means sevenfold, in the sense of seven days, i.e a weekly.

- British army sets up its '77 Brigade', of 'Facebook warriors,' skilled in psy-ops and use of social media, January 2105.

- Paris Bataclan event on 11/13/15 (US date)

- Brussels on 22/3/16 has a bomb on the tube explode at 11 minutes past 9. The date numbers add to 7+7 or 77. (Compare 'Skull and bones' Lodge number 322)

- Nice on 14/7 had 77 dead, which then finalised at 84 (multiples of 7).

- Hamburg on 22/7, 70th anniversary of blowing up of the King David Hotel.

- On 22/7 in 1946 the British HQ in Palestine, the King David Hotel, was blown up by the Zionists: to help the British understand that, they had to leave.

These numbers never seem to add up to much, I've never met anyone who could predict anything using them .. but they are unmistakably present.

Kevin Barrett quoted the opening of the Wiki section on 'The 2011 Norway attacks' which said they were 'two sequential lone-wolf terrorist attacks against the government, the civilian population, and a Workers' Youth League (AUF)-run summer camp in the Oslo region on 22 July 2011, claiming a total of 77 lives," and added: 'All those elevens, like those in 9/11, 11/22, and so on, are probably just a coincidence.'[295] Or, should one just ignore such numerology?

2. The Gunpowder Plot

It has taken four centuries for the truth about the 1605 Gunpowder Plot to emerge in the definitive *The Enigma of Gunpowder plot, 1605, The Third solution* by Francis Edwards.[296] This five-hundred page book was a culmination of Edwards' life-work, earlier books of his having investigated other Elizabethan-age plots and the character of the master-plotter Robert Cecil, the Earl of Salisbury who was, in effect, Britain's Prime Minister. It follows on from Lady Antonia Frazer's *The Gunpowder Plot* (1996) which took a LIHOP approach ('Let It Happen On Purpose'), to use a modern term, where the authorities saw the event coming, it had been plotted elsewhere maybe abroad, and they merely allowed it to proceed, claiming not to have had foreknowledge.

Webster Tarpley gave a remarkable lecture in 2007 on this topic to the old London 9/11-truth group, entitled: "From Guy Fawkes to 9/11 - 400 Years of State Sponsored Terrorism," which can be viewed on YouTube. Inspired by this, I did an interview with Rense radio, on November 5th 2008 - here is a transcript of a part of it:

> N.K.: I think Webster Tarpley's analysis of it is spot-on. Some years ago there was a report from the War Office dated from some days after the gunpowder plot, showing that the thirty barrels of gunpowder under the British House of Lords was something called cornpowder, which had decayed, it was a very low-grade type of gunpowder that would not have actually blown up. I think that is a key, and it gives us an analogy with modern fake-terror events that are used to scare everybody.
>
> Yes, and also, as Webster Tarpley brings out, the nucleus of that gunpowder plot Catesby and Winter with others, who had met the year before, they had come from a failed plot, as a rebellion of the Earl of Essex, and so they could all have been executed. In other words, the state, or British intelligence, had a handle on them, because of stuff they had

been involved in before, so they could in some degree be manipulated, and this chap Cecil was the mastermind.

Because they had been implicated, they could be manipulated to set it up. And what it led up to, (King) James I wanted some reconciliation with the Catholics and with the Spanish empire, and there were forces which didn't want this to happen, which wanted war, and as a result of this gunpowder plot, there was bitter anti-Catholic feeling, because all of the people in the plot were Catholics, and so this led to a century of war against the Catholics. It's so important to appreciate that these brewed-up terror events, their aim is war, and their aim is to get people to hate the right enemy. British people are deeply conditioned to have an enemy, to need an enemy, to hate the enemy, and to feel togetherness through having that enemy.

Rense: How much easier it is to accomplish that now with the mass media.

Here are some notes from a talk Webster Tarpley gave on the subject:

'Robert Cecil, the younger one, he's the one who does the Gunpowder Plot … when he really makes it to the top thanks to the Gunpowder Plot, he becomes Lord Salisbury. Guy Fawkes is really not the most important, he is the one who has been demonised, but the important ones are two guys called Catesby and Winter, and they meet in the early months of 1604, and they begin discussing some kind of a plot to take revenge on James I. … They had all been involved in the rebellion of the Earl of Essex. In other words, these people all could have been executed by the Cecils as a result of this attempted coup by Essex against them which failed. So you have two police informants, essentially, meeting to create a plot. Now, what did they talk about? They talk about first of all, renting a room in a basement across from the House of Lords and digging a tunnel. And they start trying to dig this tunnel, but it turns out they can't do it, because they have to go through a wall, they also have to get a guy called Sir Dudley Carlton to come in, who is later on one of Cecil's big diplomats, to help them rent this room. Eventually they find that they can't tunnel, so what they do is simply go and rent the basement under the House of Lords, and they stock this up with what looks to be gunpowder. We'll see in a minute that it's not.

They eventually recruit some other plotters, they recruit a guy called Thomas Percy, who becomes one of the leading plotters. One of the people at the time in the Autumn of 1605 is going home at 2 in the morning and he meets Percy the plotter, and he's coming out of Cecil's house. Get it? The main plotter is reporting to Robert Cecil about what's going on. So, he's a double agent.

'You've got double agents, you've also got a couple of fanatics. You've probably got Guy Fawkes as a fanatic, a dupe, a patsy in that sense. Now, a couple of weeks before November 5th, when the Parliament is supposed to meet, this Catholic nobleman Lord Mounteagle comes forward and he says to Cecil, "I just got a letter that says I shouldn't go to the opening of Parliament, because it might be dangerous," and he shows him the letter. This is called the famous Mounteagle Letter. So Cecil waits four or five days until he can meet the King. Cecil shows it to the King, and says, "Your Majesty, I got this strange letter from Lord Mounteagle, what could it mean, that we shouldn't go to the opening of Parliament? I really can't figure this out." And James said, "My God, they're going to blow up the Parliament." Now, it turns out that James I, when he was in Scotland, he was very unpopular, there were numerous attempts to kill him. And one of the attempts to kill him was allegedly a gunpowder plot. They tried to blow up James and his father, so he's used to this. Now, what you have here, of course, is Cecil wrote the letter himself, whether with his own hand, or through some agent, he had agents who could duplicate handwriting, so he gets the letter sent to Mounteagle, Mounteagle delivers it back to Cecil, Cecil takes it to the King, and he lets the King think that the King is a genius, that he is the Solomon of England, that he's the only one who could figure out such a deep dark mystery. Alright, so then they wait a few more days, and they send somebody over and they discover that it's - Guy Fawkes.'

For comparison, here is an insightful comment found in an 18th Century history:

Not long after, a conspiracy broke out of a more horrid and dangerous Nature, being the most unparallel'd Treason that ever was harbour'd in the Breasts of Men; this impious Design gave the greatest Blow to the Catholic Interest in England, by rendering that Religion so odious to the People: the common opinion regarding the Discovery of this plot, by a Letter to the Lord Monteagle, has not been universally allow'd to be the real Truth of this Matter; for some have affirm'd, that this Design was first hammer'd in the Forge of Cecil, who intended to produce this Plot in the Time of Queen Elizabeth; but, prevented by her Death, he return'd his Project in this Reign, with a design to have so enraged the Nation as to have expelled all Roman Catholics, and confiscated their Estates; to this end, by his secret Emissaries, he entic'd some hot-headed Men of that Persuasion, who, ignorant whence the Design first came, heartily engag'd in this execrable Powder-Treason; tho' this account should not be true, it is certain that the Court of England had Notice of this Plot from France and Italy, long before the pretended Discovery; upon which Cecil, who knew the whole matter several weeks before, fram'd that Letter to the Lord Monteagle, with a Design to make the Discovery seem the more miraculous, and at the same Time magnify the Judgement of the King, who by his deep Penetration was to have the honour of unravelling so ambiguous and dark a Riddle.[297]

The traditional tale suffers from the following impossible and unresolvable problems:

- 36 barrels of gunpowder is a lot. The government tightly controlled all the gunpowder in Britain, so how did Guy Fawkes and co. get a hold of it? Did they have a contact inside parliament? And how could it have been moved across London from the Tower of London to Westminster (two miles distant) without anyone seeing it?

- Would a group of Catholics have been allowed to rent a house so close to the Houses of parliament, or a cellar right underneath it? That seems most unlikely, in those troubled times.

- Why did they search the Parliament cellars on that night, for the first time in British history? What would have inspired such a search?

- Why did the soldier who shot Robert Catesby and Thomas Percy at the Holbeach House shootout receive such a large pension (allegedly 10p a day for life) as a reward? On the usual story, these men would have been better taken alive, to be tortured, and betray their co-plotters.

- Why would the Catholic plotters have wanted to blow up Parliament when it housed not only Protestants, but also all the country's leading Catholics?

- Elizabeth, James' Protestant daughter, was due to take over, if the plotters succeeded. Why would the Catholic plotters want Elizabeth on the throne?

- The aim was to change King James' policy: to make him more grateful and dependent upon Cecil, and more hostile towards the Catholics. We may compare this with today's fabricated terror events, whose organisers expect and receive salary increases, public gratitude, etc.

-

3. Letter to Lady Justice Hallett

October, 2010

Lady Justice Hallett, the Royal Courts of Justice, The Strand, London, WC2. (This letter plus copy of my book was personally delivered on 18th October, and she acknowledged it)

Dear Lady Justice Hallett,
                    Concerning the 7/7 Inquest:

On the 4th October (at the preliminary hearing), you were advised by Barrister Mr Keith that a "core tension is obviously between, on the one hand, a trying to ensure, if at all possible, that the trier of fact - namely, yourself in this context - does not reach decisions on matters as important as whether or not the Security Service were involved in a causative sense in the 7/7 bombings..." (37:7-12)

One is disturbed that this Inquest has been pressurised, a priori, to avoid what should be an absolutely central question relating to the 7/7 bombings. I wrote a book (here enclosed) arguing that the security services were indeed 'involved in a causative sense' in the events of 7/7. I respectfully submit the following few observations and comments, mainly concerning the first day of this Inquest, 11th October 2010 (references are to this day, unless stated otherwise).

Your Inquiry is prohibited under Section 11 of the Coroners Act and rule 42 in the Coroners Rules from 'the framing of the verdict in such a way as to appear to determine any question of criminal liability.'(Oct 11, 13:9-12) You could use this Rule, not to accept what you will be repeatedly told throughout this Inquest, that: '…the perpetrators are, of course, dead.' (14:1) I urge you not to view this as self-evident.

0:18-25: "Between 22 February and 22 15 June 2005, there were 41 telephone contacts between mobile phones attributed to Tanweer, Khan, and Lindsay and hydroponic outlets, that is to say places selling hydrogen peroxide. Hussain's computer at college revealed the names of two particular shops for which he had searched online, and business cards and other literature found at Alexandra Grove related to other such similar shops."

Hydroponics is a way of growing things in water not earth: small quantities of peroxide could be used as a disinfectant, but no hydroponics shop is going to sell large quantities, because it kills growing plants. I doubt whether anyone could buy tens of litres of strong peroxide unless registered as an industrial company - these lads weren't. That is surely why, in 2005, the 7/7 'peroxide allegations' against the accused all had as the peroxide source, hair-bleach lotions. If the police reckon they have these phone links, I suggest you ask them to reveal the shop(s) where the peroxide was purchased, and see if any owner(s) will testify to selling tens of litres of strong peroxide to a young Muslim? It is quite unlikely!

Also:

- Hasib Hussein was not at college. He had just got his GCSEs and was about to start at Leeds Business College.

- What business cards were found at 18, Alexander Grove? (the so-called 'bomb factory' - to which no journalists have ever been allowed access).

- What 'Literature' was found at 18, Alexander Grove? Please bear in mind, concerning this new and suspect evidence, that that flat was never occupied or rented by any of the Four.

1:5-6: "Regarding the CCTV and mobile phone evidence of the 'reconnaissance mission' on 28 June 2005, given as the second most important piece of evidence concerning the guilt of the Four: this visit to London featured, e.g. Sid Khan, photographed eating ice cream in front of Madame Tussauds. The tube stations that the photographs show they visited do not bear a great resemblance to the ones which got blown up a week later, e.g., Baker St Tube for Madame Tussauds."

2:8-13: "Documents or items belonging to Khan were found:
1) In the carriage at Edgware Road
2) In the carriage at Aldgate.
3) In Tavistock Square.
4) In the tunnel between Kings Cross and Russell Square (59:20-23)."

Is this 'finding' of Khan's remains in FOUR different places really acceptable as evidence for his presence in London? He had allegedly been blown into little pieces in a tunnel near Edgware Road station, but some unburnt ID documents in his possession are strangely preserved; his wallet (with ID) was given to Hasib Hussain to leave at Tavistock Square; and now we hear that his intact mobile phone, was recovered from the remains of the blasted Piccadilly Line carriage. How strange that Kahn's intact mobile phone - far from where he died - should have recoverable phone messages from that morning, and how odd that this has not hitherto been mentioned over the previous five years!

6:11-17.: Mr Keith told you that he had seen no evidence "that the explosions took place under the trains, nor that they were connected to fictional events aired on a Panorama programme in May 2004, nor to a fictional terrorism training exercise that had been carried out apparently that same morning by a private crisis management company."

I would be happy to provide the court with plenty of such evidence, for explosives having been under the trains. Nor can the *Panorama* program of May 2004 possibly be described as 'fictional' - it (amazingly) presented an identical template to the actual bombings fourteen months later. Nor can Peter Power's 'terror drill' which exactly synchronised in time and space (in his own words, "the very same stations") with the actual event that morning be described as 'fictional.'

7:8-9.: There was 'no mystery' Mr Keith assured your Court in the fact that "several [CCTV] frames appear to place the railings outside the [Luton] station in front of Tanweer." He meant Khan not Tanweer; and - yes, there is quite a mystery here. It has clearly been 'photoshopped'. The railings should be behind those Four and cannot be in front of them.

Mr Keith continued: "What would, we rhetorically ask, be the point in anybody fabricating CCTV evidence showing them at Luton when later CCTV evidence, not apparently fabricated or challenged, proves them to be at King's Cross? (7:10-13)"

That King's Cross CCTV is a blurred and dark image where no faces can be recognised, and why was it produced only three years later, at the 2008 Kingston Trial? A lot can happen in three years. Far from this being 'not challenged,' I find that informed sources view its authenticity as dubious.

In the 'dry run' on 28th June, with no rucksacks, the four are photographed entering that station at 8.10 am. They had to buy tickets, walk up across a platform up some stairs, cross the railway lines, and go down the steps to the platform where they caught the train. The CCTV images together prove that THIS ALL

TOOK 5 MINUTES, as one might reasonably expect (Video footage shown on 13th am):

> 08.10.07 Enter Luton station (and buy tickets), 08.14.26 Go through barriers, 08.15.07 Enter platform.

On 7/7, however, the four arrive with their heavy rucksacks at 07:22, buy their tickets (three-day returns) and catch the King's Cross train in one and a half minutes. The evidence of the dry run shows THEY COULD NOT REASONABLY HAVE DONE THIS. With heavy, liable-to-explode rucksacks they would have had to move more slowly:

> 07.21.54 Enter Luton, 07.22.29 Ticket hall, 07.22.43 Go through barriers, 07.23.27 On platform, 07.24.47 Train arrives.

I suggest, Lady, that they missed that train. When the train-times evidence from Luton to King's Cross on 7/7 was uncovered (I found this information from the official British Rail records of the day and put it in the public domain), John Reid, the then-Home Secretary altered the government narrative to fit the new facts. But, Inspector Andy Hayman in his book, "The Terrorist Hunters", still has the four on the 7:40, not the 7:25 train. For a whole year all government sources were claiming that the Four caught the 7.40 train and arrived in King's Cross at 8.23. Then I showed that train was cancelled and they may have caught the 7.42 (the delayed 7.30 train) from Luton, which only got into London at 8.39. All the CCTV photos of Hasib Hussein in King's Cross that morning (shown Oct 13th, pm) start at 8.55 am, which supports this more plausible narrative.

It appears that whoever is building the government case has come to realise that what were the established and accepted facts of the movements of the four on the morning of 7/7 make it physically impossible for them to have been anywhere near the places where the underground bombs exploded.

Lady, please consider that these men got to London too late for the terror-drills they thought they were participating in. That, in the view of an increasingly large number of people, is the key to making sense of this story.

75: 2-20: You heard two witnesses, describing the Four on the 07.24 Thameslink train from Luton to King's Cross - reminding one of the Official Report of 2006, which had two witnesses likewise describing the Four on the 07.40 train that morning. Following my discovery that the 07.40 train had not run, were these two 'witnesses' simply shifted back to the earlier train? If the two witnesses were as clear as your Inquest heard, how come all official sources believed for a whole year that the Four had travelled on the 7.40? There has to be something bogus about this testimony.

24:15-18: You heard on the morning of 11 October from Mr Keith that "During his first conspiracy trial, Waheed Ali accepted that he travelled to Pakistan with Khan in 2001 and that he, Ali, had received terrorist training when there."

I query whether your barrister has the right to slander a man who has been judged innocent by a jury of charges of terrorism. Waheed Ali (Kingston 2008 trial) categorically denied any association with terrorism, insisting his training was by way of defending the independence of an Islamic nation - mainly Kashmir - and that this was regarded as quite OK under Islamic ethics. I heard him give this testimony. Yes, it was military training, but of a kind approved by Beeston's Islamic community.

62: 2-5 Hugo Keith reaffirmed the story of the main explosive used being black pepper and peroxide: 'several kilograms of HMTD [at Alexander Grove] as well as containers containing mixtures of pepper and hydrogen peroxide'- the main explosive mix that the HMTD detonators were supposedly designed to explode.

We heard how "at least 34 milk pans had been used to boil and concentrate the hydrogen peroxide. All that remained, however, were the labels, because the pans had been presumably destroyed by the harshness of the process." (64:6-9) Boiling hair-bleach, or any other form of hydrogen peroxide in milk-pans would not concentrate it - quite the contrary - nor would it destroy milk-pans! Complicated, low-pressure, fractional-distillation apparatus would be required to concentrate it, up to the 70% level that is explosive. To suggest that those four lads knew how to handle liquid oxygen, or to write out chemical equations, or to compute the density of hydrogen peroxide (62:13-15) is to approach quite extreme limits of absurdity: your Inquest should call witnesses who knew them, before such claims are to be made. Perhaps a team of experts, from the 'Defence Science and Technology Laboratory and the Royal Centre for Defence Medicine' might be asked to testify on this matter - I surmise they would have difficulty in keeping a straight face if they are expected to support this comical narrative! Black pepper and peroxide mixture does not really explode - and will certainly not lift a train carriage off the rails.

You will be hearing testimony from the top forensics expert at the Government's explosives laboratory at Fort Halstead, Clifford Todd. Do ask him, concerning the deadly explosives allegedly found by the police at 18 Alexander Grove and at Luton car-park - and in Tanweer's car, etc. - please ask him, can he produce any analysis signed and warranted by a professional chemist, plus a signed affidavit of where they were taken from? I predict that he cannot.

Lady, if there is no murder weapon, then there is no criminal guilt. If your Inquest is telling you that the Four went down to London with black pepper and peroxide in their rucksacks, then that is about as dangerous and frightening as the Chappati-flour and peroxide 'bombs' which went off phut two weeks later, on 21st July.

It would be relevant to try and call for evidence Leeds university PhD chemist Magdy al-Nashar, who was renting the flat at 18, Alexander Grove. He left for Egypt on 5th July: the police might not like his testimony, but at least it would be the truth. Al-Nashar was arrested in Cairo and then released with no charges, though he left that flat only in the week before 7/7. Had the flat really contained all the equipment the police are now claiming - for distillation, heating, cooling, filtering, etc., with kilograms of TATP and HMTD, etc., plus notes showing plans to blow up the Underground, etc. - he would now most definitely be in jail.

Apart from the overriding fact that the descriptions by survivors of the explosions on 7/7 indicate very strongly that it was military-grade 'C4' that was used, the other explosives 'evidence' implicating the four Muslims is ridiculous and simply unbelievable.

70:12-17

We will hear evidence being read from a parking attendant who recounts how he saw a Fiat Brava parked in the station car park [at Luton] with its driver, a black male, asleep in the front seat. The parking attendant issued a parking fine at about 05.53 that morning but didn't want to waken the man as he was on his own and feared being attacked.

Are we to believe that Lindsay Germain arrived early, driving from Aylesbury, for his final suicide mission, anxiously waiting to meet his colleagues and be given his dreadful backpack - and he nods off? Can the story get more absurd? One cannot help noticing that all photos of the Four have them looking quite relaxed and happy.

Moving briefly onto the 14th, your Inquest heard of how Germain Lindsey appeared in the main King's Cross concourse somewhere between 8.20-8.40, demanding from a platform assistant to speak to the Duty Manager, adding 'It's something very important' (67:19-20). Does that sound to you like a suicide bomber? From that same testimony (Mr Fayaz Patel) we gather that "the entire Tube gate line area was congested and we'd implemented a station control to try and minimise the flow of passengers." This involved shutting escalators off, shutting the main entrance and exit points, and then periodically opening them as and when appropriate. Therefore unusual controls were being imposed on the main concourse at King's Cross. Passengers were being delayed and, as Mr Patel says later, getting angry and "abusing" staff. Mr Patel replied to Lindsay, "Well, we're quite busy at the moment because of, obviously, with the station control." So the stressful situation of managing the 'station control' was 'obvious.' This was *before* the bombs had gone off. In addition, various police community officers were coming, and note carefully Mr Patel's answers:

> Q. Do you know why they were there? A. I believe they were just passing through or they were going to a training course or something, and they heard about - and they came to help. Q. What had they heard about? A. They had just heard that there's some kind of problem or some kind of power failure or - at King's Cross.

Permit me to suggest, madam, that this was deeply related to the terror-drill that morning, alluded to by Peter Power. I suggest that Lindsay could not help noticing such unusual turbulence and 'control' - ghastly possibilities started to dawn upon him. He had agreed to participate in what he thought was a fairly innocuous terror-drill. It was indeed 'something very important' that he wished to raise with the Duty Manager; but, in the end, he was too frightened to stay.

Madam, the British justice system is traditionally adversarial, where two opposite views can be expressed, prior to judgement. That has been prohibited from happening at this Inquest. For example, you will be hearing comments about 'Mohammed Siddique Khan's goodbye video which came into their [two witnesses'] possession through Hasina Patel,' (Oct 4th, 23:1-2) but your Inquest has refused permission for Hasina Patel to give testimony concerning her husband. Permit me to remind you that no one has ever questioned the integrity or innocence of Hasina Patel - though she has been jailed and roughly handled by the police. Clearly, her testimony concerning this video (made in the closing of 2004 before Khan's prolonged visit to Pakistan) would be of more value than anyone else's.

While admiring the fairness of your conduct of this Inquest, I believe that you are in essence listening to police storytelling - however much credence you may wish to give to it - and will hear much more of the same during the next five months.

I humbly offer my service should comments upon any aspect of the 7/7 narrative be desired, from the 'unacceptable' point of view of defending the innocence of British Muslims and especially concerning the improbable chemistry that was allegedly used by the four Muslims on 7/7.

I am, yours, etc.

4.Tunisia - June 26, 2015

I visited Tunisia shortly before this event, and experienced a deeply peaceful nation, suffused with a quiet optimism. But, that country apparently did not appreciate why it needed 'AFRICOM,' a huge US military base, declining the offer on the grounds of adverse impact on its tourist industry, its main source of revenue.

Israel has a habit of knowing when and where terror is going to strike. On May 1st, 2015, the office of Israel's Prime Minister Benjamin Netanyahu warned Israeli citizens in Tunisia that they could be a target of a terrorist attack, and Israelis were advised to avoid traveling to Tunisia next weekend. This was reported in *Haaretz* newspaper, explaining that Israel's Counter-terrorism Bureau had 'updated information' on the matter. (ibtimes.com, 2/5/15)

In the middle of the holy month of Ramadan - hardly the time of year when one would expect Islamic terror - three countries experienced terror on the same day: Tunisia, Kuwait, and France, leaving 63 people reported as dead.[298] In Tunisia's coastal tourist resort of Sousse, Britons were staying at the Imperial Marhaba Hotel. A Wiki site went up quickly, saying "39 people, mostly British tourists, were killed when armed gunmen attacked two hotels," and that was soon altered to 'an armed gunman.'

The very next day, Britain's Prime Minister David Cameron told the nation who had done it. It had been perpetrated by *Islamic State Terrorists*. How did he

know that? One is reminded of Tony Blair telling the British people that Muslims had perpetrated the 7/7 event, on the very day that it had happened. It was near to the tenth anniversary of that event, and Britain's Foreign Minister declared it was "the most significant terrorist attack on the British people" since those London bombings.(BBC News, 28.6.15)

The Islamic State had claimed responsibility for the attack at the Imperial Marhaba hotel, according to SITE Intelligence Group. SITE have long been the group used to 'discover' the Al-Qaeda/Bin Laden videos, the Foley beheading videos, etc., used in official narratives. There is something fishy when Rita Katz's SITE Intelligence Group is involved.[299]

The Perpetrators

A Tunisian news agency reported how three persons, one in police uniform, arrived by boat, and carried out the shooting. One was killed, another arrested, and the third escaped. The Interior Ministry spokesman Mohammed Ali Aroui told reporters that authorities were "sure" that Seifeddine Rezgui had had accomplices. Reuters reported 'at least one gunman.'

The event, as Craig Murray commented, was "highly organised, including some gunmen who arrived by jet-ski. There were many grenades thrown, which is also missing from the BBC account.... One BBC correspondent said that he was tipped off that something was going to happen so stayed away from the beach."

The *Mail Online* (26 March) reported that two British witnesses saw a 2nd gunman. Mr Johnson, a retired police officer, says he saw a second man standing on the beach, dressed in red shorts, who was holding an automatic rifle and shooting the tourists along with the gunman in dark clothing.

Kirsty Murray was shot in both legs by a man she says was not Rezgui in a hotel corridor. But she says it was not an automatic rifle, like Rezgui was using, but a smaller weapon. Her father Neil said: 'She believes there were at least two gunmen, because she was shot at close range with a handgun. 'Both her and her fiancé have said there was more than one gunman. One person is not capable of doing that much damage anyhow.'

In the video clip of the gunman running along the beach 'we see another man running a few metres behind him, that can only be another gunman as nobody else would risk being shot by running behind him like that...'

A woman interviewee on ITN (female, age over 65) referred to two gunmen and indicated two locations from which she saw or heard gunfire. Several other witnesses also refer to explosions, presumed by stun grenades. The BBC reported that the Tunisia gunman Seifeddine Rezgui 'did not act alone' but had help in carrying out the attack.

There was a story that the man, believed to be a student, came from the beach hiding his Kalashnikov under an umbrella before opening fire on the tourists. From there he entered the Hotel Imperial through the pool, shooting people as he went.

As usual, all the blame is laid on a single 'lone nut' who is dead and cannot reply.

Fabricated Photos

"The gunman strolling along the beach is of no interest to most of the group behind him. People are not running for their lives and many are not looking at him at all. He is not casting a shadow and the day looks pretty dull. In other pictures, the sunlight is intense and the shadows dense and sharp. That means that the stroll-along-the-beach photo could not have been taken on the same day. Curious.

"In another picture, the gunman aimlessly wanders the brilliantly lit street, looking for somewhere to pray and get shot; his shadow is intense and there is a lot of 'ghosting around him that you do not seen in other pictures. The shadows cast by the gunman and the wall are inconsistent with the same sun angle. That has to be fake as well. There is a claim from a poster on the Chris Spivey site that he took a screenshot of that photo three days before the Tunisian incident occurred." ('Nick Turner')

A Dead Man Takes the Blame

"Friends told Sky News that even two days before the attack, Yacoubi showed no signs of radicalisation, visiting a cafe, and going for a walk." Those accounts were backed up by his uncle Ali al Rezgui, who told the *Telegraph* the family had seen nothing to worry them. Mr Rezgui told the paper:

> He used to use hair gel and wear the nicest of clothes, and he used to do break dancing. He even used to go to competitions and things like that in Tunis, he was well known for that here. He didn't even have a beard, and I've never seen him with anyone with a beard. We have extremists like that in Gaafour, but never have I seen him with them.

That testimony cannot fail to remind readers of the alleged London bombers (Chapter 5) who had no discernable interest in politics. The 'gunman' has been named as Seifeddine Yacoubi and as Seifeddine Rezgui. There are pictures of this Tunisian student break-dancing, that is about all we know of him. A video shows a dilapidated home, an empty fridge, of an impoverished student: and he arrived by Ski-Jet onto the beach?

Figures: The fiendish villain, with straight hair, Dracula fangs and a nose job. Compare the real Seifeddine Rezgui, a curly-haired break-dancer.

How did the 'official' picture of him come to have guns on either side, and what on Earth has happened to his nose? What impressive Dracula teeth he has grown! A real picture of him is shown for comparison. It is clear that the curly-haired break-dancing patsy had a double who was used, with straight hair.

Thirty British Deaths?

If 30 out of the 39 dead in Tunisia are British, that shows either (a) a remarkable ability to focus upon holiday Brits by 'crazed killers' or else (b) crisis actors are involved (Chris Spivey has suggested this). My impression is, there may have been real deaths on the beach, but crisis actors in the hotel scenes.

In the aftermath of these attacks, Britain's home Secretary Theresa May urged parents to report any signs of 'radicalisation' amongst children or friends to the police. This could include, she explained, 'bedroom radicalisation.'

These Tunisian events served to divert attention from Israeli arrest of the boats that were then approaching Gaza in an attempt to break the siege. One of the occupants was Dr Moncef Marzouki, a former President of Tunisia, the first president after the 2011 popular uprising. The three boats that set off on Saturday, June 27th, to break the siege of Gaza, were thus unmentioned in the MSM.

Or None?

One needs evidence of only one fake death, one crisis actor on the beach, to discredit the story given. Several videos are available on this matter which one can peruse, e.g., http://nodisinfo.com/lady-in-the-pink-bikini-proves-the-tunisian-hoax/. There is no real blood and close-ups show applied moulage to simulate bullet wounds. The British media have described this woman (let's not give her name) as being seriously injured, etc.,[300] but close-up photos fail to show her stomach or any body parts damaged, by bullet-holes or anything else. This has to indicate the complicity of British intelligence.

There's an important philosophical point here. We cannot answer the question, 'Did anyone really die?', and it's not our business to do so. It is our business to ascertain that fake actors with pretend wounds were used - which means that it was a set-up or designed event.

Mossad had enhanced its presence in Tunisia a few years earlier: "According to the Tunisian Journal, the Mossad has three primary goals for its activity in the north African country: to form spy rings for sabotage and incitement purposes, to follow the development of events in neighbouring Algeria and Libya, and to track what is left of the Palestinian groups in Tunisia as well as Islamic and Salafi movements that are active there." That's from an official Israeli source (ynetnews.com, 14.2.12). Three hundred Mossad agents became stationed in Tunisia, and their mission, in the view of Hamma al-Hammami, general secretary of the Workers' Party of Tunisia, was: 'the Israeli regime prevents any action to create strategic coalitions with parties, thus frustrating the Tunisian revolution for the benefit of the Tel Aviv regime'.[301] Did the beach-terror event have some such purpose?

Index

End Notes

1 Tarpley, *9/11 Synthetic Terror Made in USA* 4th Edn., 2008, p.59.

2 The 2006 film *V for Vendetta* by the Wachowski Brothers was based on the 1989 graphic novel by Alan Moore, which was about a Guy Fawkes night in 1997. The film's anarchist face-mask has become quite iconic.

3 Daniel Ganser, *NATO's Secret Armies* 2004, 2007 (online).

4 Richard Cottrell *Gladio: Nato's Dagger at the Heart of Europe* 2011, 2015.

5 R.D. Steele, 'Was Paris 11/13 a False Flag Event?' in *Another French False Flag?* Ed. Kevin Barrett, 2016.

6 See N.K., 'Osama bin Laden, 1957-2001' in *And I Suppose we didn't go to the Moon either* 2015 Ed. Fetzer, Moon Rock Books pp. 237-250 (also online).

7 Quoted in Francis Edwards, *The Enigma of the Gunpowder Plot* 1605: the 3rd Solution (2008) In 1969 he had published *Guy Fawkes, the Real Story of the Gunpowder Plot?* so much of his life was occupied with the topic.

8 Or, if reading this erudite text is too much, here is a transcription of a talk by Webster Tarpley on the subject: http://progressivepress.com/peaceweek/cloakandgunpowder.html

9 Francis Edwards, p.3.

10 'All four bombers were members of al-Muhajiroun, believed by American and Western intelligence services to be an al-Qaeda front organisation that recruited British Muslims.. the leader of al-Muhajiroun, Omar Bakri Mohammed, had advance warning of the 7/7 attacks ...' But alas British Intelligence had used an 'appeasement paradigm' and failed to move swiftly enough, not taking 'appropriate preventative action' that would have stopped the four Islamic extremists. Ahmed, The London Bombings (2006), p.274). Likewise his The War on Freedom (see e.g., p.224) did not question the role of Mohammed Atta as the 'lead hijacker' in perpetrating the 9/11 event.

11 Thierry Meyssan's *Voltaire Network* is here highly recommended. He wrote: "Contrary to what President François Hollande has declared, the Libyan migration is not the consequence of a 'lack of follow-through' of operation 'Unified Protector', but the desired result of this operation, in which his country has played a leading role." www.voltairenet.org/article187588.html

12 Israel Shamir wrote of Nicolas Sarkozy, former French President: 'by bombing Libya he sent more immigrants to France than any left-winger would.... Well, perhaps François Hollande, the present President, can compete with him, as his support for Syrian rebels did send a million refugees to Europe.' A Cold Summer for Europe, www.thetruthseeker.co.uk/?p=120199

13 Intro to Adam Curtis' classic BBC trilogy *The Power of Nightmares*, 2004 (online)

14 See NK & Jim Fetzer, 'Star Wars and 9/11' in The Real Deal episode 157.

15 Search for 'Rich planet TV The show that allegedly caused its removal' for my DLR interview.

16 He has since got his slot of Sky TV back, owing to many complaints that were written in by his supporters, but he's been censored: he is free to do paranormal programs about flying saucers, etc., but not politics.

17 For destruction of the seven buildings on that day, WTC 1,2,3,4,5,6 and 7, see: Judy Wood, *Where did the Towers go?* 2010. Most accounts only mention the three buildings WTC 1,2 and 7.

18 The Journal of 9/11 studies.

19 Danielle Ganser, Nato's Secret Armies, 2005, Ch.6 'The Secret War in Italy'.

20 Webster Tarpley, 'From Guy Fawkes to 9/11 - 400 Years of State-sponsored Terrorism' (online)

21 See my 'Osama bin Laden 1975- 2001' in Ed Fetzer And I suppose we didn't go to the Moon, either Moon Rock books 2015, 237-250.

22 Judy Wood Where did the Towers go? 2011

23 Covered in the 3rd Edition of my *Terror on the Tube*, 2011 'Insights from the Inquest.'

24 Craig Roberts, 'The MH-17 'Report' 13 October 2015.

25 'Cameron calls for Clampdown on Non-Violent Extremists:' www.thetruthseeker.co.uk/?p=104575

26 9/11 Activist Hands Himself in to British Police Over Cameron Remarks on "Non-violent Extremists" – it went viral.

27 A loose translation of Sentence 7 of his *Tractatus Logico-Philosophicus*, 1922.

28 See e.g., Webster Tarpley op. cit., David Ray Griffin, *The New Pearl Harbor*, 2004; Thierry Meyssan, 9/11 The Big Lie, 2002; Mike Ruppert *Crossing the Rubicon*, 2004 (a British book); Ian Henshall and Rowland Morgan *9/11 Revealed*, 2005; Barry Zwicker *Towers of Deception, The media cover-up* 2006. Re: *Moira*: "In the last section of the Iliad, Moira is the 'mighty fate' who leads destiny and the course of events."

29 The final word on Timothy McVeigh, executed for the Oklahoma bomb, is said to have been given in Gore Vidal's *Perpetual war for Perpetual Peace, how we got to be so hated* NY, 2002. Some aver that the Oklahoma bomb was a National Security Council (NSC) operation, www.newswithviews.com/Briley/Patrick17.htm, but we may never know.

30 Len Bracken, *The Shadow government, 9-11 and State Terror*, 2004 Adventures Unlimited Press Ill.

31 A Pentagon - yes, Pentagon - report a year after concluded that five separate bombs inside the building had caused the explosion, with McVeigh having a 'peripheral' role as a 'useful idiot:' Vidal op. cit., p.120.

32 Richard Serino who was the Director of Boston's Emergency Medical Services, composed this detailed and fully operation plan, entitled: 'Marathons – a Tale of Two Cities and the Running of a Planned Mass casualty Event.' View the complete sequence in James Tracy's 'Obama's FEMA Director Planned Boston Mass Casualty Event in 2008' in *And Nobody Died in Boston, Either* Ed. Fetzer & Palecek, 2015, pp.121-135. PDF is at http://memoryholeblog.com/2013/05/21/obamas-fema-director-planned-boston-mass-casualty-event-in-2008/

33 *And Nobody Died in Boston, Either* ed. Fetzer & Palecek 2015 p.43.

34 Liquid binary munitions don't actually exist, they just come out of Hollywood movies, that was part of the charm on this story: see Chapters 6&7.

35 Annie Machon, *Spies, lies and Whistleblowers MI5, MI6 and the Shayler Affair* Sussex 2005 Ch.14.(NB, she wrote it with David Shayler)

36 Daniel Ganser: 'it was actually London and Washington who had set up the secret [Gladio] networks. It was MI6 and the CIA who were operating the stay-behind armies' (2012, ref. 13), p.230.

37 Fetzer & Palecek, *And Nobody died in Boston either*, 2016, p.93

38 To quote Ole Dammegard again, concerning bodies left lying on the floor of the Bataclan theatre in Paris on 11/13/15: 'What she is, and what these bodies are, I would strongly suggest are what are called capper bodies, stunt bodies, used for film stunts, not real bodies.' *Another French False Flag?* Ed Barrett, 2016, p.252.

39 www.lifetec.com, 'mass casualty dummy.'

40 www.crisiscast.com.

41 www.21stcenturywire.com,'Casting Crisis' 20.7.16

42 *Another French False Flag* Ed Kevin Barrett, 2016, p.249.

43 http://www.arcwebsite.org/pages/votes.htm: 'Voting against Peace and Disarmament.' Around thirty of these motions were listed yearly, on average, with only 4% of votes being against them. I've here looked at the period 1972-2001. For early voting-patterns I used the SIPRI yearbook (Stockholm International Peace Research Institute), which gave more or less the same list every year, as the UN Yearbook, of all the motions on the general area of peace, international well-being and disarmament. The graph shows three-point moving averages of votes cast.

44 Source: SIPRI Yearbook 2015, Table 10.9 p.439: 'The financial value of states' arms exports', expressed in constant (2013 US dollars. Three-point moving averages are here shown, of yearly data from 2014 to 2013. The next two in this league table are France and Israel, with roughly half the yearly arms sales, i.e., around $5-6 billion p.a.

45 Robin Cook's *Guardian* article 8.7.05 about Al-Qaeda, explaining how it meant 'the database,' was printed one day after the London bombing – then he died merely weeks later, 6.8.05. He was still alive after having a heart attack while walking in the Pennines with his wife, but after being picked up by the army helicopter which happened to be in the area, he soon died. It was crucial for the Empire that no labour MP could oppose or undermine Tony Blair's phoney narrative, in the wake of the London bombings.

46 Edward Thompson, 'Notes on Exterminism, the last stage of civilization' New Left Review 1980.

47 *The Guardian*, 'UK prison population is biggest in western Europe' 8.3.16

48 See, 'Does Al-Qaeda exist?' by Brendan O'Neill http://100777.com/doc/614 . For the evolution of 'Al-Qaeda' in the mid-90s out of US/UK use of Mujahadeen recruited to fight in Bosnia, see Ahmed, 'Al-Qaeda and Western Covert Operations after the Cold War' in *The Hidden History of 9/11* Ed. Zarembka, 2006. Originally the term was Bin Laden's name for his computer file, used while employed by the CIA in Afghanistan, to co-ordinate the 'jihad' against the Soviet Union: Thierry Meyssan, 9/11 *The big Lie*, 2002, p.99. As Burke pointed out, 'The US intelligence community used the term "al-Qaeda" for the first time only after the 1998 embassy bombings' of Kenya and Tanzania. James Burke, *Al-Qaeda The True Story of Radical Islam*, 2003, p.6.

49 'For several decades there had been an unrelenting demonisation of the Muslim world in the American media.' Gore Vidal, Perpetual War for Perpetual Peace, 2002, p.4.

50 For who bombed 'Red Bologna,' see Cottrell *Gladio, NATO's dagger at the Heart of Europe*, 2015 pp.7-9, 227.

51 Tarpley, Ibid, p.60.

52 Tarpley, Ibid p.60.

53 This can be viewed online.

54 See William Blum, *Killing Hope: US Military and CIA Interventions Since World War II*, 1995.

55 EU debate over Gladio on 22 November, 1990: Ganser Ibid, p. 21.

56 Ganser, 2005 p.23.

57 Belgium, Switzerland and Italy did endeavour to take such measures.

58 Daniele Ganser, *NATO's Secret Armies, Operation Gladio and terrorism in Western Europe*, 2011.

59 The connection of the Bologna railway station bombing with Gladio remains enigmatic: see Daniel Ganser, chapter, 'NATO's Secret Armies in Europe' in *Weapon of the Strong: Conversations on US state Terrorism*, by C. Aksan and J. Bailes, Pluto Press (2012), p.224.

60 In Richard Cottrell's opus, for *Gladio* in Italy, read pages 56-64, starting "To mention the name of Aldo Moro in Italy is to invoke an aching pain at the heart of a nation.' Or to start earlier with the 1969 blast at Milan's Piazza di Fontana, at a later chapter, p.196: 'The huge blast at Milan's Piazza di Fontana that same December marked the commencement of hostilities which came to be known as the Italian years of lead.' Then, concerning the Bologna blast, 'A classic false-flag designed to throw blame on the Brigate Rosse instead blew back on its real perpetrators, the Nuclei Armati Rivoluzionaire owing homage to P2, Italian intelligence and Gladio,' p.201. 2nd edition 2015, pages 68-81, 226 & 227.

61 Some reckon the Madrid bombing of March, 2004 was an exception here in that it resulted in the left-wing socialist government of Zapatero swiftly gaining power: Chapter 4.

62 The classic Gladio textbook has to be *NATO's Secret Armies: Operation GLADIO and Terrorism in Western Europe* by Danielle Ganser 2005, which however is out of print and expensive on Amazon. In some ways more readable is *Gladio, NATO's Dagger at the heart of Europe* by Richard Cottrell. Make sure you get the 2015 2nd edition, much clearer and more enlarged than the first edition of 2011.

63 Quoted in The CIA and the Cult of Intelligence (1974) Marchetti & Marks: See Wikiquotes.

64 Machiavelli, The Art of War, quoted in Webster Tarpley, Synthetic Terror 2007, p.378.

65 Ganser, Ibid.

66 George Orwell, 1984, p. 127.

67 Michael Meacher, *The Guardian*, 'This War on Terrorism is bogus', 6.9.03.

68 This did not prevent Britain from supplying intelligence help in that war, via MI6 and SAS troops, plus bomb and napalm-delivery air flights: Mark Curtis, *Web of Deceit, Britain's Real role in the World*, 2003, 105. Cottrell, *Gladio* 2015, Chapter IX, 'A Very British Coup.'

69 Stephen Dorrill, *MI6 50 Years of Special Operations* p.799, quoted in Curtis, Ibid, p.75.

70 These are only years when bombings began, not how long they lasted (Source: https://wikispooks.com/wiki/US_Bombing_campaigns_since_1945) nor does it include repeat bombings of the same nation. William Blum, *Rogue State: A Guide to the World's Only Superpower*, 2000.

71 A brilliant 'comic' here is *Addicted to War, Why the US can't kick Militarism* (Joel Andreas, Canada, 2003) except that alas this anti-war 'comic,' used as a history text in hundreds of colleges, blames Muslims for the 9/11 event. It was first published 1992, then updated.

72 For CIA and Mossad warnings of the HSBC and British consul targetings, see:www.libertythink.com/2003/11/mi6-foreknowledge-in-istanbul-bombings.html. Cottrell gives a background to the story, Gladio 2015 p.

73 Reported and discussed on the July 7th truth campaign website.

74 I and my colleague James Stuart had ascertained this from data kindly sent to us by the Luton station assistant manager.

75 An anonymous 63-page evaluation of the 7/7 London Bombings published by the House of Commons in May, 2006.

76 Ms Patel's described the alleged will in an interview with Julie Etchingham on Sky News: NK, *Terror on the Tube*, 2011.

77 Rowland Morgan, *Flight 93 Revealed* 2006, p.95 (a companion *to 9/11 Revealed, Challenging the facts behind the War on Terror*, 2005, by Ian Henshall and R. Morgan).

78 Thierry Meyssan, 'Argentinian judicial authority rules out Islamic lead,' Global Research 28.7.06. For the Buenos Aires attacks see Chapter One.

79 http://nafeez.blogspot.com/2006/08/truth-about-terror-plot-and-new-pseudo.html.

80 Nafeez Ahmed, *The London Bombings*, 2006, *The War on Freedom*, 2003.

81 See Ahmed, 'Al-Qaeda and Western Covert operations after the Cold War' in *The Hidden History of 9-11-2001*, Ed. Zarembka 2006.

82 prisonplanet.com 'Cooked Terror Plot Recycles Politics Of Fear' 22.6.06; plus, 'Al-Qaeda plan to fly planes into London skyscrapers concocted by government lobbyists.'

83 This chapter is, to a large extent, possible because of Jim Fetzer's visit to Argentina and his liasing with Adrian Salbuchi (see interview October 2009, e.g. http://www.voltairenet.org/article162474.html).

84 Sources: http://inthesenewtimes.com 'Timeline: Israeli Embassy and AMIA bombings.1992-2006;' also thetruthseeker.co.uk/?p=74509; and Salbuchi video, 'False Flag Attacks in Argentina: AMIA and Israeli Embassy Bldgs'

85 *Asia Times* atimes.com Argentina's Iranian nuke connection by Gareth Porter

86 VoltaireNet 'False Flag Attacks in Argentina: 1992 and 1994' by Adrian Salbuchi and James Fetzer 13.10.09

87 John Paul Leonard, p.363 of *The War on Freedom, How and Why America was attacked on September 11, 2001*, Nafeez Ahmed, 2002.

88 Rense.com 'Mossad Agents Arrested In Attempt To Bomb Mexican Congress', 26.11.01.

89 Interview with Israeli writer Hamish Oz, published in the Israeli newspaper Davar on December 17th, 1982 (in Hebrew), reprinted by US journalist Holger Jensen in a 2002 article.

90 The article 'Terror' first appeared in the LEHI underground organisation journal *Hehazit* (The Front) in the summer of 1943.

91 For a sample, see: www.thegoldencalfspeaks.com 'Commands to kill gentiles in Judaism.'

92 This grave question is addressed in *The Controversy of Zion* by Douglas Reed, 1978, reprinted in 2012, a book which every politician needs to read.

93 Thierry Meyssan (of Voltaire Network) commented, 'Il est étrange qu'il faille une dizaine d'années pour se rendre compte qu'un attentat a été réalisé en plaçant un explosif dans un bâtiment et non avec un véhicule kamikaze.' Roughly translated, this means, how odd that it took them ten years to realise, there was no truck. Israel Shamir, whose geopolitical views are generally sound, has a page on the topic which begins: 'Israel's embassy in Buenos Aires, Argentina was bombed on March 17, 1992, when a pickup truck, driven by a suicide bomber and loaded with explosives, smashed into the front of the Israeli Embassy and detonated destroying the embassy.' it will hopefully have become clear that no such truck existed.

94 BBC News 26 July On this Day 1994: 'Israel's London embassy bombed'

95 The two Palestinians complained that 'an unfair trial was followed, after a long wait, by an unfair appeal. This was a political trial from day one and we are totally innocent … We were only convenient scapegoats.' www.innocent.org.uk/cases/botmehalami/index.html.

96 *Spies, Lies and Whistleblowers* by Annie Machon 2005 (David Shayler claims to be the actual author of this text, averring that his lady friend wrote it down because he was under a MI6 injunction of silence) is the only text in print on the topic of this chapter. But, see also: www.freesaj.org.uk/appeal_booklet/appeal_book.pdf and www.freesaj.org.uk/pdf/justice.pdf)

97 The silver grey Audi 100 that exploded outside the Israeli Embassy carried the number of a genuine Audi: D201 BGU; its original number plate had been B49 GNU. This car was bought on 15th June 1994 at a car auction in Milton Keynes by a man giving the name 'George 'who turned out to be Rida Mughrabi and he has never been traced. (NB, this Rida bought 'explosives' for one of those jailed, see above refs for this story.)

98 www.freesaj.org.uk/

99 Infinite Injustice, Human rights breaches and wrongful convictions of Samar Alami and Jawad Botmech, 2002, p.11.

100 In the 1980s, a micro nuke was designed called the 'Special Atomic Demolition Munition' (SADM). It yielded .01-1 kilotons blast. The standard SADM would have a core of pure Pu239 with a thin shield of UR 238, a neutron reflector. But, that would give easily-detectable radiation due to its uranium cladding. Then, the Dimona, Negev (Israel) lab developed a new 'stealth' micro-nuke with ultra-pure plutonium and no U238 reflector. Plutonium emits only alpha radiation, mainly invisible to a standard Geiger counter – Joe Vialls.

101 Experts can tell, from the blast overpressure, about the explosive used: Potassium Chlorate gives 2 psi (pounds per square inch), ammonium nitrate and fuel oil (ANFO) gives 4psi The military 'C4' explosive can yield 10 psi, while it takes well over 20psi to get bones crushed, and dead bodies lying around did have their bones so crushed. To have concrete stripped from steel wire as happened here would need around 100 psi and only a nuclear blast does that.

102 There is an analogy here with the 9/11 event in New York, where car-parks a block away had cars burning, especially the engine and electrical parts. Likewise (I suggest) the Oklahoma City (Federal Murrah building, April 19, 1995) bomb had loads of toasted cars around in the aftermath. The controversial Judy Wood opus on 9/11 comments upon the toasted car phenomenon.

103 Why not get your friends together, and watch the film –the Truth about the Bali Bombings. Part 2 outlines the huge financial benefit of the Bali bombing for Australian police and security services.

104 Section 7, 2 mins, 'Fool Me Twice.'

105 Section 7 of the Australian film 'Fool Me Twice,' in twenty parts on Youtube. (NB, earlier sections review state-terror events: section 5 the assault on the USS Liberty in 1963, section 6 the attack upon the New York World Trade Centre in 1993). For no craters in ground from car-bombs, see section 9, for blast overpressure ratio (ref. 2) see section 11.

106 'Terrorists attack NATO', *Isis Europe*, 6, May 2004, p. 7.

107 R. Minita, *Shadow War: War on Terror*, 2004.

108 Tarpley here commented: '… the terrorist attacks had failed to produce the expected effects. The Washington consensus had previously been that terrorism would infallibly stampede the voters of any country into voting for the incumbent, but this time the anti-Bush challenger was the beneficiary,' Synthetic Terror, 2008, p.400.

109 *International Herald Tribune*, 'Mixed Verdicts in Madrid terror bombing Trial', 30.10.07. Compare comment by Richard Cottrell: 'Certainly the show trial of 28 accused conspirators failed to produce a shred of evidence of Al Qaeda provenance.' *Gladio*, 2015, p. 339.

110 *The Guardian* 31.10.07 '21 Guilty, Seven Cleared over Madrid train bombings'.

111 Wiki, 11 March 2004 Madrid attacks, TV interview on Libertad Digital. As Richard Cottrell explained: 'The story circulated in the media that one backpack contained screws and nails intended to serve as shrapnel. However, autopsies proved that none of the train bombing victims had been struck by sharp metal projectiles, the equivalent of shrapnel.' *Gladio*, 2015, p338.

112 Those who had allegedly supplied the explosives were found to have links with a senior police bomb squad: Ian Henshall, *911 Revealed*, p.188; www.vialls.com/myahudi/madrid.html.

113 *El Mundo* of 6 May, 2004; Tarpley, p.401.

114 www.vialls.com/myahudi/madrid.html - this Joe Vialls article can still be viewed on archive.org: go, e.g., back to 2006.

115 Prosecutor Olga Sánchez: Un factor "cabalístico" en la elección de la fecha de la matanza en los trenes EL PAÍS – Madrid – 10/03/2005 "gran carga simbólica y cabalística para los grupos locales de Al Qaeda". Al Qaeda is (supposedly) an Arab movement, who would hardly have used Kabbala?

116 Wiki 'Controversies about the 2004 Madrid train bombings'

117 Frank Gaffney, 'Spain's Terrorgate?' 18.5.05 Report on the Madrid daily *El Mundo* 16.5.05 account of its research, *National Review*.

118 Or, see my post "Jury Rejects State Charges against 7/7 Ripple Effect's Muad'Dib" on www.terroonthetube.co.uk

119 http://www.julyseventh.co.uk/J7-Inquest-Submission/05.Explosions_Immediate_Aftermath.pdf Its reference 26 has been deleted - to the Intelligence & Security Committee 2009 Report, 'Could 7/7 Have Been Prevented?'

120 'Former Mossad Agent Accidentally Admits They Did the 7/7 London Bombings', asheepnomore.net.

121 For a detailed account of how Israel had a major hand in planning, arranging and perpetrating the 9/11 event, see my '9/11 and Zion: What was Israel's Role' online: or my book 'Who did 9/11?'

122 'Since about November 2004, the US FBI, but not other US agencies, has been refusing to use the London Underground' – Tarpley, Op. Cit., p.462 - i.e., the FBI had little or no idea when it was going to happen.

123 MacGregor is here discussing an article, anonymous, reviewing the London bombings, which he conjectures was written by Aumann: http://mtrial.org/201009-who-did-london-77-hard-proof

124 Jeff Gates, How Israel Wages Game Theory Warfare' *Foreign Policy Journal*, August 2009.

125 *Gladio*, 2015, p.341.

126 On 13.8.06 *The Sunday Mirror* disclosed in 'EXCLUSIVE: BABY BOMB' story that one couple who might have been intending to take part in this plot, might also have been intending to take their new baby on board in their suicide flight, in order to be able to conceal the explosive in the baby's bottle! Mothers boarding at Heathrow with young babies were thereafter obliged to drink from their baby's bottle before boarding flights, in order to demonstrate that they were not planning to blow up the plane.

127 'Britain's airline terror plot: Questions that need to be answered' World Socialist Web 11.8.06, www.wsws.org/articles/2006/aug2006/lond-a11.shtml.

128 www.takeourworldback.com/short/liquidbombhoax.htm (anon).

129 http://en.wikipedia.org/wiki/2006_transatlantic_aircraft_plot.

130 Ibid.

131 Craig Murray, *The Guardian*, The UK Terror plot: What's Really Going On? 15 August, 2006, archived at www.oilempire.us/blair-scare.html.

132 For Col. Wylde on the fake explosives, see: www.propagandamatrix.com/articles/September2006/180906_b_terror.htm.

133 http://nafeez.blogspot.com/2006/09/ex-uk-intel-official-says-liquid.html (Sept 18, 2006) Ahmed, 'August terror plot is a 'fiction' underscoring police failures'; Col. Wylde, 18 Sept

134 *Daily Mail*, 23 Dec 2006.

135 Thomas Greene 'Mass murder in the skies: was the plot feasible? Let's whip up some TATP and find out', theregister.co.uk, 17.8.06.

136 Meyssan, op. cit.

137 BBC News, August 21, 2006.

138 Rense.com 'Latest Terror Threat – More Government Foreknowledge', By Joel Skousen, World Affairs Brief, 12.8.06.

139 http://en.wikipedia.org/wiki/Ammonium_nitrate.

140 *Guardian*, June 3rd 2008, 'Airline accused wanted to 'cause disturbance' at airport'.

141 Peter Osborne, *Use and Abuse of Terror*, 2006, p.25. The 'Ricin plot' was also cited in the anonymous *Official Account* of July 7th as an instance of Islamic terror: pp.30, 34. See also Lawrence Archer & Fiona Bawden, *Ricin! The Inside Story of the Terror plot that Never Was* 2010, p. xi.

142 Scott Creighton, 'Umar Fizzlepants Update' 9.1.10 willyloman.wordpress.com [deleted by Wordpress]

143 Ian Crane was formerly President of the London 9/11 truth movement, and has since organised the 'Alternative View' conferences: http://www.ianrcrane.co.uk/

144 *The Guardian*, 'US plots retaliatory strikes against al-Qaida in Yemen over plane bomber'

145 Lack of any epicentre of this blast, was described by Olé Dammegard at: newsinsideout.com by A. L. Webre, 3.8.15 at 34 minutes.

146 Cottrell, *Gladio*, 2015, p.425.

147 See Infowars.com 'Norwegian Police confirm drill identical to Breivik's attack' 26.8.11. For a translation from Norwegian see www.cryptogon.com/?p=24540 29.8.11 (from *Aftenposten*)

148 Torstein gave an address to our '911 Keeptalking' group in London, in October 2011, and much of the present text came from discussing the matter with him. He lives in Oslo near to the site of the blast and heard it.

149 Compare the (anonymous) 'Red Ice Creations' narrative 'Oslo Bombing 7-22-11 – Inconsistencies'. At 7 minutes: no trace of crater or blackening of ground can be seen, where the explosion was supposed to have taken place. At 24 mins, film of a crowd first-arrivers on the scene after the blast, wondering where the bomb had been: 'to me it's like, everybody's looking around, trying to figure out where it's been coming from, the main explosion, even the camera man is panning around…'

150 Stated in the Breivik court case: 'The Uncanny Valley and Art Making as Forging Evidence In the New World Order Part II,' The Paulstal Service, at 8 minutes.

151 Åsne Seierstad, *One of Us, the Story of a Massacre and its Aftermath* 2015.

152 Gordon Duff, *Veterans Today*, 18.8.11 'Norway: Berwick in Constant Contact with Police During Massacre.'

153 But NB it was claimed by Åsne Seierstad that 'The police had established that the bomb had been made exactly as Breivik described in the manifesto. They had carried out a test detonation of the same type of bomb, and Holden [lawyer at the trial] again showed pictures.' *One of Us* 2013 p.436.

154 Richard Cottrell, *Gladio*, 2015, p.432.

155 *Gladio*, 2015, p437.

156 See video 'Kent Freedom Movement investigate the Woolwich false flag psy ops,' viewed 25 thousand times, where we visited Artillery Road soon after the event. Deb Williams was with us, and she grew up around Artillery road, her insights were vital for out narration. The KFM has since folded up.

157 'See Woolwich Defies common sense" – Morris.

158 http://kentfreedommovement.com/video/woolwich-massacre-deception-exposed-special-edition-22-may-2013

159 *The Independent*, 24 May 2013, Michael Adebowale and Michael Adebolajo

160 September Clues, 'Woolwich 'terror event' This is an old 9/11 truth site still going, based on the thesis that real planes did not crash into the Towers on that morning. It's generally the best one for fabricated terror events.

161 See comments by Nafeez Ahmed, 28.5.13 'The Cutting Edge'

162 Aangrifan, 'Woolwich: Adebolajo was paid by MI6'

163 Earlier KFM video link, Part 2, 4 mins

164 http://nodisinfo.com/what-is-in-this-woolwichstrange-yellow-bag/

165 25.3.13 'Woolwich attack: confusing, horrific, bizarre – the horror that made literally no sense'

166 *Mirror* 'Woolwich Attack Video' 24 May.

167 Aangrifan site, May 24th 'Woolwich'

168 Before its News 25 May 'Woolwich hoax'

169 *The Mail*, Dramatic Final Seconds of DLR's Life' 25.11.13.

170 The archive www.ancestry.co.uk has no record of the birth or death of anyone of that name, not would Manchester hospital confirm his birth. No one has produced a birth or death certificate that identifies Mr Lee Rigby.

171 Lyn Rigby, *Lee Rigby, A Mother's Story* 2016, p.59.

172 Halifax Courier 'Murdered soldier Lee Rigby was married in Halifax'. 24.5.13

173 The book *Lee Rigby, a mother's story* by Lyn Rigby shows someone wearing army fatigues on 3rd page of the colour pictures: one might not guess this was the same person.

174 On the 3rd anniversary of his death, BBC News: 'Family of Murdered Lee Rigby release home video,' half a minute long, of a young man dancing, drumming and in a smart uniform: a machine-gunner?

175 It was a Boeing 747 that had just taken off from Kennedy airport, believed to have been shot down by a US Navy sub. It was full of passengers, there were no survivors. Many witnesses reported a bright object streak up from the ocean and hit the aircraft.

176 see the authentic flight data at: http://www.flightradar24.com/data/flights/mh17/

177 See e.g., my 'Nine Keys to 9/11', Key No. 8 (on (www.9/11forum.org.uk): the American Airline planes AA11 and AA77 were not registered as flying that day.

178 Or, as Veterans Today put it: "You can't fire a Buk missile in broad daylight with no witnesses" 13.10.15

179 http://rt.com/news/173672-malaysia-plane-crash-putin/

180 For details of this Spanish air-traffic controller's report, posted the day after, see: 'Spanish Air Controller: Ukraine Military Shot Down Boeing MH17', http://slavyangrad.org/

181 Global Research Eric Zusse, 'Evidence Is Now Conclusive: Two Ukrainian Government Fighter-Jets Shot Down Malaysian Airlines MH17. It was Not a 'Buk' Surface to Air Missile' August 2014

182 21 July, Prison Planet: Whistleblower: U.S. Satellite Images Show Ukrainian Troops Shooting Down MH17

183 Washington Times, 18 July 2014: "Pro-Russia rebel commander suggests passengers died days before Malaysian flight." For Infowars mulling over the bodies-drained of blood on the ground see www.infowars.com/rebel-leader-says-many-of-the-dead-bodies-in-mh17-werent-fresh/

184 YouTube, 'Hacked emails 'False flag to occur in Ukraine''

185 Crisis actors appear after the event http://nodisinfo.com/ukrainian-crisis-actors-zionist-mh17-hoax/ with fake corpses lying around http://nodisinfo.com/synthetic-gore-real-dead-bodies-mh17-hoax/ and forged passports http://nodisinfo.com/mh17-passport-staging-proves-hoax-nodisinfo-video/

186 On 9/11, the fate of flight United Airlines 93 was somewhat comparable, whereby a plane probably without passengers was blown out of the sky in Pittsburgh, Pennsylvania: see 'The Mystery of Flight 93' by the author, online. Operation Northwoods was a scheme devised by Lemnitzer and his Joint Chiefs of Staff in 1962 but not allowed by JFK, which only became public knowledge in 1999 with publication of *Body of Secrets* by James Bamford.

187 Gerhard Wisnewski's Yearbook (Jahrbuch) for 2015: a summary of his MH17 thesis there, was given (in German) in Kopp Online, 245.1.15.

188 The final report of October 2015 was 'Crash of Malaysia Airlines flight MH17.'

189 Comment on video: 17 July, 2014 'Are they Wagging the Dog?'

190 See more at: 'Countries agree to MH17 prosecutor team' 28.7.14

191 Duff, 'Media Control and a Rigged Report, MH17 - Kiev shot MH17 down and the Dutch, part of the NATO gang responsible, are part of the problem and fully culpable for the crime as predicted' VT, 13.11.15

192 P.C. Roberts blog, 'In the West respect for truth no longer exists' 19.8.14

193 See "FOX Network predicts MH17 bloodless, decomposed bodies four days prior to July 17th" 19th July, theunhivedmind.com

194 The Piazza Fontana in Milan was destroyed by a bomb on 12th December 1969, killing 16 people, signalling the start of Gladio terror in Italy; the 1980 Bologna station bombing took 85 lives.

195 Compare with fake digital images used on front page of London's Evening Standard of 9.3.03 with toppling of Saddam Hussein statue in Bagdad: the Empire wanted cheering crowds to greet their 'liberation' of Baghdad but there were none. A US Marines psy-op involved tearing down the statue, with a few dozen people assembled, mostly flown especially in for the occasion, made to look like a big crowd.

196 See comment by Webster Tarpley, in: *We are not Charlie Hebdo*, Ed. Barrett 2015, Chapter 'Charlie Hebdo: A Classic Exercise in NATO Discipline': "It was pure heresy, one of the biggest breaks with the Anglo-Saxon lockstep since the death of de Gaulle."

197 Press TV, 'Paris attack designed to shore up France's vassal status': Roberts 10th Jan.

198 But NB see my post http://terroronthetube.co.uk/related-articles/police-collusion-in-norway-terror-attacks/

199 See my 'Fukushima as fabricated terror' www.thetruthseeker.co.uk/?p=35234

200 Kuala Lumpur Tribunal's genocide prosecution of Israel in November 2013.

201 http://terroronthetube.co.uk/2015/01/01/black-hand-takes-down-malaysian-plane/#more-4732

202 Sandra Barr, 'Charlie Hebdo False Flag x2' truthseeker444.blogspot

203 Source: his nephew Philippe Baron de Rothschild, see Kevin Barrett, p.203, 'A List of Charlie Hebdo suspects', in We are Not Charlie Hebdo, ref. 21.

204 I asked Sanda Barr if there had been any real deaths in the CH event (see discussion below her article, ref.27) and she replied: "I am not altogether sure Nicholas, best guess no, no one was killed in the making of the event, but I have to say, the French crisis actors are a bit better than the US & UK ones." (!)

205 as alleged by 'Lasha Darkmoon' (pseud): 'Madame Rothschild – "I know who was behind the Paris attacks!" the truthseeker.co.uk 12.1.15

206 Brandon Martinez, 11.1.15, Voice of Palestine, on CH event..

207 *Veterans Today*, 'Zionists linked to "Charlie Hebdo terrorists' escape: A spectacle staged by Sayanim?'

208 Police Commissioner Involved in Charlie Hebdo Investigation "Commits Suicide," *Global Research*.

209 Noted originally at Jimstonefreelance.com,.8.1.15

210 For Israeli foreknowledge, see my Terror on the Tube, behind the Veil of 7/7, 2012, pp. 52, 73-74 and 100.

211 forbiddenknowledge.tv, sky-news-you-can-see-the-blood-on-the-ground-which-has-been-put-there

212 See video, 'Charlie Hebdo, Observez, voyez vous la même chose? Donnez votre avis dans le respect.'

213 See video 'Busted!!! Paris shooting cops shooting blanks' www.thetruthseeker.co.uk/?p=109889.

214 New police powers included the ability to keep people in their homes without trial, search the homes of people without a warrant from a judge, and the power to block any website that is deemed a problem.

215 Brandon Martinez, nonalignedmedia.com 'Decoding the Paris Attacks.'

216 See video in French, 'Paris Attacks A Chilling Coincidence ENG Subtitles. 'It quotes Patrick Pelloux as well as Dr Pierre Carli, head of the Paris SAMU, the emergency services.

217 For discussion, see video, "The elusive Paris attack" by 'Professor Doom' At 15 min, we are shown ambulances gathered together in central Paris in early evening for the drill.

218 www.challenges.fr/, 'Comment le Samus s'est préparé aux attentats simultanés de Paris', 15.11.15.

219 See film of drill on ABC News 'Paris Attacks: New Updates, At Least 100 Reported Dead' at 22-23 mins.

220 Daily Mail, 14 November: "Earlier on Friday, the German national football team had been evacuated from their hotel in Paris due to a bomb threat."

221 It was sold on 9/11 to the billionaire Arnaud Lagardère (Lagardère Group, Hachette, Larousse, France Telecom, Vuitton, Lazard, Vivendi Universal, etc). The largest Lagardère Group stockholder is the Emir of Qatar (a major ISIS sponsor), so the new owners may not have felt a very strong loyalty to France.

222 *The Guardian* 17th November 'Something from Dante's Hell' NB this police report strangely omits mention of the well-filmed police shootout in the building right next to The Bataclan, 10 pm.

223 Interview Takimag.com 14.5.16.

224 The November issue of the Paris music mag 'Rock Folk' had the Friday 13th EODM concert at the Bataclan in its 'agenda' for the month.

225 'Panamza,' 'United Hatzalah, le groupe israélien présent à la fois au Bataclan et à l'aéroport de Bruxelles', at egaliteetreconciliation.fr 25.3.16.

226 See close-up of dummies in video 'Paris Attack Hoax 11/13/15'(Nov. 26), at 5-6 minutes.

227 interview with Olé by Kevin Barrett, in *Another French False-Flag*, 2016, p.252.

228 Thanks to September Clues for spotting this

229 See analysis by Dr Eowyn, http://fellowshipoftheminds.com/tag/bataclan-attack/

230 The Observer, 15th November.

231 P. C. Roberts' blog, 'French Security Left Blind During Paris Attacks', Nov 15.

232 Nobody Died at Sandy Hook, 2015, Dennis Cimino chapter, 'The Nexus of Tyranny: Tucson, Aurora & Sandy Hook,' p.202.

233 See Craig Murray blog 'Shoot to Kill and News Management': death of Hasna Ait Buolacehn, 18th November. But, NB, a Moroccan woman has claimed that 'stolen identity' photos of her have been used for HAB – reminding one of the 9/11 hijackers. As a result, she could not go outside and was living in fear.

234 His mother said he must have done it out of 'stress' (Daily Mail, 16 Nov.) which might not sound like a regular cannabis user.

235 Tony Cartalucci Global Research.

236 See Spivey on absurdity of the given narrative: http://chrisspivey.org/qui-qui-poo-poo/

237 Breitbart.com 'Special Forces And Police On Standby For Multiple Terror Attacks In London' 20.3.16

238 For Olé Dammegard's account of this eyewitness testimony, see his interview with A. L. Webre, Newsinsideout 1.6.16, starting 38 minutes, for 20 minutes: he there displays a clear memory of what we were told.

239 For a reconstruction of where everything happened in that airport lounge, see: 'Location, location, location (Brussels Bombing Hoax)'

240 See 'Brussels Bombing Hoax / False Flag - Construction In The Airport' by The Paulstal service.

241 *Global Research* is a Canadian 'truth' site, run by the discerning 9/11 scholar Professor Michael Chossudovsky.

242 One needs to view the colour images here: search Google Images for 'Brussels crisis actor on phone' and 'Bataclan crisis actor on phone'

243 Jetairwars.com, select 'flight schedules'

244 Haaretz.com 22.3.16 'Israeli Science Minister Links Brussels Attacks to Europe's 'Foolish' Rebukes of Israel'

245 For an analysis of this fraud, see Michael Chossudovsky, 'Is the ISIS Behind the Brussels Attacks? Who is Behind the ISIS?' *Global Research*, 22 March.

246 *The Guardian*, 'Islamic State claims attacks at Brussels airport and metro station', 22 March.

247 TheUglytruth.blogspot.com, 2012, Mark Glenn

248 For pictures see nodisinfo.com, 'The Fake Wounded of the Brussels Hoax Terrorist Attack' 23.3.16

249 See Youtube video 'Brussels Bombing Hoax - CNN Sellout Giulia Paravicini'

250 Barrett, *Veterans Today*, 'Israel Celebrates Successful 9/11 Operation on Purim Holiday,' 1.3.13

251 The above-mentioned eyewitness A.W. recalled a group of twenty or so black-clad Hasidic Jews at the boundary between Counters 1 & 2 and the rest of the departure lounge, as if they were there to stop people from wandering into the nearly-empty space; and he surmised that these could have been the 'United Hatzalah' group. For Olé Dammegard recalling this testimony, see his interview with A. L. Webre, Newsinsideout.com 1.6.16, 53 mins.

252 Haaretz.com 22 March 'Brussels Attacks.'

253 [Pointed out by Redsilver] 'Munich Mall Shooting and Nice attacks conspiracy busted open' (image used with his kind permission). I've taken the phrase 'the joker' from him.

254 www.cafebabel.it: Italian reporter Anita Westrup gets the call from Gutjahr at 11.14.

255 www.pamelageller.com, '**GRAPHIC** Raw FOOTAGE of Nice Terror Attack', 14 July. Compare with 2nd video of the dummies' in 'Nobody died in the Nice Terror Attack', by Johnny Gatt, 23 July.

256 These are all better viewed in colour: see video 'Nobody died in the Nice Terror Attack', by Johnny Gatt, 2 mins.

257 She gave her source as 'Jester twitter' which doesn't sound very French.

258 The *Daily Mail* averred that the lorry 'mounted pavements at high speed and ploughed through crowds.'

259 We see laughing crowds on the 'Place Macena' (a road with tram lines on it), as they were running away from the beach: see 'Nice Attack: Follow up & New Information' by Serebra Sana 25.7.16, first minute; or her 'Nice Attack: More Crime Scene Breakdown + Analysis' 20.7.16.

260 www.lelibrepenseur.org/, 15th July. That displays the video he made the next day, speaking in Arabic. Later it published an open letter by him, about how his life was being ruined by the publicity, he had received death-threats and did not dare return to France.

261 Salman Hossain, henrymakow.com, 'Zionist Fingerprints on Nice Terror Hoax,'20.6.16.

262 Salman Hossein, Ibid.

263 video, Serebra Sana, 'Nice Attack: Truck + Heroes - Detailed Analysis' 19.7.16 (but NB, this video is one hour long).

264 For media reports on these 'heroes' see Serebra Sana, Ibid, also her 'Nice attack: Follow up and New Information.'

265 Ibid, 27 minutes

266 Serebra Sana: 'Hero Emerges and its "Gecko Guy"'!!!'22.7.16

267 www.rt.com: 'Beyond a massacre: France deliberately bombed Syrian civilians after Nice attack' 20 July.

268 Serebra Sana, 'Nice attack, another Bombshell,' 7.8.16

269 See e.g., 'Munich McDonalds Shooting Hoax'

270 www.investmentwatchblog.com, 28 July: 'The same guy who caught the Nice event also was on the spot in Munich to video it…'. NB This is a fairly mainstream site that

would not normally carry 'conspiracy' issues.

271 Investmentwatchblog.com, 24 July, 'Smoking Gun: Nice and Munich Terror Attacks Linked To CIA and Mossad.'

272 Scott Alexander, 'An Olympic sized Scam, the Munich Shooting' 1.8.16 Fetzer blogspot.

273 See video, 'the KFM investigate the London 322 "terror Attack".'

274 *The Guardian's* account of events had the car mount up onto the pavement after that sign, however the kiosk selling postcards and tourist trinkets is at the start of the bridge before it, and that was allegedly hit.

275 See video, 'Witnesses exposed as crisis actors, London 3/22/17'.

276 In Melbourne a few months earlier 20 January a car had mounted a pavement and ploughed into pedestrians, with four reported dead, so the events were similar.

277 For more detailed images of these scenes, search Google images for, e.g., 'Westminster terror dummies.'

278 See O.D.'s site, 'Light on conspiracies.'

279 See interview with O.D. by K.B., in *Another French False Flag, Bloody Tracks from Paris to San Bernardino,* Ed. Kevin Barrett, 2016, 249-257, p.249.

280 Metro, 29 March: 'Khaleed Masood was a family man, says BBC interviewee.'

281 I spoke to Paulo Fiora, who was there and saw things happening, peering through the House of Commons railings. He saw the 'perpetrator' allegedly shot lying on the cobblestones, with his eyes languidly wandering around, so he did not look as if he were in pain. He (and also a friend he was with) did not notice any bullet-marks on his shirt. He has given interviews on the subject, with Jim Fetzer and Lambremont Webre.

282 Paul Craig Roberts, *The Boston Marathon Bombing After Four Years, 15.4.17g*

283 Professor Danielle Ganser, Director of the Swiss Institute for Peace and Energy Research, lectures on this topic at the University of Tubingen.

284 Laura Knight-Jadczyk , *9/11 The Ultimate Truth,* Red Pill Press, 2006, p.407.

285 Peter Oborne, *The Rise of Political Lying,* 2005, pp. 6,227.

286 P.C. Roberts, '9/11 and the Orwellian Redefinition of "Conspiracy Theory,"' Prison Planet, 20/6/11.

287 I argued that they did go to the moon in 'Did they go to the Moon? Doubts about Apollo' (*And I suppose they didn't go to the Moon, either* Ed Fetzer and Palecek, Moon Rock Books 2015, pp.25-36). However in online debates I've had on this topic (e.g., on *Windows on the World*), it is far from evident that I win the argument! We are all increasingly in a condition of 'cognitive dissonance' on this topic.

288 25 September, 2011: Kevin Boyle, 'Conspiracy Theory conference.'

289 On the 'Conspiracy Day', Mr Aaronovitch pulled out and after an impromptu vote of those present he was replaced by Mr Ian Crane, formerly Chair of Britain's 9/11 truth movement.

290 Let's quote here Olé Dammegard: 'Show me a picture of ISIS, and if there is any vehicle visible I can guarantee it will be a Toyota.' He was discussing 'product placement' in modern SFT events: interview with A L Webre, Newsinsideout.com, 1.6.16, at 38 mins.

291 Mail online 20.8.14

292 JFK Address to US Newspaper Association April 27, 1961

293 John Michell, *How the world is made, Sacred Geometry,* 2009, p.112.

294 The significance of this title (by film-maker Kevin West) was not generally appreciated: it alluded to the Tom Stoppard play 'Rosenkrantz & Guildenstern Are Dead.' This play, based on the two Hamlet characters, began with one of these two tossing a coin repeatedly. It kept coming up heads, violating the laws of probability. I and Tony Farrell devised a similar ploy to show the likelihood of the Peter Power drills on the morning of 7/7 being at the same stations at the same times: 23 heads in sequence, I computed.

295 For English readers: 22 November was the JFK assassination date.

296 Reprinted by Progressive Press, CA in 2008.

297 Higgons, A Short View of the English History 1735, p.207.

298 Tony Cartalucci, 'America's Co-ordinated Multinational Ramadan Attacks,' *Global Research* 1.7.15

299 Born into a wealthy Iraqi Israeli family, Rita Katz' father was arrested on charges of espionage for Israel, and hanged. The family escaped to Israel where she served in the IDF. Then in 1997 she emigrated to the US where she co-founded the SITE institute, a private intelligence firm. It has specialised in 'discovering' the latest Al-Qaeda/Bin Laden intelligence tapes. In 2007, it issued the Bush administration with a not-yet released OBL video. In 2008 she changed it to The SITE Intelligence Group and moved to Fort George, Maryland, conveniently near the NSA, the world's largest spy agency. Carelessly, she allowed her new company to have the same IP address as another Mossad asset, MEMRI, viz. 67.19.162.130.

300 E.g., *Mail Online*, 29 June 2015, 'Tragic homecoming: wife in a coma'

301 pravdareport.com 'Mossad mercenaries'

- Yevgeny Zamyatin - We
- HG Wells - Modern Utopia
- Christopher Bollyn - Orlando Falkelly
- John Mitchell - How the World is Made
- 911 - The new pearl harbour